THE NUCLEAR
TERRORIST

THE NUCLEAR
TERRORIST

HIS FINANCIAL BACKERS AND POLITICAL PATRONS
IN THE U.S. AND ABROAD

ROBERT GLEASON

A TOM DOHERTY ASSOCIATES BOOK

NEW YORK

THE NUCLEAR TERRORIST

Copyright © 2014 by Robert Gleason

A Forge Book
Published by Tom Doherty Associates, LLC
175 Fifth Avenue
New York, NY 10010

www.tor-forge.com

Forge® is a registered trademark of Tom Doherty Associates, LLC.

The Library of Congress Cataloging-in-Publication Data is available upon request.

ISBN 978-0-7653-3812-9 (hardcover)
ISBN 978-1-4668-3756-0 (e-book)

Forge books may be purchased for educational, business, or promotional use.
For information on bulk purchases, please contact Macmillan Corporate and
Premium Sales Department at 1-800-221-7945, extension 5442,
or write specialmarkets@macmillan.com.

First Edition: April 2014

Printed in the United States of America

0 9 8 7 6 5 4 3 2 1

For Tom Doherty, who made this book possible

SPECIAL THANKS TO:

Linda Quinton—a gifted publisher and a great friend

Susan—again and always

Jerry Gibbs—for over five decades of irreplaceable friendship

For we wrestle not against flesh and blood, but against principalities, against powers, against the rulers of darkness of this world, against spiritual wickedness in high places.

—Ephesians 6:12 (King James Bible)

CONTENTS

CONTENTS

ACKNOWLEDGMENTS

Sessalee Hensley—for encouraging me to write about these terrifying subjects; Christine Jaeger—for her help with all my books; Kelly Quinn and Whitney Ross, two of the finest young editors and individuals I've ever known; and Lee Lawless, writer, editor, rock star . . . and, of course, friend.

Junius and Hilde Podrug—for so much friendship and support.

Doug Greenlaw, Alice Gleason, Simon Basse, Blaine Heric, Janis Kinsey, Gary Nuspl, Larry and Tina Beaver, Pat and Cathy Hinger, LaVerne Dunlap, and all my Michigan City, Indiana, friends. Also, Bernard Lootens, historian, mentor, friend, and the world's preeminent expert on Arnold Toynbee.

To Jaime Levine, the editor's editor; Helen Chin, for labor above and beyond the call of duty; and for Kevin Sweeney, who put Humpty back together again.

Maribel and Roberto Guierrez—I will never forget.

And once more to Herbert M. Alexander, 1910–1988. Wherever you are, old man, I've got your back.

Introduction

I will show you fear in a handful of dust.
—T. S. ELIOT, *THE WASTE LAND*[1]

A few years ago, the History Channel featured me in a special on nuclear terrorism, and during the pre-show interview a producer wanted to know what frightened me most about the subject.

"That it's so eminently feasible," I said.

To illustrate my point I told him that nuclear terrorists were already plying their trade in Pakistan. During the last decade terrorists had begun attacking Pakistan's nuclear facilities.[2]

"What prevents those terrorists from visiting the U.S.?" the producer asked.

"And melting down the Indian Point nuclear power plant near New York City?" I asked him back. "Or setting off nuclear explosions in the Sandia National Laboratories near San Francisco?"

"What would stop them?"

"Very little."

My nickname at the History Channel became "the Prince of Darkness."

Unfortunately, Pakistan's nuclear terrorists are growing more competent, more deadly. And they are more dedicated. Over the past several years, units made up of al Qaeda and the Pakistani Taliban have focused their efforts on those regions where their potential nuclear collaborators are located and where most of the country's atomic assets are deployed—Pakistan's northern and western sectors as well as the areas around Islamabad and Rawalpindi.[3]

This new generation of al Qaeda and Taliban terrorists has already attacked and blown up portions of Pakistani nuclear facilities, and they are also taking on Pakistan's most heavily fortified military installations. These cadres are disciplined, fearless, and highly skilled. Their alarmingly successful raids have shown us that Pakistan cannot protect its nuclear sites. The United States cannot defend its own nuclear sites either, since, as we shall see, America's nuclear facilities are far easier to break into and destroy than Pakistan's. The devastation of U.S. nuclear installations would be, for these fighters, a relative cakewalk.[4]

Some experts believe that the Special Service Group (SSG), the Pakistan army's elite commando unit, have trained these al Qaeda/Taliban terrorists, since these teams are so impressively professional.

- One of their first attempts was a 2007 raid on a nuclear missile base south of the Pakistani capital where they killed eight people.[5]

- In August 2008, terrorists entered and blew up parts of a Wah Cantonment facility, which was believed to be a nuclear weapons assembly plant.[6]

- In December 2008, suicide bombers next attacked a school bus outside Pakistan's Kamra Airbase—which was thought to be a nuclear weapons storage facility.[7]

- In October 2009, terrorists, disguised in army uniforms, invaded the Pakistan General Army Headquarters in Rawalpindi. In this brutally professional, painstakingly planned assault, nine soldiers and nine militants were killed along with two civilians, even as the militants took forty-two hostages.[8]

- In Basra in March 2010, terrorists blew a hole in the military base's wall and entered, killing six soldiers and wounding fifteen before twenty-five of their own fighters were killed.[9]

- In 2011, in one of their most daring and meticulously organized raids, black-clad terrorists stormed and occupied the Mehran Naval Air Force base in Karachi, which is only fifteen miles from a reputed nuclear weapons storage site near Masroor. They not only knew the locations of the base's surveillance cameras, they also knew how to neutralize them. In this operation, fifteen attackers killed eighteen military personnel and wounded sixteen. They also set fire to several state-of-the-art warplanes with rocket-propelled grenades.[10]

- In July 2012, militants assaulted a military base near Wazirabad in Punjab, killing seven security personnel.[11]

- In August 2012, dozens of terrorist attacked an army installation, again near Wazirabad, killing eight soldiers. The press reported that many of the victims were decapitated.[12]

- On February 2, 2013, *The New York Times* reported that Tehrik-e-Taliban Pakistan militants killed nine Pakistani soldiers and four government-hired mercenaries—possibly more—in an assault on an army base in the Khyber-Pakhtunkhwa Province. The militants were equipped with military machine guns and rockets; they also murdered ten civilians. A spokesman for the terrorists said they were avenging the drone assassinations of two Tehrik-e-Taliban leaders.[13]

The raids on the Rawalpindi General Army Headquarters and the Mehran Naval Base were amazingly sophisticated. The terrorists' equipment and expertise included such tactics and materials as in-depth reconnaissance, diversionary explosions, the counterfeit tagging of vehicles, critical knowledge of their enemy's numbers and defenses, the penetration of a half-dozen security perimeters, detailed maps, military personnel disguises, falsified documents, and high-powered weaponry. Utterly ruthless, those terrorists who weren't killed during the raid attempted or succeeded in blowing themselves up.[14]

It *Can* Happen Here . . .

In his book, *The Last Refuge: Yemen, al-Qaeda, and America's War in Arabia,* Gregory Johnsen, a noted al Qaeda expert, has argued that the organization is alive and robust. Johnsen explains that Saudi al Qaeda and Yemeni al Qaeda merged into al Qaeda of the Arabian Penisula and that the merger was a turning point. Since then that organization has expanded exponentially. In 2009, Johnsen said, al Qaeda

---

of the Arabian Peninsula had 200 to 300 active terrorists. Now the State Department puts that number at a few thousand and that their growth is still enormous despite the drone assassinations.[15]

Johnsen also wrote that al Qaeda will continue to attack America. Al Qaeda not only issues these threats publically, since 9/11 they have launched three separate attacks against the U.S. Their most notable attempt was on December 25, 2009, when an aspiring suicide bomber tried to blow up an airliner as it approached Detroit. Johnsen predicts their increased numbers will help them with future attacks. "When [al Qaeda] tries again—and it will—the organization will be able to draw upon much deeper ranks," he wrote in a *New York Times* op-ed piece.[16]

Johnsen believes part of al Qaeda's anti-American motivation comes from U.S. drone attacks. While drone attacks have obviously decimated the al Qaeda leadership, they have also catalyzed the organization's recruitment of new terrorists. The drone attacks in Yemen, Johnsen demonstrates, have killed significant numbers of civilians—numbers which some U.S. officials seriously understate, deny, or ignore.[17] Moreover, many drones, armed with Hellfire missiles, fly as low as two thousand feet and are visible on the ground with the naked eye. Yemenis and Pakistanis can look up and watch these Hellfire drones wheeling overhead, searching for their targets, never knowing when and where they will strike. The drones are an indelible reminder that the U.S. believes it has a right to observe and kill them, anytime, anywhere. Nor are all the drone deaths terrorists. As

Johnsen says, the numbers of civilian drone deaths are "significant."

If Yemeni drone attacks are fueling al Qaeda's desire for revenge against the U.S., the strikes are also provoking Pakistani rage with an even greater vengeance. As of the writing of this book, Pakistan has experienced approximately ten times as many drone strikes and fatalities as Yemen. The total number of Pakistani drone strikes at this moment is 366. Total Pakistani drone strike fatalities so far are between 2,537 and 3,581. Up to now, the number of Yemeni drone strikes is between 43 and 53. Yemeni drone strike fatalities, as of the writing of this book, are between 228 and 325.[18]

That Pakistan's government officials and workers can't be trusted makes the war against nuclear terrorists almost impossibly difficult. America's then ambassador to Pakistan, Anne W. Patterson, expressed this frustration in a WikiLeaked memo, in which she said she did not worry about Pakistani terrorists stealing nuclear bomb-fuel as much as she feared government employees smuggling it out, peddling it to terrorists, or constructing a crude terrorist nuke themselves . . . and, as we shall see, building a crude but powerful nuclear device is not particularly complex.[19]

At the highest levels, the mistrust between the United States and Pakistan is mutual. The American and Pakistani leaders view each other as irreconcilable enemies; in Pakistan, fear of the U.S. verges on the pathological. They are so afraid that the United States—and India—will learn the location of the nuclear weapons, they transport them from storage site to storage site in anonymous delivery vans, acting out a nuclear version of "musical chairs." Unfortunately, this system also increases their vans' and their bombs' vulnerability to terrorist hijackers, to whom sympathetic workers, or even officials, might have given the vans' schedules and itineraries. Pakistan's leaders, however, fear that the U.S. or India will steal their bombs more than they worry about their own indigenous terrorists stealing the bombs and detonating them on Pakistani soil . . . perhaps in a terrorist coup attempt.[20]

During the pre-interview, I told the History Channel producer with whom I was working that the terrorist attacks on Pakistan's nuclear facilities and military bases also bothered me to no end and that such attacks should have terrified the American president as well. The attacks demonstrated that Islamist nuclear terrorists could practice their catastrophic craft in America as well as in their homeland. Compared to Pakistan's installations, U.S. nuclear security, as we shall see, is preposterously lax.

Furthermore, the consequences of a nuclear power plant attack and its subsequent meltdown would be intrinsically unmanageable. If these Pakistani terrorists melted down the Indian Point nuclear facility near New York City, the evacuation zone would cover communities totaling 20 million people. San Francisco—near the Sandia nuclear weapons lab—would be another prime target.

If they could do it *there*, they could do it *here*.

Islamist terrorists have already targeted U.S. nuclear power plants. The 9/11 terrorists had considered taking out the Indian Point nuclear power plant, and a man, Sharif Mobley—who was connected to al Qaeda terrorists and who is also a U.S. citizen— worked at six U.S. nuclear power facilities. According to *The New York Times,* Sharif had "unescorted access to the interior of the plants," so he might very well have been gathering intelligence on those plants for future assaults. He had also frequented known terrorists, including Anwar Awlaki, an American-born al Qaeda chieftain, who was on the U.S.

government's hit list and whom the U.S. killed on September 30, 2011 in a drone strike.[21]

In 2010, Mobley was captured in Yemen. Although he has not been convicted of terrorism, he did shoot and kill one Yemen agent, then wounded another in a Yemen prison hospital.[22]

Perhaps most troubling is that during Mobley's six years of nuclear power plant employment, he spoke openly of his jihadist beliefs and referred to his fellow non-Muslim workers as "infidels." His extremist views were known within the plants but no one contacted the Nuclear Regulatory Commission or the Federal Bureau of Investigation. The lapse in nuclear security appeared to be systemic, and Senator Charles Schumer (D-NY) demanded an inquiry. The report documented severely flawed procedures for detecting and exposing potential terrorists in the employment of the nuclear industry, and the problems were national in scope.[23]

After Sharif Mobley was apprehended in Yemen, President Obama did nothing additional to protect U.S. cities and their nuclear facilities against people like Mobley and Pakistan's terrorist teams. Obama seemed to believe that these enemies would not strike U.S. nuclear installations. If so, his assumption was fatuous. By that line of reasoning, al Qaeda could not have flown to New York City and flattened the towers at the World Trade Center.

By that logic, the events of 9/11 never happened.

I also told the History Channel producers about the lack of physical security at U.S. nuclear power plants. Those installations cannot effectively defend themselves against terrorist assaults. The Nuclear Regulatory Commission holds the federal government responsible for the defense of nuclear power plants, not the plants themselves or the private security firms which they hire. The nuclear industry, however, has successfully prevented the federal government from truly protecting U.S. nuclear power plants. The industry seems to fear that upgraded security would lead to more stringent regulations, inspections, and increased expenses. As it stands, plant personnel are neither trained nor equipped to confront the sort of formidable force which attacked the United States on 9/11—a team totaling nineteen professionally trained killers.[24]

Even worse, melting down nuclear power plants is so surprisingly simple, Sharif Mobley might well have been overtrained. Once terrorists commandeer the control room, they can set the fuel rods on fire in minutes—and that method actually means they are melting down a power plant the hard way. They don't have to enter the control room at all. As Japan's Fukushima Dai-ichi nuclear disaster in 2011 taught us, if terrorists merely disable the plant's cooling system, they could incinerate the power plant's reactor cores and storage pond encasements. A few well-placed bombs would cut off the water needed to cool the reactor and toxic waste pools. Once the fuel and spent fuel rods caught fire, extinguishing those fires would be an interminably difficult operation. Fukushima proved that.[25]

Most Americans do not understand how costly such meltdowns are or how many decades a cleanup would take. A major plant disaster can irradiate and render uninhabitable as much as 27,000 square miles—an area the size of New Jersey, Connecticut, and Maryland combined. A study done in the 1960s by the Brookhaven National Laboratory and the Atomic Energy Commission concluded that a major nuclear power plant meltdown could contaminate "an area . . . equal to that of the State of Pennsylvania." Cleaning up the 2011 Fukushima meltdown will take forty years.[26]

If the nuclear power plant was located near a large urban area, the total cost to taxpayers could be as much as $11 trillion—70 percent of America's Gross Domestic Product (GDP).[27]

I told the History Channel producers that the Obama administration's failure to properly secure our nuclear facilities, like that of the previous Bush administration, ought to disturb everybody. That failure indicates that neither of those administrations understood how doable nuclear terrorist strikes truly were. (Why we haven't been hit thus far is a subject we will discuss later at some length.) Obtaining nuclear bomb-fuel is relatively simple. Russia still has six hundred tons of weapons-usable nuclear bomb-fuel, and as the storage sites are so numerous and spread out, Moscow cannot adequately control their security . . . particularly given Russia's pervasive corruption.[28]

Most people, moreover, do not understand how improperly safeguarded U.S. nuclear bomb-fuel storage sites are. The U.S. nuclear weapons labs have occasionally run tests in which undercover security workers sneaked into the labs and attempted to steal nuclear bomb-fuel. According to the best evidence, 50 percent of the time they succeed—even though the testers often told the weapons lab's security officers in advance when, where, and how the operation would be conducted. In one such exercise the mock-terrorists trundled the nuclear bomb-fuel out of Los Alamos—birthplace of the atom bomb—in a Home Depot garden cart. They were apparently curious to test how much nuclear bomb-fuel they could steal, so they loaded the flat-bedded garden cart with canisters of nuclear explosive canisters, then walked openly out of the front gate.[29]

During tests at the now closed-down Rocky Flats facility—a U.S. nuclear weapons lab sixteen miles from Denver and ten miles from Boulder, Colorado—disguised terrorists gained access to the twenty tons of bomb-grade fuel stored there and beat the guards 80 percent of the time.[30]

An 82-Year-Old Nun Breaks into the Oak Ridge Nuclear Bomb-Fuel Site . . .

"Sister Megan Rice, 82," *The New York Times* reported in August 2012, "a Roman Catholic nun . . . and two male accomplices [ages 63 and 57 respectively], have carried out what nuclear experts call the biggest security breach in the history of the nation's atomic complex, making their way to the inner sanctum of the site where the United States keeps crucial nuclear bomb-fuel parts and fuel."[31]

The three pacifists—late at night, equipped with bolt-cutters and flashlights—had cut through three to four security fences as well as through barbwire. Ignoring motion detectors and surveillance cameras, they crossed the compound and stopped at the Highly Enriched Uranium Materials Facility, part of the Oak Ridge Y-12 installation. Sometimes called the nuclear establishment's "Fort Knox," this $500 million building is surrounded by guard towers. The major storage facility for the country's bomb-grade highly enriched uranium, it contains over one hundred tons of bomb-grade highly enriched uranium, enough to build thousands of Hiroshima-style bombs. As we shall see, the material is so explosive real terrorists could have detonated it inside the building once they got their hands on it. Sister Megan and her pacifist friends reportedly splashed small amounts of human blood and hung banners on the facility walls. One banner contained the words: "Swords into plowshares. Spears into pruning hooks," citing Isaiah.

According to one report, they spray-painted the walls with peace slogans, such as "Woe to the empire of blood" and "The fruit of justice is peace." They then sang peace songs such as "Down by the Riverside" and "Peace Is Flowing Like a River."[32]

The New York Times reported that the pacifists "apparently spent several hours in the Y-12 complex before they were stopped by a lone guard." Even though they set off "numerous alarms and sensors," the security personnel seem to have ignored them.[33]

Guards were suspended, other personnel reassigned, patrols increased, and a specialist was brought in to evaluate Y-12's security. Nonetheless, security at the facility could continue to deteriorate. The *Knoxville News* reports that the "break-in at Y-12 came just days after WSI, the government's security contractor in Oak Ridge, confirmed plans to eliminate about 50 security jobs in Oak Ridge—including 34 security police at Y-12."[34]

In 2007 the head of the National Nuclear Security Administration was dismissed after security lapses were detected. Little has seemed to change. The Department of Energy's Inspector General's report on the break-in stated that the three reached their objective because of "multiple system failures on several levels." These failures included refusal to respond to alarms, broken surveillance cameras, and poor communications. An unidentified government source said that some of the cameras weren't operational and others were incorrectly positioned.[35]

Many people felt the trio should have been commended for alerting the Energy Department to critical holes in its nuclear security system. More than three thousand citizens petitioned Attorney General Eric Holder to grant the three pacifists leniency. In the case of the 82-year-old nun, Sister Megan, a long sentence would be a death sentence. Nonetheless, Holder's Justice Department charged and convicted the three of multiple felonies, including sabotage and terrorism. As of the writing of this book, each could receive up to thirty-five years in prison. Ironically, Attorney General Holder is the same man who, according to *Frontline*'s documentary "The Untouchables," had failed to thoroughly investigate Wall Street executives who profiteered off the subprime derivative mortgage scandal of 2008. According to the documentary, Holder's Justice Department presided over no major indictments and convictions of those directly responsible for the subprime meltdown. Holder had no problem, however, prosecuting an 82-year-old nun who had the temerity to expose the grossest kinds of security lapses at U.S. nuclear storage sites.[36]

I told the History Channel producers that our politicians did not grasp how relatively simple it was to assemble a Hiroshima-style terrorist nuke, and that bothered me as well. Fabricating nuclear bomb-fuel is complicated, but once the terrorists had it, a horrifically powerful terrorist nuke was "something even a high school kid could make," to quote Luis Alvarez, the man who built the Hiroshima bomb's triggering mechanism. Nuclear physicist Frank von Hippel has demonstrated that if a person simply dropped a hundred-pound grapefruit-size chunk of bomb-grade highly enriched uranium (HEU) onto another chunk from a height of six feet, he could produce 50 percent of the Hiroshima yield. If he placed a smaller chunk in a short piece of cannon barrel—and the United States has thousands of old cannon barrels left over from the Civil War—and blasted one chunk into the other with extra high explosive, he could conceivably produce the Hiroshima yield.[37]

Does Iran Have a Nuclear Weapon?

If Iran spent the money and expended the effort necessary to steal nuclear bomb-fuel, they would have at least one bomb, and it is only prudent to assume they do. Moreover, Iran's Hezbollah would have found it far easier to obtain bomb-grade HEU from Russia's far-flung storage sites than other terrorist organizations. After all, Russia built Iran's Bushehr nuclear power plant, and the Iranians have paid Russia huge sums already and continue to pay them handsomely for that assistance. Iran has powerful allies at the pinnacle of Russia's atomic energy ministry, Rosatom, and cobbling together a crude terrorist nuke is a fairly straightforward process.

Iranian terrorists would find such a nuke preferable to a bomb fueled by their own nuclear bomb-fuel factories. Since the stolen nuclear bomb-fuel would be fabricated abroad, nuclear forensics would not reveal Iranian DNA or detect a Persian fingerprint. Retaliation against Iran would be complicated, since we would probably have no evidence that they were the guilty party.

Nor is bomb-grade plutonium or highly enriched uranium—as opposed to their impure oxides and compounds, including nuclear waste—that difficult to manipulate. Terrorists could safely handle either if they had no open cuts on their skin. Plutonium emits only alpha rays, which are effectively blocked by healthy undamaged skin. For that reason, both fissile bomb-fuels are relatively easy to smuggle into the United States. They can also defeat radiation detectors with surprisingly little shielding.[38]

During his first term, President Obama said his scariest nightmare was the nuking of a single U.S. city. I told the History Channel producers even that statement troubled me because it revealed an inadequate understanding of our nuclear terrorism nightmare. A single nuking was in no way America's worst nightmare scenario. So much nuclear bomb-fuel has been available for so long that truly ambitious terrorists would find no shortage of ineffectually guarded nuclear explosive. They would not necessarily have to stop at a single detonation. They might choose to stockpile enough nuclear bomb-fuel to arm half a dozen panel trucks, each with a Hiroshima- or Nagasaki-style terrorist nuke, which they could then set off in half a dozen major American cities.

If such a nuclear device exploded in front of the New York Stock Exchange, it would devastate the global economy for decades to come.

Nor, in all likelihood, would the ultimate perpetrators be tracked down. Disintegrated by the blast, the suicide bombers would leave no forensic evidence. To avoid retaliation—quite possibly nuclear retaliation—state sponsors and associates would hide behind masks of silence and anonymity . . . and leave no clues.

Nuclear power advocates, such as Barack Obama and George W. Bush, have never acknowledged that nuclear power reactors—with low-tech enhancements—are de facto nuclear bomb-fuel factories. A 1977 Oak Ridge study proved that just by using the equipment from an old dairy or winery, low-tech terrorists could construct a primitive but effective nuclear bomb-fuel reprocessor in six months. In another month they could reprocess enough plutonium from the nuclear power reactor to build the Nagasaki bomb. A 1998 Los Alamos study demonstrated that it was not always necessary to reprocess the fuel from a nuclear power reactor to power a one-kiloton nuclear blast.[39]

Nonetheless, President Obama enthusiastically supported nuclear power, and that support has frightened me inordinately. Nuclear power has always been the Trojan Horse inside of which the nuclear proliferators have hidden. Nonetheless, the Obama administration sought to facilitate the sale of nuclear power reactors to Saudi Arabia. Fifteen of the nineteen 9/11 hijackers were Saudis and while Hillary Clinton was secretary of state, she stated in a Wiki-leaked memo that Saudi Arabia is the premier financier of Islamist terrorism in the world, saying, "Donors in Saudi Arabia constitute the most significant source of funding to Sunni terrorist groups worldwide." She also complained that Saudi officials refused "to treat terrorist financing emanating from Saudi Arabia as a strategic priority." Still, the Obama administration continued its attempts to assist in selling the Saudis these de facto nuclear bomb-fuel factories . . . even as he and his state department officials were poring over Secretary Clinton's incendiary e-mails.[40]

Perhaps most frightening of all is the fact that too often high-ranking officials have made money off the corporate financiers of nuclear rogues. Donald Rumsfeld, for example, was a board director at a Swiss firm which tried to sell nuclear reactors to North Korea. Dick Cheney was CEO of Halliburton when it did business in Iran and Iraq. Halliburton's business dealings could have financed those nations' nuclear industries. The Bush administration was heavily staffed with oilmen, who enriched themselves off the Middle East's petrol-wealthy nation-states, most notably Saudi Arabia, which was al Qaeda's number-one paymaster, even as that country was (and still is) funding Pakistan's nuclear weapons program.[41]

That people in high places can personally traffic with those who wish us harm, perhaps nuclear harm—is truly frightening. Lenin once said that when the Bolshevik-terrorists came to hang the West's capitalists, those whom they wished to dispatch would sell them their own death-ropes. Thankfully, that transaction was never consummated, but had Lenin substituted "nuke" for "rope," he might have been genuinely prophetic.

We have sold our enemies enough nuclear know-how and technology to blast our major cities and nuclear sites into bloody oblivion.

But enough of that for now.

We will get to all of these issues later and in greater detail.

PART I

BARACK OBAMA: A STUDY IN NUCLEAR DENIAL

1

OVER 100,000 NUCLEAR SHIPMENTS— A CHERNOBYL ON WHEELS[1]

Too much nuclear bomb-fuel has been too available for too long, and, as we have seen, once sophisticated terrorists acquire it, fabricating a small Hiroshima- or a Nagasaki-style nuclear device is not overwhelmingly difficult. If they have thirty-five pounds of highly enriched uranium (HEU), a small group of unskilled people with low-tech equipment can build a Hiroshima-style terrorist nuke.[2]

Unfortunately, rather than confronting nuclear proliferators, aspiring nuclear terrorists, and most importantly their paymasters, the administrations of George W. Bush and Barack Obama . . . enabled them.

Obama's nuclear proliferation policies reflected Bush's to a disconcerting degree. In fact, as we shall also demonstrate later, at times he pursued the Bush policies with greater tenacity than Bush did—a tenacity that his supporters did not anticipate.

"Until we can make certain that nuclear power plants are safe . . . I don't think that's the best option," Obama had said in one campaign speech. "I am not a nuclear energy proponent," he claimed another time.[3]

Consequently, his almost monomaniacal support of nuclear power left many of his supporters dumbfounded.

We will discuss Obama's apparent mind-change, but for the moment, let us examine his seeming disregard for the nuclear proliferator's threat—and by extension that of the nuclear terrorist. President Obama never treated nuclear proliferation as a serious problem. Instead of reining in nuclear proliferators, at home and abroad, he sought to retail nuclear power reactors—every proliferator's holy grail—by offering them to some of the most unreliable nations in the developing world, including Saudi Arabia, India, the United Arab Emirates (UAE), and even Iraq.[4]

Before Egypt erupted in flames in 2011, it announced that it would issue a tender for building four nuclear power plants. Its minister of electricity, Hassan Younes, told Reuters that the United States expressed interest in building nuclear power reactors for them, too. What the Egyptian rebels, rioters, and administration partisans would have done with three or four completed nuclear reactors during their revolution is painful to contemplate.[5]

Throughout his political career, Obama never acknowledged nuclear power proliferation's dark side—it is the perfect cover for developing nuclear weapons and once the nuclear reactors are built nothing short of a military invasion can definitively destroy that nation's nuclear weapons program. Iran and North Korea are cases in point. But instead of fighting nuclear proliferation, Obama became that industry's most effective advocate since Dwight David Eisenhower, who created the global nuclear proliferation industry with his "Atoms for Peace" speech—something we will discuss in detail later.

Obama also seemed indifferent to the threat nuclear waste posed to the nation.

Given the almost incomprehensible virulence of spent fuel, one would think that Washington would have outlawed its creation and shut down the industry's current reactors as soon as their licenses expired.

Not so.

Instead, in 1987, President Ronald Reagan convinced Congress to begin building a central repository for that industry's soaring

Preternaturally Poisonous for . . .
250,000 Years!

The most overwhelmingly toxic substance on Earth, people do not have to ingest or even touch nuclear reactor waste in order to die from it. Standing in its presence will kill a person. Moreover, nuclear waste remains poisonous for as long as 250,000 years—longer than Homo sapiens have been in existence. Sequestering this waste in secure, isolated, leak-proof storage facilities over so many thousands of centuries has proven to be an absurdly quixotic quest. The nations of Earth have too much waste, and produce too many tons of it each year to make safe storage achievable. Humanity cannot even contrive warning signs—which would prove decipherable in a quarter of a million years—for their waste dumps.[6]

edifice of radioactive refuse—which, during the Obama administration, weighed over seventy-five tons. The industry adds to that quantity 2.2 tons annually and were those endlessly lethal rods all packed together like sardines, they would take up 160,000 cubic feet. Of course, were they thus crammed together, they would also chain-react.[7]

Reagan's permanent storage site for this nuclear nightmare was to be Yucca Mountain, less than a hundred miles northwest of Las Vegas. Washington eventually spent over $11 billion on the Yucca

---

400,000 Tons of Nuclear Waste—
No Permanent Storage Plan in Sight

By the time of Obama's presidency, the nuclear nations had produced almost 400,000 tons of high-level radioactive waste. Were it all compressed, its total volume would come to 750,000 cubic feet—except, as we said, it would burst into flames. The world creates an additional ten thousand tons of such waste annually. Given nuclear waste's immense volume, tonnage, toxicity, and growth rate, one would think that the planet would have found a permanent repository for it by now, or would have put the industry out of its misery.

The world has tried to find that vault of eternal rest. For sixty years, people have tried. However, the human race hasn't found it yet, and in all likelihood never will.

Even the most ardent nuclear hawks cannot describe a definitive storage system that is currently feasible.[8]

---

storage site—a deep stainless-steel-lined mine shaft bored into the mountain, and the Bush administration estimated that were the United States to finish it, the total cost would run $90 billion. To pressure the Department of Energy (DOE) into finishing the facility on time, Congress ordered the completion of the Yucca Mountain site by 1998; failure do so required $1 billion a year in fines and penalties, payable to the nuclear industry. Since 1998, U.S. taxpayers have ponied up $1 billion a year in tribute to the nuclear power industry.[9]

Why did U.S. citizens have to pay such extortionate late fees to the nuclear power companies? Why didn't the nuclear utilities build their own geologic repositories and not the government? Why did taxpayers and utility rate-payers have to finance and underwrite virtually 100 percent of nuclear power's costs, all the while bearing its eternal fiscal and physical liabilities?

Obama offered no answer to these questions.

It was as if the nuclear power's hawks were corporate socialists, who believed that U.S. taxpayers worked for the industry.

Even so, a storage site had to be found. Nuclear physicists agreed almost unanimously that the most secure resting place for America's waste would be a geologic repository deep inside of a mountain. The solution wasn't perfect by any means. Over so many hundreds of millennia, the storage sites would be subject to flooding, earthquakes, even sabotage; if nothing else, simple plain deterioration and leakage. Still "a deep geologic repository" was the only answer scientists could come up with, which was why in 1987, President Ronald Reagan and the U.S. Congress agreed on such a storage site: the tunnels of Yucca Mountain.[10]

Sequestering so many tons of frighteningly flammable waste necessitated a mountainous amount of storage space. The Department of Energy would have had to bore forty miles worth of tunnels, each of which would have to be at least twenty-five feet in diameter, after which the country would have to spend several decades hauling waste into that stony labyrinth. Even before the DOE filled it up, however, it would have to find and open up another forty miles worth of twenty-five-foot-in-diameter tunnels in which to stow what its nuclear plants had again accumulated, after which the DOE would have to honeycomb another mountain with another endless maze of nuclear mine shafts.[11]

On and on, ad eternam, ad infinitum.

Or until the entire nuclear industry disappeared into one vast, apocalyptic meltdown or the industry ran out of mountains to despoil.

Obviously, most Americans feared—even hated—the Yucca Mountain repository . . . for good reason. Not only was the site itself a seismic hazard, transporting the spent fuel to Yucca Mountain would be a potential "Chernobyl on wheels." The caravans of boxcars—one-third of which would pass through metropolitan Chicago—would be an open invitation to terrorists.[12]

So when Obama took office, he came up with a plan that would allow the nuclear power industry to expand and at the same time alleviate voters' fears of Yucca Mountain. He wouldn't move the seventy-five tons of toxic waste. He'd leave it right where it was—in power plant cooling pools, on the plant grounds—guarded by rent-a-cops. It would stay there until someone figured out what to do with it. In other words, he would kick the can down the road.[13]

Obama's rationale for this storage system was specious in the extreme. America's toxic fuel pools at the reactor sites held 400 percent more nuclear waste than they were built to store. It was as if Obama was trying to cram four hundred pounds of waste into a hundred-pound bag.[14]

Badly Trained, Poorly Armed Rent-a-Cops
for Protection

Obama did place a comparatively small quantity of spent-fuel rods into "dry casks"—steel containers, encased in concrete, filled with an inert gas such as helium. But this temporary fix was expensive—over $1 million per cask—and the life-span of these containers was measured in decades not millennia. Then the casks would have to be cracked open, the rods removed, and the deadly, intractable problem of what to do with them would have to be addressed all over again . . . at great cost, with immense difficulty, and no small risk. Casks only kicked the can down the road and for a relatively brief period.[15]

Moreover, the rods still emitted radiation and are still hot. The air around casks is sometimes 90 degrees. Because of the heat they give off, they are kept aboveground and are dangerously exposed. They are an inviting target for terrorists, such as the brutally professional teams that have been blowing up Pakistan's nuclear facilities, and the nineteen terrorists who attacked the United States on 9/11. Since these casks are also housed, like the cooling ponds, on the premises of the nuclear power plants, they have been dependent on the nuclear industry's badly trained, poorly armed rent-a-cops for protection.[16]

Transporting the spent fuel would be a forbiddingly difficult task. When the plan was still on the drawing board, experts estimated the nuclear energy would need 100,000 individual shipments to load the waste into Yucca Mountain and that the operation would take decades. The shipping routes would take it throughout forty-three states. Wherever that central storage site was located, the country's nuclear refuse would have to travel though most of the United States. The storage sites were just too spread out.[17]

Would those transport vehicles be safe from terrorist attacks? Security at U.S. power plants and weapons labs had proven to be abysmal. Why would transport security on over 100,000 shipments be any better? At any one of the myriad stopping points, a terrorist could slip a bomb into one or more of the nuclear transport vehicles.[18]

And as we have said, one-third of those toxic waste-trains would pass through Chicago.

As we discussed, in the 1980s the Reagan administration passed a law guaranteeing the nuclear power industry the creation of a centralized, permanent nuclear waste repository. The law stated that if the federal government failed to build the repository by 1998, the U.S. taxpayers would owe the nuclear power companies fines and penalties for that failure. The U.S. taxpayers have consequently shelled out hundreds of millions of dollars a year, have paid $2 billion in all to these nuclear companies, and unfortunately the penalties are going up. Nor does transporting nuclear power's intensely radioactive fuel and its toxic waste to a permanent, centralized site—an interim site is against the law—appear even remotely feasible. The waste and the fuel first have to be packed into protective casks, which are massive. Typically constructed of steel and surrounded by concrete, the containers stand over two stories high, are eleven feet in diameter, weigh 180 tons, and can become warm to the touch. Those casks aren't meant for shipping though. In order to transport these silo-size cylinders, they have to be lighter. The maximal tonnage for truck casks is 26 tons, and for rail car casks 125 tons, so the concrete must be removed in order to ship them. For transport purposes, the casks also have to be smaller.

The overall diameter for truck casks must be reduced to 6 feet and their length is 20 feet. The overall diameter for rail casks must be 8 feet, their length 25 feet. These are still big, very heavy objects, however, and their transportation requires powerful, highly specialized equipment, including cask-lifting cranes and in many cases rail lines, most of which the U.S. has not built and installed in sufficient quantities at these sites. The country also lacks the custom-built trucks and rail cars into which the casks would have to safely fit during the course of the casks' journeys—over 100,000-plus cumulative shipments in all. These containers are, for now, literally too hot and heavy to handle and ship safely.[19]

Moreover, at a number of the storage sites the reactors have been shut down. The unused reactor fuel has to be loaded into casks and stored on site. However, since these installations are no longer generating power and profit, the companies have cut back on security. At these locations taxpayers have to pick up the security tabs. The Department of Energy is, as of the writing of this book, sitting on 2,800 tons of such nuclear fuel—which is of course different from nuclear waste—stored at nine different sites. Over all, the DOE is storing casks filled with nuclear waste and rejected reactor fuel at 120 sites.[20]

Obama Never Knew How Dangerous the Pools Were

The Nuclear Regulatory Commission (NRC) stated that power plant cooling ponds could safely store spent-fuel rods for up to one hundred years, then proceeded to extend dozens of nuclear power plant licenses and issue four new licenses based on that assumption. A Washington, D.C., appeals court, however, determined that the commissioners had never researched the long-term safety and durability of those pools. *The New York Times* reported that the commission had not analyzed the storage ponds individually. The NRC never calculated the risk of cooling water leaking out of the ponds or the threat of the fuel rods catching fire.

The court also wrote: "The commission apparently has no long-term plan other than hoping for a geologic repository." The court pointed out that the U.S. government might never create a deep, safe, politically acceptable geologic repository and that "possibility cannot be ignored." The judges went on to say that if the Department of Energy could not find a safe, permanent storage site, nuclear waste would be sequestered in those storage ponds at the nuclear power plants forever.

As we have said, the reason the NRC had claimed— without any evidence or facts—that the pools would be safe for a hundred years was, according to *The New York Times,* "to extend the operating licenses of dozens of power reactors in recent years and to license four new ones."[21]

2

SAFE, EASY-TO-HANDLE NUCLEAR . . .
PLUTONIUM

n 2009, Barack Obama suspended George W. Bush's attempts to resurrect the reprocessing of nuclear waste. Some nuclear power advocates criticized Obama for that action, arguing that reprocessing would solve the waste-storage problem. Most nations, however, do not reprocess spent-fuel rods. The United States stopped doing so in 1976 after India demonstrated that it could fuel and detonate nuclear weapons by using reprocessed nuclear power plant waste. At that point President Gerald Ford suspended plutonium waste reprocessing in the United States, and the next year President Jimmy Carter banned it outright, encouraging other nations to do the same. Ronald Reagan lifted the ban after taking office, but he also stopped the building of civilian reactor reprocessors. The operation was too expensive, and the nuclear industry could not afford them. In fact, nuclear power's skyrocketing construction, financing, spent-fuel storage, and insurance costs made the development of nuclear power plants and nuclear reprocessors economically infeasible.[1]

Nonetheless, reprocessing's advocates have always argued that reprocessing waste was desirable because it reduced it to a relatively safe powder. Still, most of the nuclear nations—twenty-one out of thirty-one—refused to go that route. The ten nations, which continued to reprocess, argued for the most part that their nuclear industries were established well before the ban and were already dependent on reprocessing.[2]

One reason the other twenty-one nations did not reprocess waste was its exorbitant cost. Since nuclear power was already far more expensive than, for example, gas turbine-generated power, the additional cost of reprocessing spent fuel cut heavily into nuclear power's bottom line. A study from The Keystone Center, composed in part by nuclear power executives, stated: "Reprocessing as currently practiced is several times more expensive than a once-through fuel cycle system," and the study concluded that "reprocessing of spent fuel will not be cost-effective in the foreseeable future."[3]

Another reason why most nations don't reprocess is that it doesn't solve the waste disposal problem. Reprocessing only neutralizes a small amount of the toxic waste. Most of the waste remains massively lethal. It must ultimately be sequestered—eventually in a geologic repository, a solution that has so far proven a political impossibility worldwide.[4]

Bush's championing of nuclear reprocessing made no sense—except to other nuclear power enthusiasts. They advocated reprocessing, because its corporate welfare potential was limitless: Reprocessing would require prodigious government subsidies, if it were ever to be viable. It also created the illusion that the bulk of nuclear waste could effectively be detoxified, and of course it can't.[5]

Even worse, reprocessing was exactly how governments separated out plutonium and uranium, and then converted it to bomb-fuel. In fact, almost four hundred tons of plutonium—enough for more than forty thousand bombs—had already been extracted from waste by the world's nuclear reprocessors. Because the United States had stopped reprocessing, it hadn't been burdened with the hard and hazardous task of securing hundreds of tons of additional plutonium, to say nothing of the extortionate expense. Since the reprocessed fuel was relatively safe to handle, it was also easier to steal than current plutonium waste, which is the most toxic substance on earth. Moreover, after smugglers stole the reprocessed plutonium and uranium, tracking the thefts would be next to impossible.[6]

The United States ran a reprocessing facility from 1966 to 1972 in West Valley, New York, and disposal of the unreprocessed waste was a nightmare. Workers were exposed to shocking levels of radiation, and after thirty years of waste disposal and decontamination, the ultimate cleanup was estimated to cost over $5 billion and would take a total of forty years. Furthermore, the cost of building the facility was not included in those figures. In effect, the Department of Energy had turned the site into a massive money pit and toxic waste dump.[7]

Moreover, reprocessing at the installation was prohibitively complex. While the site had the capacity to reprocess 330 tons of spent nuclear waste per year, in reality, the facility could only handle less than one-third of that amount—a total of 640 tons of waste after six years.

Were the United States to reprocess all of its nuclear waste, the global quantity of separated plutonium and uranium would have soared to over eight hundred metric tons and the U.S. would still not know what to do with the vast bulk of lethal waste which reprocessing would not have neutralized.[8]

3

A FINANCIAL APOCALYPSE

When Obama took office, the global financial markets still viewed nuclear power unfavorably. He and the world faced ballooning deficits and a critically urgent need to cut costs. Nonetheless, Obama upped the financial ante on Bush's 2005 Energy Policy Act. In fact, Obama matched Bush's nuclear power allocations, asking Congress to budget over $18 billion for nuclear power plant construction. He eventually asked for a total of $54 billion.[1]

Citibank had analyzed the cost-effectiveness of nuclear power construction after Obama took office. Private nuclear power developers, its report said, faced critical risks in five areas—planning, construction, power price, operations, and decommissioning. The report concluded that nuclear power was financially untenable in all five areas for private firms.[2]

In its paper, "New Nuclear—The Economics Say No," Citibank accused nuclear power's proponents of blinding themselves to the magnitude of nuclear power's liabilities. Focusing solely on the private investors' "planning risk," the nuclear power lobby ignored nuclear power's other unsustainable costs, the Citibank report said, which the nuclear utilities would pass on to taxpayers.[3]

"[T]he risks faced by developers . . . are so variable," the Citibank study stated, "that individually they could bring even the largest utility company to its knees financially."[4]

Electricity consumers could also bear the costs. It's happened in the past. As Peter Bradford, a former member of the Nuclear Regulatory Commission, said, "[Electricity customers] spent tens of billions of dollars saving nuclear power plant owners from large losses, even bankruptcy" during the 1990s.[5]

Furthermore, Citibank considered only a tiny fraction of nuclear power's total costs. The insurance industry's refusal to issue full-coverage policies to nuclear power companies meant that the nuclear industry would be totally liable in the event that security failed and terrorists melted down one or more nuclear power plants and the adjacent waste storage pools. Since nuclear power firms everywhere lack the resources to cover truly catastrophic losses, the U.S. taxpayer would again have to bail out the industry—just as the Japanese taxpayers will cover the crushing bills from the disaster at the Fukushima I Nuclear Power Plant for the next forty years.[6]

Six major investment companies confirmed Citibank's assessment of nuclear power's financial risks, and the Government Accountability Office (GAO) agreed with Citibank's scathing assessment, estimating that if Obama did guarantee $54 billion in nuclear plant construction loans, at least 50 percent of those loans would fail.[7]

Over $27 Billion Worth of Bad Nuclear Loans

The 50-percent failure rate for Obama's nuclear industry loans was a Government Accountability Office (GAO) estimate, which the Obama administration tried hard to ignore and forget. The press, however, would not let them. After Obama launched that program, a reporter told Energy Secretary Dr. Steven Chu about the GAO's estimate. Those defaults would come to over $27 billion worth of red ink. Dr. Chu said he had not known of that study when he signed off on the loan guarantee package.[8]

By one estimate, a combined-cycle gas-turbine power plant could be built in four years for as little as $742.4 million and did not require that governments underwrite insurance, construction loans, plant decommissioning, and eternal waste storage. Critics of nuclear power say that a nuclear power plant requires eight to twelve years of construction. For example, the new Finnish Olkiluoto 3 nuclear power plant is expected to take nine years to complete, and it could take longer than that. The French Flamanville nuclear power plant is also taking at least nine years and is costing $11 billion.[9]

As the Flamanville nuclear power plant demonstrates, construction costs can run $8 billion to $12 billion—most of which would have to be guaranteed by the U.S. government. Furthermore, these amounts are only the tip of the iceberg. During nuclear power's last eight-year building stint, the basic construction costs were as much as four times the initial estimates.[10]

In other words, the money needed to actually build a nuclear power plant could easily outstrip the estimates by 400 percent. Such an increase would make the construction of a nuclear power plant forty to sixty-four times more expensive than the construction of a gas turbine power plant.

Solartopia . . . *for Real?*

Toward the end of this book, we will describe how relatively efficient and inexpensive some of the alternate energies have become, particularly several of the solar power options, most notably the solar-and-wind hybrid systems. Walmart—which is famous for cutting costs—has confirmed the cost-effectiveness of these systems through its actions as well as its words. It has been increasing its reliance on alternate energy systems for quite some time, and it has announced that it will power its United States stores and facilities with 100 percent green energy by 2020 . . . for largely economic reasons. We will examine these issues later in detail.

These estimates, of course, ignore the incalculable sums, which liability insurance, plant decommissioning, and toxic waste disposal will cost. Historically, nuclear power has sometimes generated sky-rocketing electricity bills as well.[11]

These American critics were not alone in their financial assessments. European nations had cut funding for nuclear power after calculating that its expense per kilowatt-hour was higher than that of renewable energy operations . . . particularly after the costs of spent-fuel storage were factored in. The European nuclear power plants under construction—such as Finland's Olkiluoto project—faced explosively high, utterly unanticipated construction costs.[12]

In their push for more nuclear power construction, both the Bush and Obama administrations also ignored the cost-of-money issues. Capital expenses devoured up to 80 percent of the construction budget, because of the protracted building time and vertiginous interest rates.[13]

During the global economic downturn, financial institutions were already tightening their risk-management criteria, and the consequent credit constriction could easily drive nuclear power costs into the stratosphere. In that case, the U.S. taxpayers would face the unpleasant choice of footing even more extortionate nuclear finance charges and interest rates or abandoning the unfinished power plants and choking on the flood of red ink.[14]

In the end, the bills for nuclear power were so exorbitant that only a government could pay them—a scandal which the Bush and Obama nuclear apologists never discussed publicly because that discussion would have instantly revealed the industry for what it is: a corporate welfare glutton and fiscal black hole.

Shortly before the Fukushima tsunami, the Union of Concerned Scientists (UCS) concluded that nuclear power was so expensive that in some instances "buying [non-nuclear] power on the open market and giving it away for free would have been less costly than subsidizing the construction and operation of nuclear power plants."[15]

Peter Bradford—a former member of the Nuclear Regulatory Commission (NRC)—said that employing nuclear power to solve America's energy problems was like buying "caviar to fight world hunger."[16]

$1 Billion in Nuclear Power Bills for . . . *No Electricity?*

Nuclear power's hidden costs can be huge. Even though the San Onofre Nuclear Power Plant had been shut down for over a year due to faulty steam generators and steam tubes, the power company still reportedly charged its rate-payers approximately $1 billion. These bills were for electricity which customers never received.[17]

Prospects for the reactor are bleak. After over a year, the power company reputedly complained that the reactor's manufacturer had no long-term plan for fixing it or replacing the defective parts. The company then decided to permanently shut down the two San Onofre reactors.[18]

A $25 Billion Nuclear Power Plant?

The Voglte Nuclear Power Plant is getting a special accommodation from the Georgia legislature, which has enabled it to bill its customers for "reasonable" costs while the plant is under construction and which also provides Voglte with a safe, fixed profit margin. Florida had a comparable law, which allowed some nuclear power firms to receive regulated profits on nuclear power stations *before* they were under construction. One yet-to-be-built Florida nuclear plant was projected to cost nearly $25 billion. The Florida law has subsequently been modified.[19]

Nuclear Power: The Terrorist's
Nuclear Bomb-Fuel Factory

Citibank and the Government Accountability Office never considered nuclear power's proliferation risks abroad. Their analyses did not include the fact that every rogue state—including nations such as Pakistan, India, North Korea, and Iran—manufactured their nuclear bomb-fuel with the same kind of reactors and centrifuges that their nuclear power firms developed and used.

"During my eight years in the White House," Al Gore said, "every nuclear weapons proliferation issue we dealt with was connected to a nuclear reactor program."[20]

And now sixteen nations in the Middle East and Africa are planning to go nuclear.[21]

Nor did Obama ever discuss publicly the costs nuclear power would impose on the U.S. taxpayers if terrorists successfully melted down a nuclear power plant near a major U.S. metropolis. As we have said in the preface, German estimates for such an attack run as high as $11 trillion—70 percent of the U.S. gross domestic product.[22]

4

THE NUCLEAR REGULATORY COMMISSION (NRC): THE FOX IN THE NUCLEAR CHICKEN COOP

Earlier we discussed how susceptible nuclear weapons labs and bomb-fuel storage sites are to theft. Neither the Bush nor the Obama administrations has ever acknowledged that weakness. They also have never admitted how poorly protected U.S. nuclear power plants are. In the case of those facilities, Bush and Obama only needed to look at how America's nuclear power plants had fared during their force-on-force, mock-intruder tests, and they would have understood how defenseless U.S. power plants were.

In 1991, the Nuclear Regulatory Commission (NRC) began a series of these force-on-force exercises in which bogus terrorists attempted to invade nuclear power plants. Nuclear power companies performed terribly, flunking twenty-seven out of fifty-seven tests. In other words, almost 50 percent of the time, the terrorists won. The tests demonstrated that in a real attack, the mock-intruders could have dramatically damaged the reactor core and created radiological release . . . that is, an American Chernobyl.[1]

The tests were so embarrassing for the nuclear industry that they discontinued them in 1998. However, public indignation and Congress forced the NRC to bring the tests back. The nuclear power industry's record did not improve, and between 2000 and 2001, the nuclear power plants flunked six out of eleven mock-intrusion trials. In other words, the terrorists won over 50 percent of the time. In the real world, those plants would have been staring at critical meltdowns.[2]

After 9/11, the NRC devised a new kind of force-on-force testing, which the owners were to conduct at each plant every three years and which the NRC was to observe. The Union of Concerned Scientists (UCS), however, could not adequately analyze any such tests: They were secreted under a blanket of classification, and they did not require plant fortification against 9/11-style kamikaze aircraft strikes.[3]

During the last public discussion of these mock-intruder tests, the NRC admitted that they were unable to properly analyze the tests because the nuclear power industry disagreed with them sharply over the evaluation of the results. The Union of Concerned Scientists argued that if the NRC wasn't administering severe penalties to those nuclear plants that fail these tests, these plants would also never be properly secured.[4]

Despite the proven lack of protection at U.S. nuclear power plants, the NRC and the nuclear industry refused to seriously upgrade security against eventual terrorist attacks on the industry's facilities— even after 9/11. They argued that terrorist attacks are a government problem, not an industry problem. At the same time, however, both the NRC and the nuclear industry fought off any attempts to protect nuclear facilities with federalized guards.[5]

One possible reason why the industry and the NRC resisted enhancing power plant security could be that the costs of such enhancements could be passed on to the companies. Also, if the public saw how much protection nuclear power plants really needed—if people saw military-trained personnel fortifying these nuclear sites with surveillance technology and multiple defensive perimeters—the public might come to understand the threat that these facilities pose to their local communities.

A Culture of Harassment and Intimidation

Can the NRC become an effective nuclear watchdog? Not given its corrupt, collusive culture. The Union of Concerned Scientists explained:

"[N]early 50 percent of NRC staffers in a recent survey reported feeling unable to raise safety concerns without fear of retaliation and nearly one-third of NRC staffers who had raised safety concerns felt they had suffered harassment and/or intimidation as a result."[6]

Unfortunately, an attack on a U.S. nuclear power plant would not be that difficult to pull off. In tests, the mock-intruders had no problem entering the control room, and once in charge of the control room, terrorists could melt down a reactor in minutes.[7] Fukushima demonstrated that to melt down a nuclear power plant, terrorists did not even have to reach the control room. If they blew up the cooling pumps and intake pipes they could melt the plant down.[8]

The National Academy of Sciences panel determined that if terrorists succeeded in draining the water from a spent-fuel pool, they could quickly provoke a horrific nuclear fire. If a large aircraft slammed into the nuclear plant's control building—a structure that is not built to withstand such assaults—the crash could easily cause a core meltdown and incinerate those nuclear waste pools.[9]

Even worse, some experts have concluded spent-fuel meltdowns were more lethal, costly, and difficult to manage than even a reactor meltdown.[10]

Such a massive disaster could force the evacuation of an area as large as 27,000 square miles, which is more square mileage than New Jersey, Maryland, and Massachusetts combined. In addition, the United States has thirty-five boiling water reactors whose spent-fuel pools project several stories above the earth instead of being buried in thick, concrete containment structures, making them especially vulnerable.[11]

The Union of Concerned Scientists charged for decades that the U.S. Nuclear Regulatory Commission has been far too soft on the nuclear power industry and did not enforce safety standards.[12] Yet even the NRC was concerned that the new generation of reactors was far too fragile. The NRC issued a scathing indictment of Westinghouse Electric Company, a nuclear reactor company that was recently bought by the Japanese company Toshiba. It attempted to sell its new plant, the AP1000, worldwide, even though the NRC believed it would not survive a jet plane crash, which a 2009 NRC rule required. Moreover, none of America's 104 reactors met that NRC requirement, and over two dozen weren't even as strong as the Chernobyl power plant reactor, which in 1986 suffered an apocalyptic meltdown.[13]

And the threat of such a terrorist attack is real. FBI director Robert Mueller testified before the Senate Select Committee on Intelligence that nuclear power plants were an "area we consider vulnerable [to terrorist attacks] and target-rich."[14] Even worse, terrorists do not lack opportunity. Robert Kennedy Jr. found that there were at least eight relatively easy ways for terrorists to melt down a nuclear power plant. He sailed boats up the Hudson River twice to point out to observers the lack of security around nuclear power plants situated on that waterway.[15]

The U.S. government struggles with disaster response. The government's ineffectual response to Hurricane Katrina in 2005, the Deepwater Horizon/BP oil disaster in 2010, and Hurricane Sandy in 2012 underscored the country's essential helplessness in the face of such overwhelming catastrophes. These events highlight how incapable the U.S. government would be in responding to a nuclear power meltdown.

New evidence also surfaced that if terrorists were to target U.S. nuclear power reactors with a Stuxnet-type computer worm—the kind with which saboteurs attacked Iran's Bushehr reactor—they could provoke a Chernobyl-type meltdown. We will discuss this new threat in more detail later.[16]

All this for an industry that is, in the long term, cataclysmically expensive. Ralph Nader described nuclear power as an "insanely dirty and complex way to boil water to generate steam for electricity."[17]

Still the Bush and Obama administrations never explained to the public the stunning feasibility of terrorist attacks, their mortal consequences, and the interminable, illimitable costs they would leave in their wake.

5

The most significant source of funding to
Sunni terrorist groups worldwide.
—SECRETARY OF STATE HILLARY CLINTON
ON SAUDI ARABIA[1]

President Obama is worse than his last several predecessors on nuclear power proliferation. He has come closer than any president since Richard Nixon to making nuclear power proliferation a reality. In South Carolina and Georgia, he provided guaranteed government-backed loans to support the first construction of nuclear reactors in over thirty years.[2]

He was more committed to proliferating these nuclear bomb-fuel refineries to rogue states than his predecessors. His administration has agreed to build two nuclear power plants for India and to allow them to "reprocess U.S.-originated nuclear materials," according to Reuters.[3] The Obama administration is also seeking nuclear reactor sales to Saudi Arabia. The Global Security Newswire quotes a U.S. State Department representative as saying, "We are negotiating [nuclear trade] agreements [with Saudi Arabia]."[4]

Having long ago spurned the Treaty on the Non-Proliferation of

Nuclear Weapons, or the Non-Proliferation Treaty (NPT), India was by definition a rogue state, so to make the sale, Obama also had to defy the NPT. Undeterred, Obama did so, and agreed to build nuclear reactors in India. Moreover, Obama's undersecretary of state for political affairs had signed an agreement, which would authorize India's reprocessing any nuclear waste, which as we have discussed, creates a nuclear proliferation problem.[5]

Obama's reactors would immediately enable India to increase nuclear bomb-fuel production. The more nuclear power plants that the United States sold to India, the more unrestricted reactors India would have available from which to reprocess nuclear waste into nuclear bomb-fuel.[6]

The Obama administration—like the Bush team before them—was also attempting to sell high-tech, first-use delivery systems to India, which include 126 new jet fighters, six C-130J cargo planes, and ten C-17 troop transport aircraft. Many of them could be reconfigured to drop or launch nuclear weapons. The Obama team could eventually sell India as much as $80 billion in high-tech offensive weapons. Obama himself flew to India, hoping to close the deal. Until Bush took office in 2001, U.S. military sales to India had been banned. Under the Bush and Obama administrations, however, these deals were considered major financial coups.[7]

All this . . . even though India had fought at least one war with Pakistan which almost went nuclear.

For decades certain Saudi royals were Osama bin Laden's and al Qaeda's chief financial contributors. Fifteen out of the nineteen 9/11 terrorists were Saudis, and as Amnesty International annually documents, Saudi Arabia is one of the world's major human rights violators; its abuse of women's rights is a perennial Amnesty outrage. As we have discussed, Hillary Clinton—Obama's secretary of state in his first term—reported in a classified dispatch that Saudi financial aid to global terrorists was still an urgent national-security problem, writing that Saudi residents "constitute the most significant source of funding to Sunni terrorist groups worldwide."[8]

Nonetheless, like the Bush administration before him, Barack Obama seemed to disregard the Saudis' history of funding Islamic terrorism. Instead the Obama administration was negotiating nuclear trade agreements with the Saudis, who said they planned to build sixteen nuclear power plants, spending over $112 billion.[9]

Obama inexplicably ignored the fact that providing the Saudis with a nuclear reactor program and a mother lode of high-tech offensive weaponry would accelerate an arms race and proliferate nuclear reactors—that is, nuclear bomb-fuel producers—throughout the Middle East.

Obama was also negotiating the biggest Saudi arms sale of all time—a sale that could come to over $60 billion worth of cutting-edge jet fighters and military helicopters. The Obama sale would include eighty-four new F-15 fighters and seventy more upgraded F-15s. The choppers consisted of seventy Apaches, seventy-two Black Hawks, and thirty-six Little Birds. In a $30 billion naval deal for the Saudis, Obama would supply them with surface vessels and littoral combat ships, designed for maneuvering in coastal waters. Many of these air and naval delivery vehicles could be enhanced and reconfigured to launch nuclear weapons.[10]

The Obama administration also contemplated the sale of Terminal High Altitude Area Defense (THAAD) missile defense systems with the Saudis, which are designed to neutralize short- and intermediate-range ballistic missiles either above or below the atmosphere."[11]

Obama inexplicably ignored the fact that providing the Saudis with a nuclear reactor program and a mother lode of high-tech offensive weaponry would accelerate an arms race and proliferate nuclear reactors—that is, nuclear bomb-fuel producers—throughout the Middle East.

A Saudi Atom Bomb?

Iran seems unswervingly dedicated to acquiring nuclear weapons, and Prince Turki al-Faisal, a former Saudi intelligence director and U.S. ambassador, has stated that the Saudis are equally determined to match an Iranian nuke. "We cannot live in a situation where Iran has nuclear weapons and we don't," the prince was quoted as telling high-ranking North Atlantic Treaty Organization (NATO) officers in the United Kingdom. "It's as simple as that. If Iran develops a nuclear weapon, that will be unacceptable to us and we will have to follow suit."

Many in the U.S. Congress fear the threat of nuclear proliferation by the U.S. nuclear industry and have introduced a bipartisan bill that would enable Congress to block such State Department–negotiated nuclear agreements. The Obama State Department opposes the bill, saying it would make the sale of U.S. nuclear technology to other countries more difficult. At this point, it is unclear whether such a bill will be voted on or what the outcome would be, but the Obama administration is resolutely resisting it.

"Nuclear cooperation with Saudi Arabia?" an unnamed congressional source said. "Maybe that's why the nuclear industry and the administration don't want Congress to have the right to approve all new agreements." . . .

"After publicly insisting that Saudi Arabia must get the bomb if Iran does, anything Saudi Arabia promises in the way of nuclear restraint would have to [be] taken with a ton of salt," said Henry Sokolski, executive director of the Non-proliferation Policy Education Center.

Sokolski and other nonproliferationists are, among other things, concerned about nuclear dominoes falling throughout the Middle East.[12]

The Obama administration was reported to be interested in selling power reactors to Egypt—right up to the moment that a civil war tore that country apart.[13]

WikiLeaks revealed that the United Arab Emirates (UAE) were significant funders of Islamist terrorism.[14] The Obama administration, however, backed their plans to build four nuclear power plants. The U.S. firm ConverDyn signed a uranium fuel contract with them, and the Export-Import Bank of the United States (EX-IM) authorized a $2 billion loan to the UAE with which to buy American construction services and technology to build the plant.[15]

As we have discussed, the list of Arab nations seeking nuclear power reactors also came to include Iraq. Even though Iraq had no functioning government, the Obama administration agreed they should have a nuclear power program, which had the potential to, of course, become a clandestine nuclear bomb-fuel program. When the United Nations (UN) resolution was passed, Vice President Joe Biden—as UN Security Council president for that month—said that the UN was green-lighting an Iraqi civilian nuclear program "in recognition of Iraq's commitment to non-proliferation."[16]

As of the writing of this book, an Iraqi government was still in turmoil. The Shiite, Sunni, and Kurdish political parties were fighting nonstop. Enemies of Prime Minister Nouri al-Maliki charged at one point that he did not want a functioning government and wanted to rule the country unilaterally.[17]

6

We but teach bloody instructions.

—WILLIAM SHAKESPEARE, *MACBETH*

(ACT 1, SCENE 7, LINES 8–9)

During Obama's first two years, the global nuclear industry faced an unprecedented threat. An aggressive—and at the time anonymous—nation used a newly minted, hyper-sophisticated cyber weapon to destroy nuclear reactors and nuclear centrifuge systems via their computerized controlling systems. Named Stuxnet, this computer worm attacked a specific high-tech computer that ran nuclear power plants' automated control systems. It focused on those systems manufactured by the German firm Siemens. That same computer system could also be used to run other components of a national energy system, including pipelines, refineries, electrical grids, and conventional power plants, as well as a variety of factories and mills.

Its primary emphasis, however, was Iran's nuclear program; experts pointed out that 60 percent of the worm's computer attacks were in Iran.[1]

This threat was unique. Without human guidance, Stuxnet could differentiate between an infinite assortment of ultracomplicated industrial computer systems until it found the system it wanted to infect and destroy. It would then wait until the time and conditions were properly aligned for its assault.[2]

This malicious software—known in the industry as malware—was singularly complex. Hackers and even nations had previously engaged in computerized mischief and espionage but had never attacked a country's energy/manufacturing sector bent on systematic destruction. The world had never before seen a potent cyber superweapon aimed at demolishing energy industry control systems, specifically those of a nation's nuclear industry control systems. The private security firms investigating the worm believed that only a nation with a large team of scientists and technicians could have designed, built, and deployed it, and the fact that a Siemens-built nuclear control computer had been singled out meant that the world was entering a new phase of nuclear war: a cyber war targeting specific nuclear reactor computers in which Stuxnet was the first shot over the bow.[3]

Which nation had drawn first cyber blood? "Myrtus"—the name of one of the malware's files—was an allusion to the Book of Esther. In that book Israel preemptively struck Persia—which today is known as Iran—thereby preventing an invasion. Experts pointed out that the malware contained allusions to Iran's 1979 execution of the head of its Jewish community. These same experts, however, also noted that those references were ambiguous and could be mere computer jargon.[4] Other experts wondered whether the United States might have launched or supported the attack. The United States received less than 1 percent of the attacks, which—given the vastness of the U.S. computer network, the distributive nature of the Internet, and the diffuse nature of the attacks—was minute. Still, the worm struck the U.S., and the United States Cyber Command (Cybercom) had been created to detect and defuse exactly this kind of attack. Yet, through-out the first five months of the attack, America's Cybercom was con-spicuously silent. Over and over, private security firms with far fewer resources scooped the U.S. government's experts with their analyses of the worm and their recommendations on how to combat it. In fact, the U.S government merely echoed these private reports, particularly those of Symantec. The United States was unaccountably slow in issuing its reports, which often came out days after the private re-ports were first published. The U.S. government's statements were also released in less detail.[5]

The United States even refused to provide its own firms with useful instructions for repairing the damaged computers and for protecting their industrial control systems from future Stuxnet assaults. It was possible that government officials feared Iran would use these in-structions to repair their damaged computers and to protect their own nuclear program from future cyber assaults. Since the United States and its allies were vehemently opposed to Iran's nuclear program—and these are the nations with the greatest motivation to destroy that program—that line of reasoning was persuasive.[6]

While Iran had denied that the cyber attack impeded their nu-clear program, many experts dismissed those claims as bravado. Iran's nuclear program slowed markedly after the first attacks began in 2009 and has been plagued by problems and delays ever since.[7]

This new form of nuclear warfare carried with it frightening impli-cations. Worms, such as Stuxnet, would be uniquely difficult to spot and analyze. Locating the malware's creator and distributor would be next to impossible. Stuxnet was not even transmitted through the Internet. It entered nuclear reactor computers through vulnera-bilities in laptop software. Infected memory sticks inserted into USB ports spread the worm to the reactor's huge computerized control-ling systems.[8]

This cyber superweapon was almost unstoppable. Its presence and ultimate destruction would not be discovered until it had reprogrammed and wrecked the nuclear computer. It had the potential to sabotage and destroy nuclear reactors worldwide, and because it did not travel through the Internet, the victim nations would not have the ability to trace it back to its perpetrator. Like a successfully detonated terrorist nuke, this new breed of cyber weapon left no fingerprints.[9]

In short, the cyber superweapon had the makings of an untraceable nuclear reactor killer that could shut down other major energy and industrial systems as well. It was only prudent to assume more ingenious, more devastating worms would target the computerized control systems managing other nuclear industries around the world, including the U.S. nuclear industry. The United States had simply too many enemies who wanted to see America's nuclear industry severely crippled.[10]

And computer scientists said Stuxnet could be replicated. "[Stuxnet is] like a playbook," said Ralph Langner, an independent computer security expert in Hamburg, Germany, who was among the first to decode Stuxnet. "Anyone who looks at it carefully can build something like it." Mr. Langner was among the experts who feared that the assault had inaugurated a brand-new form of industrial warfare.[11]

Even worse, some experts believed the Stuxnet worm might be more lethal than experts had originally surmised. Iranian and Russian technicians at the Bushehr nuclear power plant issued a report stating now that the reactor was infected, the Stuxnet worm could have the potential destructive force of "a small nuclear bomb" and could result in a Chernobyl-type catastrophe.[12]

Three *New York Times* reporters argued in a detailed, heavily documented article that Israel and the Obama administration—with perhaps inadvertent assistance from the United Kingdom and Germany—created and spread Stuxnet. They also proved that the target was Iran, explaining that "one small section of the code appears designed to send commands to 984 machines linked together" and that "the Iranians had taken out of service a total of exactly 984 machines that had been running the previous summer." The journalists reported that the Israelis had assembled a system of centrifuges identical to the Iranians' on which to test their cyber worm. The U.S. Department of Homeland Security had teamed up with the Idaho National Laboratory to examine the cyber vulnerabilities in the sort of Siemens computerized controlling systems which ran the Iranian nuclear centrifuges. The two organizations had begun this cyber attack study one year before the Stuxnet worm was discovered. The reporters also had statements from "a number of computer scientists, nuclear enrichment experts, and former officials" backing their assertion that Israel and the United States had cyber-attacked the Iranian nuclear program.[13]

Eventually, members of Obama's own national security team—who had sat in on the meetings at which Stuxnet was developed and its attacks executed—described these discussions to *New York Times* reporter David Sanger. Stuxnet was designed to monitor and report back on Iran's reactor computers as well as eventually disabling the centrifuges. The operation, they said, was nicknamed "Olympic Games," and its astonishingly powerful cyber weapon contained a code that was fifty times as big as the usual computer worm.[14]

Cyber infrastructure protection begins with the companies that own and operate these complex computer systems. Nonetheless, energy firms have been loath to underwrite sophisticated industrial security programs—particularly the kind of in-depth protection required to stop a 9/11-style assault and or a Stuxnet-type attack—as if such systems were an unnecessary expense. They refuse to finance elaborate and expensive cyber defenses as well as government testing of those defenses already in place. Nor has the U.S. government forced corporations to adopt serious cyber safeguards.

The U.S. nuclear establishment is almost universally ill-secured. In the cases of both physical and cyber protection, the nuclear industry's attitude seems to be that if the terrorists melt their plants down, the public will pick up the tab. It has happened before. Russia is still receiving money from over twenty-eight nations for a new twenty-two-ton steel shell, which is needed to seal off the nuclear abyss of Chernobyl.[15] In Japan, Tokyo Electric Power Company (Tepco) also handed off the Fukushima meltdown bill to the Japanese taxpayers. A remittance which will eventually total many trillions of dollars, that disaster will not only burden taxpayers and rate-payers for decades to come, it will do incalculable damage to Japan's economy.[16]

Most energy firms have only upgraded their computerized control systems every ten to fifteen years, some plants less frequently, and most of their systems allow unauthorized uploads.[17] Unfortunately, the Obama administration has not forced the nuclear energy industry to address these security vulnerabilities.

The United States has needed to prepare for Stuxnet's counterattacks. Richard Clarke—the former antiterrorism czar under presidents George W. Bush and William J. Clinton, as well as the cyber warfare adviser to George W. Bush—wrote in his book, *Cyber War,* that China had already sown America's electrical grid with silent cyber bombs that could be set off at the time of a major U.S.–China crisis. Other experts have accused Russia of similar hostile cyber actions against the United States. In 2007, McAfee, Inc., charged China with launching cyberattacks against India, Germany, and the United

States. In 2007, an unknown country penetrated all the U.S. military and high-tech agencies, from which it stole massive amounts of information—terabytes of data. That same year, military agencies in Russia cyber-attacked Estonia's banks, ministries, and media.[18] In early 2009, China allegedly created a cyber-spy network known as GhostNet, which peeked into the private and governmental documents of 103 countries, including many in America. That same year China cyber-attacked America's Google and twenty other companies.[19]

So the 2009–2010 Stuxnet nuclear attack was not the first assault on record. It was, however, the first one aimed at bridging the divide between the digital world and the real world by not just undermining, but actually destroying an industrial, infrastructural target.

Moreover, the nation with the most to fear from a Stuxnet-style worm was the United States. The U.S. had more critical high-tech, computer-run targets in its energy/manufacturing sector which were vulnerable to those ferocious cyber weapons than any nation on earth. As Ralph Langner, who was one of the first experts to discover Stuxnet, wrote, "Any U.S. power plant, including nuclear, is much easier to attack than the heavily guarded facilities in Iran." Nor would the attack require, according to Langner, "a long-term campaign with a sophisticated disguise" to devastate, say, New York's Indian Point nuclear power plant.[20]

The United States does not have any shortage of enemies who wish her cyber harm. The U.S.–Israel malware attack appeared to have delayed Iran's nuclear centrifuge program by eighteen months, and while that was to the good, Obama had also unleashed Macbeth's "bloody instructions, which being taught, return to plague the inventor."[21]

Americans could only guess what kind of "bloody instructions" awaited them down the road.

> "The Sin Ye Do by Two and Two
> Ye Must Pay for One by One."
> —Rudyard Kipling, "Tomlinson"

United States officials and computer experts claim that Iran has already learned its bloody instructions. In retaliation for the Stuxnet worm strikes on Iran's nuclear program, Iran formed the Islamic Revolutionary Guard Corps—their cyber corps, for short—to defend its energy industry from further cyber assaults. The cyber corps seems to have engaged in offensive warfare as well. Computer specialists have already traced a new series of possibly devastating assaults on U.S. energy firms back to Iran.[22]

Iran's goal seems to have been the destruction of data and the computerized commandeering of the systems that control important energy systems, such as oil pipelines. One official suggested that "someone is looking at how to take control of these systems." Iran has also launched a series of less sophisticated cyber assaults on U.S. financial institutions.[23]

7

WHAT JAPAN'S NUCLEAR CATASTROPHE TEACHES US

On March 11, 2011, the Fukushima I Nuclear Power Plant experienced a 9.0-magnitude earthquake, followed by a tsunami. The plant's reactors, their spent-fuel storage pools, and their cooling systems were not designed to survive such an extraordinary assault. Its sea barriers were built to stop tsunamis up to nineteen feet high, not forty-six-foot walls of water.[1]

The quakes and the waves destroyed the plant's cooling system and its external pumps. The cooling water in the reactors and the pools boiled away. A significant portion of both its reactor fuel and its waste decayed, overheated, and caught fire.[2]

Hydrogen explosions detonated in reactor buildings 1, 3, and 4; partial core meltdowns occurred in reactors 1, 2, and 3; some of the spent-fuel rods may have even ignited. Far more radioactive leakage reached the sea than at Chernobyl, some of it contaminating kelp later found on the California coast.[3] The Japanese authorities eventually concluded that at least one of the reactors suffered a meltdown before the tsunami hit.[4]

Unfortunately, the disaster at Fukushima I, also known as Fukushima Dai-ichi, was not unique. The nuclear nations suffered three major catastrophes between 1976 and 2011, and the world had suffered fifteen bona-fide meltdowns since the early fifties—in other words, one every four years. In the year before the Japanese disaster, the United States almost experienced fourteen potential Fukushima Dai-ichis—"near misses," as the Union of Concerned Scientists described them.[5]

The barely averted 2002 disaster at the Davis-Besse Nuclear Power Stations along Lake Erie had the potential to rival Chernobyl, and the United States avoided that cataclysm through blind luck.[6]

Japan's former nuclear regulatory agency—the Nuclear and Industrial Safety Agency—had been notorious for colluding with Japan's nuclear industry, which had routinely lavished largesse on the regulators after they exited the agency. Under the policy known as *amakudari*—"descent from heaven"—regulators often found employment in the very industries they once policed. Critics derided the Japanese regulators as "lapdogs," not "watchdogs."[7]

Too many U.S. members of the NRC—under both Obama and Bush—also joined the nuclear power industry after having spent years allegedly regulating it. One recent member left the commission after nearly ten years to join a firm, a division of which the NRC was charged with regulating. By going to work for the very firm that they were entrusted to regulate, members of the U.S. Nuclear Regulatory Commission create the impression of a potential conflict-of-interest because there would be suspicions that they did not come down as hard on the companies as they should have. After all, they may have hoped to land lucrative jobs with them in the future.[8]

A Japanese whistle-blower named Kei Sugaoka—who had worked for General Electric in Japan—told Japan's Nuclear and Industrial

Safety Agency about a hidden cracked steam dryer in the Fukushima Dai-ichi plant . . . the same nuclear plant which, eleven years later, was to melt down so catastrophically. Had the agency publicized his findings, Tokyo Electric Power Company (Tepco) would have been forced to perform expensive repairs. Instead, the regulators helped Tepco conceal Sugaoka's findings, which included serious splits in the shrouds covering the reactor cores. The firm made no repairs until 2003, when their misfeasance was at last exposed.[9]

The regulators—in violation of Japan's whistle-blower protection law—revealed Sugaoka's identity to the nuclear power industry. They immediately blacklisted him, banning him from future employment in that industry.[10]

When Tepco requested a ten-year extension of the forty-year-old Fukushima Dai-ichi reactor's license, the regulators—after a cursory inspection—approved it. The review, however, overlooked a number of major problems. In one instance, the diesel generators—which backed up the number 1 reactor—suffered from stress fractures. In another instance, one reactor was so deteriorated that the shock of the earthquake caused it to melt down before the tsunami hit.[11]

Prior to the tsunami, those stress fractures also exposed the generators to corrosion from both sea and rainwater. After examining the number 1 unit for less than three days—an amount of time that experts regarded as far too short—the agency granted the extension. Not long afterward, the firm admitted it had failed to inspect thirty-three pieces of cooling-related equipment, including pumps and generators. Tepco confessed to covering up flaws and doctoring data for over a decade, and the regulators admitted that "maintenance management was inadequate" and "the quality of inspections was insufficient."[12]

Nonetheless, these ravaged reactors had passed inspection only a month before the disaster hit. The tsunami flooded out those salt-corroded engines.

The Nuclear Regulatory Commission's own advisory committee attacked the NRC for compromising reactor safeguards. By lowering safety standards, the NRC had increased the likelihood that America could experience a Fukushima Dai-ichi . . . especially when one considered that twenty-three U.S. plants were now subject to Fukushima-style pressure buildup in their containment shells. That kind of pressure buildup helped to melt down the Fukushima reactors.[13]

Critics charge the U.S. Nuclear Regulatory Commission with the same kind of incompetence and corruption that had plagued the Japanese nuclear industry for so many years. In 2007, candidate Barack Obama, before his election to the presidency, stated that the nuclear power industry had taken the NRC hostage. Vice President Joe Biden had also voiced similar assessments, and the evidence that the NRC had systematically overlooked equipment defects was voluminous.[14]

The fourteen "near misses" at nuclear power plants in the United States that took place a year before Fukushima—which the Union of Concerned Scientists (UCS) had reported on—were due to pure negligence. The UCS reported that in twelve of those close calls, the NRC had allowed the plants to operate despite a proven history of radioactive leaks, plant fires, broken pumps, corroded pipes, flooding, and dysfunctional safety equipment. Electrical failure, mechanical failure, and human ineptitude were common.[15]

The UCS found seriously damaged reactors throughout the country—from Maryland to Virginia, to North Carolina, to Ohio, to Illinois, to Nebraska, to California, to Arkansas, to Alabama, to Florida.[16]

Fire did an enormous amount of damage at Fukushima Dai-ichi, and it is a major problem for nuclear power plants everywhere. Among the many terrible disasters it can inflict is the destruction of the control-room cables, which the operators need to cool the reactors. At Fukushima Dai-ichi, when those cables were disabled, the plant operators could not activate the cooling pumps and valves. The reactors and storage pools consequently melted down. Even so, the NRC—just as Japan's negligent regulatory agency had always done—often ignored the nuclear industry's pervasive fire hazards. The NRC routinely disregarded defective fire alarms, fire barriers, fire doors, sprinklers, and unshielded cables—only a few examples. Nor were such problems and oversights unimportant. During the sixteen years preceding Fukushima Dai-ichi, the nuclear power industry experienced 153 nuclear power plant fires. Some of those fires—including the 2009 electrical fire at Washington's Columbia Generating Station and Arizona's Palo Verde Nuclear Generating Station electrical explosion—wiped out the reactors' cooling pumps. The agency ignored fire violations at the South Carolina H. B. Robinson Nuclear Power Plant and ignored reports that the plant lacked the necessary fire suppressors and detectors . . . until its high-voltage cables exploded, knocking out a cooling pump and disabling the plant's power grid. After that incident, the plant was given two years to address these problems. When the plant was several years late in fulfilling this obligation, the NRC extended the deadline to 2016.[17]

The NRC was never naïve about the threat of fire. In 1975, at the Browns Ferry Nuclear Plant in Alabama, the cables caught fire and burned through hundreds of other cables, shorting out equipment and wreaking havoc throughout the plant. The consequences were so grave the NRC significantly tightened its fire-protection rules . . . but then relented and allowed the industry to either disregard or circumvent those regulations. This happened even at Browns Ferry, where, in 2005, inspectors cited the Alabama plant for fire hazards, including vulnerable electrical cables, but then looked the other way. In 2009, inspectors reported that Browns Ferry had done nothing to address the problems and took no action to do so between 2006 and 2009, and at the time of the Fukushima Dai-ichi meltdown, the NRC had still done nothing to enforce its orders and to correct these plant failures.

Inspectors found similar violations at the Calvert Cliffs, H. B. Robinson, Turkey Point, and Indian Point nuclear plants and again, the NRC ignored the multiple dangers, continually extending the deadlines for repairs. At Indian Point, which is less than thirty miles from New York City, Eric T. Schneiderman—New York State's attorney general—stated in a petition that Indian Point had breached fire-control regulations in 275 areas, particularly by not installing fire detectors and for failing to properly protect cables.[18]

The NRC, under Bush and Obama, was so indifferent to fire hazards at America's nuclear power plants that the commission did not even keep lists of the fire security breaches at the plants. By law, a nursing home had to have more fire prevention equipment than a nuclear power plant.[19]

The Obama administration never appreciated the threat posed by the poorly secured spent-fuel rods stored in relatively fragile containment pools, too many of which are mounted aboveground, as were the Fukushima containment pools. As we said before, when Fukushima's cooling system shut down, spent-fuel rods ignited just as the reactor fuel had, and many experts argue that those spent-fuel rods, once aflame, could well present an even greater threat to the United States than that of reactor meltdowns. They certainly had at Fukushima.[20]

The NRC was equally negligent in its analyses of the fire threat that the storage ponds posed. In fact, in 2012, a Washington, D.C., appeals court challenged the NRC authorization of cooling pools as long-term nuclear waste fuel repositories. The NRC never examined them individually and never evaluated the risk of them leaking or catching fire. Nonetheless, the NRC pronounced the nation's nuclear pools safe for one hundred years and, based on that trumped-up pronouncement, extended dozens of nuclear power plant licenses and issued four new licenses, all the time not really knowing where or how the power companies would one day store their waste.

The judges also attacked the NRC for refusing to acknowledge that Congress might never agree to a "deep geologic repository," and the spent fuel would, therefore, be kept in unsafe storage ponds in perpetuity. After all the government, in the end, rejected Yucca Mountain, which had been the country's agreed-on site for decades and which had also been a terrible idea. The truth was the world had no safe, rational way to store and secure nuclear waste for a quarter of a million years.[21]

An American Chernobyl . . . Almost!

Critics charge that the NRC is more concerned with promoting nuclear industry profits than protecting the public,[22] and in 2002, the NRC opted to protect Davis-Besse's bottom line instead of safeguarding the public's health and well-being. Investigators charged them with refusing to order the shutdown of a defective reactor out of concern for both the firm's profits and the industry's overall reputation for safety and reliability. In fact, at Davis-Besse, the United States came frighteningly close to a full-scale Chernobyl-style disaster. Plant workers discovered a pineapple-size cavity in the reactor head. Nonetheless, instead of shutting the plant down, the NRC allowed the plant to continue operating for forty-five days after the year-end extension date. That decision could easily have resulted in a plant disaster. The 2002 incident was only one of six major Davis-Besse incidents in a ten-year span.[23]

Critics of the Vermont Yankee Nuclear Power Station, whose plant design was similar to Fukushima Dai-ichi's, for years charged it had leaked radioactive tritium into the soil and groundwater through a complex of subterranean pipes. Entergy Corporation—the firm that owned Vermont Yankee—responded by denying that such a labyrinth of pipes existed. Nonetheless, the NRC granted Vermont Yankee's request for a license extension only a day before the Fukushima cataclysm.[24]

The NRC would not force the nuclear industry to upgrade its plants. The industry subsequently foisted far too much unreliable, out-of-date nuclear technology on the American public. Over the decades, the NRC had extended the licenses of seventy-one U.S. nuclear plants—almost 70 percent of the nation's nuclear power plants—from forty years to sixty years. This was an increase in expected reactor longevity of 50 percent.[25]

Meanwhile, all the time the NRC was granting these dozens of nuclear plant extensions and issuing these new licenses, the commissioners had never realistically determined where they would put the mountains of toxic waste, which the nuclear industry was producing yearly.[26]

The NRC's inspector general reported that 28 percent of U.S. nuclear power plants never told regulators about defective parts that could provoke serious safety problems. Even worse, American nuclear power plants were filled with one-of-a-kind facilities, many with unique, specially made parts.[27]

The Office of the Inspector General (OIG) determined in 2004 that the U.S. Nuclear Regulatory Commission had failed to upgrade its surveillance and enforcement of nuclear plant security since the Davis-Besse incident.[28]

Obama and his advisers were to the nuclear industry what George W. Bush and his oil-rich entourage had been to the petroleum industry.

A Corrupt, Collusive Culture

For years NRC staffers had told the Union of Concerned Scientists that some of the NRC managers were forbidding inspectors to write up safety violations. When NRC experts filed written objections to a plant's safety performance, staffers said that NRC managers—when evaluating a plant's safety performance—simply ignored them. The UCS report argues that the NRC has had a corrupt, collusive culture and how it has been run by too many managers who harass and intimidate staffers out of raising plant security and safety issues. At one point the UCS concluded that the NRC culture was so corrupt, it needed to be monitored and studied. Until its safety culture became one of honesty, objectivity, and integrity, the NRC itself would be a major obstacle to nuclear power safety in the United States.[29]

Arnold "Arnie" Gundersen, a nuclear-power whistleblower, said, "If you still believe the NRC is a nuclear watchdog, you are probably still sending your money to Bernie Madoff."[30]

Obama's Nuclear Collusion

After the Fukushima nuclear disaster, President Barack Obama asked the NRC to determine whether U.S. nuclear power plants were safe and secure. His newfound faith in the NRC's truthfulness contradicted his earlier skepticism.

Four years earlier he had denounced them as a captive of the industry that they were assigned to watch over, but after taking office, he quickly climbed into bed with the commissioners. His first chief-of-staff, Rahm Emanuel, had been an investment banker whose firm was instrumental in raising the $8.2 billion for the corporate merger which produced Exelon Corporation. Obama's number one political adviser, David Axelrod, was a paid adviser to Exelon. His energy secretary, Steven Chu, was one of academe's most prominent nuclear power advocates. Even after the meltdown of Fukushima Dai-ichi—a nuclear power plant that regulatory misfeasance had turned into a fiscal and medical nightmare—Dr. Chu announced that federal regulators should not postpone construction of new U.S. nuclear power plants because of Fukushima . . . despite the NRC's corrupt, collusive track record. As for Obama, Exelon's employees had deposited huge sums in his campaign coffers for years—at least $395,000. It seems to have been money well spent. *The New York Times* reported:[31]

"[Exelon] was chosen as one of only six electric utilities nationwide for the maximum $200 million stimulus grant from the Energy Department. And when the Treasury Department granted loans for renewable energy projects, Exelon landed a commitment for up to $646 million."

8

And Hell followed with him.

—REVELATION 6:8

No nation on earth could cope with nuclear cataclysms. Just as in Japan, a major U.S. power plant meltdown would produce mass confusion, even chaos. Washington had never had effective programs for dealing with meltdowns. The rules and regulations, the lines of communication, and overall authority for managing a major meltdown had been kept deliberately vague in order to accommodate the vastly varying resources of the different counties harboring nuclear power plants. Grundy County, Illinois, for example, was responsible for setting up and handling Chicago's disaster management systems if the Dresden Nuclear Power Plant suffered catastrophic damage. The difference was that 48,000 people live in Grundy County, and 7 million in Chicago, leaving Grundy untrained, understaffed, and underfunded to handle such an event. No single agency would be in charge.[1]

Some critics argued—as if justifying this industry ineptitude—

that the industry could do nothing, that nuclear devastation couldn't be managed or controlled.

The U.S. health care system was also incapable of managing a nuclear power plant disaster and its consequences. The United States still did not know how, when, or whether to evacuate those living near a nuclear meltdown any more than the Japanese did at Fukushima or the Russians did after Chernobyl or the U.S. did after Three Mile Island. In fact, in all three meltdowns, the initial response of these three nations' leaders was to lie about the seriousness and lethality of the three mega-meltdowns.[2]

During Fukushima, the U.S. government, under Obama, was inconsistent in its instructions to Americans in Japan versus its citizens in the US. When the Japanese initially told those people living within a ten-mile radius of Fukushima to relocate, the Obama administration, rejecting the Japanese order, told Americans staying within a fifty-mile radius to leave. The Union of Concerned Scientists proved that Obama's advocacy of the fifty-mile danger zone was correct. If the New York Indian Point Nuclear Power Plant melted down, the unevacuated residents living within a fifty-mile radius of the disaster could be looking at as many as 562,000 near- and long-term deaths from cancer.[3] Nonetheless, Obama's evacuation policy for those Americans living near U.S. power plants contravened his guidelines for Americans trapped in a Japanese nuclear disaster. In the United States, his guidelines were the same as Japan's: you only evacuate the surrounding area if you live within a ten-mile radius.[4]

Still, if Indian Point melted down and the surrounding tri-state population followed the guidelines Obama gave the Americans living near Fukushimi Dai-ichi, the nearby citizens' evacuation radius would be fifty miles. That danger zone would encompass twenty million people. If the Indian Point Power Plant melted down, how could the country evacuate the twenty million people living near it, a population which would include most of New York City?

The answer is, the country couldn't.

Even worse, one-third of America's population lives within fifty miles of a nuclear power plant.[5]

The United States, like Japan, had fundamentally underestimated the menace of radiation poisoning after a plant disaster. No amount of radiation is safe. Multiple doses of radiation are cumulative in their toxicity. Repeated exposures to moderate doses of radiation can easily equal a single exposure to a massively lethal dose. Moreover, inhaled radioactive particles do far greater damage to people than radiation that hits the skin, and people who live near nuclear power plants in crisis could not avoid breathing the radioactive particles infesting the air. And, of course, spent fuel remains lethal for up to 250,000 years.[6]

A Dramatic Increase in . . . *Permissible Cancer*: Or, a Public Health Policy Only Dr. Strangelove Could Embrace

Obama also authorized a major increase in the permissible levels of radiation in the soil and in the drinking water after a radiological incident. These new permissible radioactive levels would raise the long-accepted 1 in 10,000 cancer rate in people who were exposed to these levels to one in twenty-three persons. Jeff Ruchs, the executive director of Public Employees for Environmental Responsibility (PEER), wrote that the change was "a public health policy only Dr. Strangelove could embrace."[7]

Lacking adequate nuclear catastrophe insurance, the Japanese taxpayers had to cover Fukushima Dai-ichi's costs—not only Tepco's plant damage bills but also reparations to injured and aggrieved citizens as well. Like Japan, America's 104 nuclear power plants also have no realistic insurance coverage nor could they afford the coverage if it existed.[8]

Fukushima's cleanup will take at least forty years. Decontaminating the radioactive buildings, equipment, storage tanks, and reactors will require high-tech robots that the world has yet to design, let alone build.[9]

The catastrophic accident insurance for the world's 443 nuclear power plants is grossly inadequate. The most socialistic business enterprise on the planet, nuclear power ultimately depends on taxpayer bounty. Meanwhile, taxpayers do not understand how prodigious their financial liabilities can be.[10]

So what would be a realistic expense estimate for an Indian Point nuclear disaster? Located approximately thirty miles from New York City, the cost could easily approach or surpass that of Germany's worst-case cost estimate of $11 trillion ... which, as we discussed, would bankrupt America. Furthermore, Indian Point was alleged to be one of the nuclear industry's worst violators of the NRC regulations—regulations that the collusionary agency refused to enforce.[11]

Even worse, Indian Point has been on nuclear terrorists' target lists since before 9/11.[12]

Which was one of the many reasons why banks would not finance the full construction costs of new nuclear power plants. It is also one of the reasons why insurance companies will only insure them for a small fraction of the total amount of fiscal liability that a serious meltdown would incur.[13]

Meanwhile, Japan will stagger for the rest of the century under the economy-busting tax bills, which Fukushima so unceremoniously dumped onto the shoulders of that nation's citizens. That the world fails to heed the lessons of Fukushima is a mistake we may all live to regret.[14]

A New Fukushima Tsunami of Strontium-Poisoned Wastewater

As of the writing of this book, the Fukushima nuclear power plant is getting swamped by another kind of inundation—groundwater, which is deluging its wrecked reactor buildings. Those facilities turn water extremely radioactive, and it threatens to flood the all-important cooling system. In the meantime, workers must pump strontium-infused water out of the facilities and into huge storage tanks, which hold as much water as 112 Olympic-size pools. Fukushima is in serious danger of overflowing those tanks. Officials fear that subsequent flooding could poison the ocean.[15]

The *New York Times* quoted Tadashi Inoue, a nuclear power expert who helped create the plan for the Fukushima cleanup, as saying: "Tepco is clearly just hanging on day by day, with no time to think about tomorrow, much less next year." In fact, some experts believe the flooding is up to 400,000 gallons of aquifer water a day and that the torrent is already poisoning the ocean.[16]

A Fukushima Apocalypse?

Tepco is attempting the removal of over 1,300 spent fuel assemblies . . . which are crammed closely together, weigh a total of 400 tons, and are stored in the cooling pool of Fukushima's number 4 reactor. Ten meters by twelve meters, the pool is constructed out of concrete and its base is situated eighteen meters aboveground. Each rod weighs approximately 660 pounds and is fifteen feet long.

The procedure is problematic. The fuel assemblies have to be extracted from their underwater storage racks, then placed in a heavy steel chamber. The transfer must be performed underwater, after which the chamber must be relocated to a pool in an intact building.

Nor do the conditions at Fukushima favor such an operation. During the initial disaster, an explosion blew the roof off the installation housing the assemblies. The structure was left in danger of collapse, its walls bulging, possibly tilted and sinking. The reactor was badly damaged and the fuel assemblies may be as well. Saltwater—some of which was used to cool the spent rods—also corroded the facility and equipment. For a time the pools were exposed to the air. The cranes and machinery designed to remove the spent rods were wrecked. Moreover, extraction and relocation of the rods is not only a difficult and sensitive operation, the work is usually guided and aided by computers. Reuters quoted Toshio Kimura, a power-plant technician, who had worked at Fukushima for over a decade, as saying:

"Previously it was a computer-controlled process that memorized the exact locations of the rods down to the millimeter and now they don't have that. It has to be done manually so there is a high risk that they will drop and break one of the fuel rods."

In other words, the technicians will be working in relative darkness.

No company has ever attempted the removal of so many fuel rods under such catastrophic conditions on such a colossal scale. The risks will be enormous, and it will take over a year. Among other things, if a fuel assembly was cracked, or if one bundle banged hard enough against another to ignite it or if one got jammed up and caught, the pool could have a huge radiation release. Arnie Gundersen, a U.S. nuclear engineer, said that cooling ponds are designed to counteract heat from nuclear decay, not from a nuclear chain reaction. "The problem with a fuel pool criticality," Gunderson said, "is that you can't stop it."

The nuclear waste in the pool has 14,000 times the amount of Cesium 137 unleashed by the Hiroshima bomb. Nuclear experts Mycle Schneider and Antony Froggat warn that a full release from unit 4 "could cause by far the most serious radiological disaster to date."

If the removal program utterly failed, if the fuel rods caught fire and went critical, if Fukushima's underground aquifer was terminally contaminated, personnel would have to abandon Fukushima. No one could remain near reactor 4 nor reactors 1, 2, 3, 5, and 6. No one would be there to manage the cooling operations of any of those reactors. The entire site would be in danger of an apocalyptic radiation eruption. If Fukushima's radioactive contamination required the evacuation of the nuclear power stations along Japan's east coast, the consequent fires and detonations at those abandoned plants could render half of Japan unlivable. The forced relocation of forty million people, including the city of Tokyo, could become a reality. Depending on windage, and the duration and severity of the cascading disasters, deaths throughout the Northern Hemisphere could number in the millions, or even the billions.[17]

9

BACK FROM THE ABYSS

Given everything we've learned from the Fukushima debacle and Obama's nuclear policies, what course should the United States pursue? Bernie Sanders—independent senator from Vermont—compiled a list of five recommendations:[1]

- A special independent presidential commission to review the safety of America's nuclear reactors and waste sites.

- A moratorium on the NRC's licensing and re-licensing activities.

- Overturning the federal law requiring the government to indemnify the nuclear power industry.

- Redirecting Obama's request for an additional $36 billion in nuclear power subsidies to improve renewable energy technology and energy efficiency.

- Granting states and those people living "in the vicinity of nuclear power plants...a meaningful role in deciding whether or not the safety risk is acceptable."

Wise as Sanders's recommendations were, they fell on deaf ears in both the Obama White House and the Republican-controlled Congress. They were never enacted as legislation. Opposition was too great.

[Y]et repented not of the works of their hands, that they should not worship devils, and idols of gold, and silver, and brass . . . Neither repented they of their murders . . . nor of their thefts.

—Revelation 9:20–21

PART II
A HABITATION OF DEVILS

1

TRADING WITH THE NUCLEAR DEVIL

Many books have been written about the George W. Bush administration. None of them, however, addresses that administration's gravest failing. Once they were out of office, too many members of the Bush team—rather than confronting the nuclear proliferators—worked for firms which made money off their oil-rich backers. Examples of them trafficking financially with "the enemy" are legion:

- According to the Associated Press on October 9, 2004, Dick Cheney, in the 1990s as chairman of Halliburton, advocated lifting U.S. sanctions against Iran. The AP reported that his firm's subsidiaries increased their business with that country. In 2002 Cheney said that Iran was "the world's leading exporter of terror."[1]

- Dick Cheney's Halliburton rebuilt Saddam Hussein's oil industry in the 1990s—even though Cheney would later claim Iraq was developing nuclear weapons. Through this Halliburton reconstruction program, Cheney's firm helped Saddam earn the dollar revenues that Cheney later asserted were financing a nuclear weapons program in Iraq.[2]

- Like Dick Cheney, Donald Rumsfeld voiced his opposition to those nations described by George Bush as "an axis of evil." Unfortunately, that same Donald Rumsfeld had also been a director at Asea Brown Boveri (ABB). While on the board, that firm sought permission to sell nuclear reactors to North Korea under the highly controversial U.S.–North Korea Agreed Framework project. It gained that permission, and contracted for those sales, although the deal later fell through. We could find no evidence that Rumsfeld opposed the sale.[3]

- In the 1980s, Rumsfeld participated in an effort to sell Saddam Hussein, a nuclear-ambitious tyrant, a Bechtel Corporation oil pipeline.[4] The oil revenues which that pipeline might have produced could have bankrolled Saddam's 1980s fledgling nuclear program—a program that was thankfully destroyed by George H. W. Bush during the 1991 Gulf War.

Only a Matter of Time and Intent . . .

Donald Rumsfeld's firm's attempt to proliferate nuclear reactor technology to a rogue state had serious military implications. Nuclear power reactors *are* nuclear bomb-fuel factories to the extent that their waste can be reprocessed into bomb-grade plutonium with relative quickness and ease. Before leaving office, George Tenet, director of the Central Intelligence Agency (CIA), remarked that converting a nuclear reactor to a nuclear bomb-fuel reactor was not that hard. The conversion was only a matter, Tenet said, of "time and intent."[5]

Cheney's Iraqi Oil-Map Meeting: The Ultimate Hostile Takeover

In early 2001, Vice President Dick Cheney convened the major U.S. oil industry executives. At the meeting, Cheney presented them with an Iraqi map, displaying all of Saddam's oil fields and facilities. (This map is available on the Internet.) With the map was a list of the foreign firms to which Saddam was parceling off those oil sites. No U.S. oil companies were listed on the map. As we shall see, many experts believed Iraq's oil reserves to be far larger than the current incomplete geological estimates.

Cheney's map arguably depicted the most valuable oil reserves on Earth, and they were oil reserves denied to U.S. firms—unless the U.S. expropriated them for those U.S. firms.[6]

- In proselytizing for the Iraq War, National Security Advisor Condoleezza Rice notoriously announced on CNN that the United States did not "want the smoking gun [evidence of Saddam's nuclear weapons program] to be a mushroom cloud." Rice had been less vocal in explaining how—two years earlier, as a senior board director at Chevron Corporation—her firm was one of Saddam's top oil customers. Chevron allegedly purchased much of its Iraqi oil illegally. As part of a settlement with New York's U.S. Justice Department and the SEC, Chevron reputedly agreed to pay out $25 to $30 million in fines. Rice's firm was among Saddam's top paymasters. Rice would later claim Saddam spent a portion of Iraq's oil revenue on a nuclear weapons program.[7]

- During the Iran-Iraq War, President George H. W. Bush secretly authorized over $5 billion worth of federally insured loans to Saddam Hussein with which the tyrant purchased arms and expanded his fledgling nuclear weapons program.[8]

- In *House of Bush, House of Saud*, Craig Unger documented Saudi dispersals to the Bush family and their close associates totaling over $1.475 billion. He also reported that immediately after the 9/11 attack, the Bush team ordered a planeload of powerful Saudis—including some of bin Laden's relatives—to be secretly and illegally spirited out of the United States, even though, as former CIA director George Tenet wrote, their relative Osama was at the time America's preeminent nuclear threat.[9]

- Moreover, the Bush administration deleted twenty-eight pages of incriminating intelligence on the Saudis in the 9/11 Commission's Final Report. Dissenting members of the committee—both Republicans and Democrats—reported that almost all of the material was blacked out not because their content breached national security but because they delineated an embarrassing financial relationship between several important Saudis and al Qaeda.[10]

- The Saudis bankrolled much of Pakistan's nuclear weapons program—and consequently Pakistan's global nuclear black market—making the Bush team's financial dealings with the Saudis even more troublesome.[11]

- Nor was "trading with the enemy" a recent phenomenon. In the 1930s and 1940s, George W. Bush's family had traded with the "enemy of enemies." Prescott Bush (George W.'s grandfather) managed the Third Reich's most lucrative investment account in the United States. Prescott Bush's client, Thyssen Steel, helped to underwrite Adolf Hitler's rise in Germany. Thyssen's support for Hitler went all the way back to the 1923 Munich Beer Hall Putsch. Helping to rebuild Hitler's arms industry, Thyssen Steel was also a major backer of Hitler's regime and World War II.[12]

Note: Prescott Bush eventually became a Republican U.S. senator from Connecticut.

Slave Labor Financiers?

The role of the Bush dynasty in the bankrolling of the Third Reich came to light in sixty-year-old declassified documents from the files of the Treasury and Justice departments and the former Office of Alien Property, which were deposited with the U.S. National Archives and the Library of Congress. A lawsuit by two Auschwitz survivors—who sued the Bush family for Prescott Bush's alleged financing of a slave labor Auschwitz coal mine in which they toiled—also produced new evidence of Prescott Bush's early financial relationship with the Third Reich.[13]

2

THE IRAQ WAR:
NUCLEAR DIVERSIONS,
PETRODOLLAR DREAMS

I

The Bush team argued that the United States invaded Iraq to stop Saddam from developing, spreading, and detonating terrorist nukes. George Bush and Condoleezza Rice notoriously warned the world that the "smoking gun" evidence of Saddam's nuclear program might be "a mushroom cloud." Vice President Cheney took Bush and Rice one step further, announcing on *Meet the Press* on March 16, 2003, that Saddam already possessed "reconstituted nuclear weapons"—actual weapons, not simply programs or activities.[1]

These assertions were horribly damaging. The Bush team's exaggerations about an Iraqi nuclear weapons program distracted the United States from the real nuclear traffickers operating out of Pakistan, China, and Russia. The Bush team's focus on Iraq also kept them from confronting nuclear proliferation and its oil-rich paymasters in the Middle East.

The Bush team's disregard for Iran's nuclear weapons program had serious consequences in the Sunni Arab world. In response to Shiite Iran's nuclear expansionism, thirteen Middle Eastern Sunni states—Saudi Arabia, Egypt, Morocco, Algeria, Jordan, the United Arab Emirates, Turkey, Kuwait, Oman, Qatar, Yemen, Syria, and Tunisia—announced that they were developing nuclear programs. *The New York Times* reported: "[Eighty-five] percent of the Gulf States—all but Iraq—have declared their interest in nuclear power. By comparison, 15 percent of South American nations and 20 percent of African ones have done so." While these Middle East nuclear aspirants argued that their nuclear programs were strictly peaceful, too many nuclear programs around the world concealed covert nuclear arms programs in the past. Nuclear power had historically been a ruse behind which rogue regimes prepared, developed, and built their nuclear weapons.[2]

A Middle East Game Changer

Israel's acquisition of nuclear weapons in the late 1960s did not terrify these thirteen Middle Eastern states into seeking nuclear reactors nor did Pakistan's acquisition of those arms. Only after Iran built its nuclear bomb-fuel centrifuges did these thirteen states seek reactors. Despite their complaints about Israel's nuclear weapons program, these states feared Israel's nuclear weapons less than Iran's Shiite bomb. Shortly after Prince Saud al-Faisal, the Saudi foreign minister, failed to talk Iran out of its nuclear ambitions, Saudi Arabia announced its intention to go nuclear . . . despite possessing the most plentiful, low-cost oil on earth.[3]

Bush's obsession with Iraq prevented him from effectively combating Iran's nuclear expansionism.

The Saudis' desire to build sixteen nuclear power plants is especially suspect. They have a portentous history of financing both terrorism and nuclear proliferation in Iraq and Pakistan. They allegedly financed Saddam Hussein's nuclear program in hopes of acquiring several nuclear weapons after he had manufactured them.[4]

Saudi Financing of Pakistan's Nukes

Bruce Riedel writes in his article "Saudi Arabia: Nervously Watching Pakistan": "Pakistan has received more aid from Saudi Arabia than any country outside the Arab world since the 1960s. For example, in May 1998 when Pakistan was deciding whether to respond to India's test of five nuclear weapons, the Saudis promised 50,000 barrels per day of free oil to help the Pakistanis cope with the economic sanctions. . . . Official aid is matched by large investments from Saudi princes and from religious institutions. . . ."[5]

Before the Iraq War blasted oil profits for the world's oil producers into the stratosphere, Iran and Russia were in dire financial straits and far more susceptible to economic carrots and, if necessary, to coercive economic sanctions. Russia never wanted a nuclear-armed Iran, and Iran's Russian-designed Bushehr reactor project was still in its infancy. Russian leaders were subject to financial pressure as well, insisting that they built Iranian reactors solely for the money. Prior to the Iraq War, Russian officials stated publicly that if American businesses would negotiate comparable contracts with them, they would shut down the Bushehr reactor. The Global Security Newswire reported:

"Economic concerns are driving Russian nuclear cooperation with Iran and the assistance will most likely continue unabated unless the United States makes an effort to compensate Moscow for the business it would lose, according to Russian and U.S. lawmakers. . . .

" 'We definitely do not want Iran to have nuclear weapons,' said Mikhail Margelov, chairman of the Russian Federation Council's Foreign Affairs Committee . . . to the U.S. House International Relations Committee. . . .

" '[O]ur nuclear sector needs contracts and if the United States of America, if other partners and antiterrorist coalitions can offer such contracts . . . that will, I think, limit [our nuclear industry's] cooperation with Iran.' "[6]

Ariel Cohen, a research fellow at the Heritage Foundation who participated in the congressional hearing, said that the United States should have considered an economic program that would have ended Russia's nuclear assistance to Iran and that would have limited or eliminated Russia's nuclear cooperation with the unstable states and/or terrorist-friendly nations, which Russia also feared.[7]

II

During the invasion, the Bush team declined to secure Iraq's alleged "nuclear weapons sites," some of which contained radioactive canisters of highly toxic—albeit nonfissile—materials. "Had the Iraqis possessed WMDs [at these nuclear sites]," Michael Gordon and Lieutenant General Bernard Trainor (United States Marine Corps, retired) wrote in *Cobra II*, "and terrorist groups been as prevalent in Iraq as the Bush administration so loudly asserted, the U.S. forces might well have failed to prevent the WMDs from being spirited out of

the country and falling into the hands of the dark forces the administration had declared war against."[8]

The hundreds of WMD (weapons of mass destruction) sites,
which the United States had claimed to have pinpointed, were ignored, appearing to refute Bush's claim that they posed a threat to the
U.S.[9]

The Bush team acted as if their first operational priority had been
to seize, secure, and then sell off the Iraqi oil fields, the most lucrative
sites going to U.S. oil firms. White House economic adviser Larry
Lindsey, applying a cost-benefit analysis to the coming Iraq War, explained: "We can afford it. When there is regime change in Iraq, you
could add three to five million barrels [per day] to the world's supply."
He added that "successful prosecution of the war would be good for
the economy." Deputy Secretary of Defense Paul Wolfowitz—who
once enthused that Iraq "floats on a sea of oil"—applied a similar cost
analysis to Iraq's reconstruction: "The oil revenue of [Iraq] could bring
between 50 and 100 billion dollars over the course of the next two or
three years. We're dealing with a country that could . . . finance its
own reconstruction, and relatively soon."[10]

The Defense Department concurred, predicting in late 2002 that
Iraq soon could increase its production from 2.5 million barrels per
day to more than 5 million—assuming adequate investment. The
State Department's Future of Iraq Project organized and mandated
an Oil and Energy Working Group to expedite that end. As one oil
company exec told *The New York Times* in February 2003, "For any
oil company, being in Iraq is like being a kid in FAO Schwarz."[11]

Donald Barlett and James Steele explained in *Time* magazine why
Iraq was such a singularly exciting prize: "Not only does [Iraq] have
the potential to become the world's largest producer . . . no other
country can do it as cheaply. That's because, for geological reasons,

Iraq boasts the world's most prolific wells. In 1979, the year before Iraq's oil fields were devastated by the first of three wars, its wells produced an average of 13,700 bbl. each per day. By contrast, each Saudi well averages 10,200 bbl. . . . Consequently, production costs in Iraq are much lower . . . That's why everyone in the business had cast a covetous eye on the country. And why each one of the world's major powers and international consortiums has an agenda for Iraqi oil.

"A measure of Iraq's potential: only seventeen of eighty discovered oil fields have even been developed." Such an achievement, Barlett and Steele remind us, would mean lower oil prices for consumers but less money for the world's oil producers, including transnational leviathans such as Chevron Texaco and ExxonMobil, whose profits are, by any standards, prodigious.[12]

All of the Bush team's actions thundered "Oil!" The Pentagon planned to seize and secure Iraq's oil fields and facilities "as rapidly as possible," a top Pentagon official told reporters on January 24, 2003. A Special Forces unit conducted their first operation in Iraq—an assault on an offshore Persian Gulf loading platform—and they secured two Iraqi oil terminals, which could transfer two million barrels a day to oil tankers. When the U.S. army reached Baghdad, troops raced not to power and water plants, or hospitals and schools (to protect them from saboteurs and looters), but went immediately to the Ministry of Oil, which they promptly encircled with a heavily armed cordon sanitaire. They occupied the Rumaila oil field in the south so expeditiously that Saddam's troops only set nine oil wells ablaze. In the north, the U.S. airborne units took the Kirkuk oil fields so quickly they found the fields essentially undamaged. In Kuwait, by contrast, Saddam's forces ignited 650 wells,[13] all the while ignoring the so-called WMD sites.

Seven months before the 2003 Iraq invasion, Cheney said in a speech to the Veterans of Foreign Wars: "[In] a seat at the top of 10 percent of the world's oil reserves, Saddam Hussein could . . . be expected to seek domination of the entire Middle East, take control of a great portion of the world's energy supplies, [and] directly threaten America's friends throughout the region. . . ."[14]

In the run-up to the war, an unnamed "senior defense official" explained that General Tommy Franks and his staff had "crafted strategies that will allow us to secure and protect those (oil) fields as rapidly as possible . . ." In other words, many within the Bush administration advocated the appropriation and preservation of Iraq's oil. Later Paul Wolfowitz would argue they wanted oil revenue for Iraq's reconstruction. Gordon and Trainor documented in COBRA II, however, that the Bush administration ignored reconstruction planning and blocked the troop deployments necessary to implement such plans.[15]

Even more damaging, Brigadier General Mark E. Scheid reported that several months before the United States invaded Iraq—when the U.S. had barely begun its 2001 incursion into Afghanistan—Defense Secretary Rumsfeld told a team of military strategists to develop the logistics for invading Iraq. When they also devised proposals for how to secure and rebuild Iraq after the invasion, Rumsfeld ordered them to stop. When they continued working on those plans anyway— believing that the army needed to prepare for such contingencies— Rumsfeld became irate. He said he would fire the next person who wrote up post-invasion security and reconstruction plans. He also told General Scheid—then Colonel Scheid—that "we would not do that because the American public will not back us if they think we are going over there for a long war."[16]

Did the Bush administration plan to commandeer Iraq's oil industry before invading Iraq? Bush's treasury secretary Paul O'Neill seemed to think so. He was so outraged by the Bush administration's alleged plans to seize Iraq's oil that he let Ron Suskind interview him for his book, *The Price of Loyalty*. O'Neill provided Suskind with nineteen thousand documents, even though he declined both credit and remuneration.[17]

During their interviews, O'Neill told Suskind of one document entitled "Foreign Suitors for Iraqi Oilfield Contracts" and also mentioned a map of those oil fields. Judicial Watch obtained the list of foreign suitors for those fields as well as the map of Iraq's oil fields. A link to the Iraqi oil map and the chart containing the list of foreign suitors is contained in the following end note.[18]

Throughout 2001, Dick Cheney held a series of secret meetings with top oil company executives representing firms and countries friendly to the United States, including ExxonMobil, BP, Conoco Phillips Company, Shell, and those of other major companies. The content of those meetings was secret, but as *The Independent* noted, we do know "at the time, Cheney was poring over a map of 'Iraqi oil fields, pipelines, refineries, and terminals' and charts detailing 'foreign suitors' for Iraq's abundant oil and gas reserves. It's not known what was being discussed by the task force and the oil companies, but it probably wasn't solar power."[19]

O'Neill did not tell Suskind what Cheney said at all those oil company meetings but O'Neill did tell him that the Bush team had plans for all that Iraqi oil—"plans for how the world's second-largest oil reserve might be divided among the world's contractors . . ."[20]

Of course, the Bush administration's rhetoric ignored the petrodollar dreams, which many critics believe inspired the war. Instead the specter of a smoking gun transmogrifying into a nuclear mushroom cloud became their battle cry and casus belli.[21]

3

THE SAUDI NUCLEAR THREAT

I

ormer Middle East CIA station chief Robert Baer characterized
U.S. business dealings with Saudi Arabia as "sleeping with the
devil." For two decades the Saudis were the preeminent financiers
not only of al Qaeda and its Taliban hosts but also of Pakistan's
nuclear weapons program.

This Saudi support of al Qaeda was reportedly documented in the
twenty-eight pages that were blacked out of the official 9/11 intelligence report. Senators Richard Shelby (R-AL) and Bob Graham
(D-FL), who read the full uncut 9/11 intelligence report, confirmed the
Saudis' unholy alliance with terrorists. They stated that 95 percent of
the report's classified material deserved to be declassified and that the
only reason for the censorship was to spare the Saudis embarrass-
ment over their involvement with al Qaeda and its allies. Senator Pat
Roberts—former Republican chairman of the Senate Intelligence

Committee—confirmed Shelby's assertion, saying on CBS's *Face the Nation* that part of the material "was redacted to protect the Saudis." Other high-placed officials corroborated their analysis.[1]

Terrorism expert Yossef Bodansky, in his biography of bin Laden, *Bin Laden: The Man Who Declared War on America,* reports on the Saudis' support of bin Laden at a 1996 meeting in Pakistan. Robert Baer, former CIA Middle Eastern station chief, reports that a Saudi royal, Abd al-Aziz, in 1997, coordinated a $100 million aid package for the Taliban even though they were harboring and safeguarding bin Laden. Nor was al-Aziz any ordinary Saudi potentate. Baer wrote shortly after 9/11, "[King] Fahd's favorite wife, Jawhara al-Ibrahim, and her . . . son [Aziz] . . . actually run Saudi Arabia."[2]

Osama bin Laden fought the Russians in Afghanistan for the duration of that war—from 1979 to 1989. Among his many duties, he often brought men from the Saudi kingdom to Peshawar on the Pakistan/Afghan border and from Peshawar to the Russian/Afghan front, where they would fight. The money bin Laden moved went to the Islamist enemies of the USSR—mujahideen who were fighting the Soviets in the Afghan mountains and deserts. In some cases, they were Saudi allies; in other cases, they were terrorist armies fighting for radical causes with which the royal family could not afford to identify itself. Bin Laden gave the royal family plausible deniability.[3]

In the summer of 1998, however, the United States was pressuring Pakistan to help them hunt down bin Laden and perhaps extradite him back to Saudi Arabia where he could stand trial for terrorism. This request—and the fear that the Saudis might cave in to the United States—created an uproar among the Taliban in Pakistan. Prince Turki al-Faisal met with the Taliban and Pakistan's ISI (Inter-Services

Intelligence) leaders in Kandahar to quiet the furor and forge a diplomatic accord.[4]

Yossef Bodansky—the former director of the Congressional Task Force on Terrorism and Unconventional Warfare—described in his highly prophetic biography, *Bin Laden: The Man Who Declared War on America,* the agreement Prince Turki negotiated with the Taliban and ISI:[5]

> The agreement stipulates that bin Laden and his followers will not use the infrastructure in Afghanistan to subvert the Saudi kingdom, and the Saudis will make sure that no demands—including American [demands]—for the extradition of individuals and/or the closure of [terrorist] facilities and camps are met. Prince Turki also promised to provide oil and generous financial assistance to both the Taliban, Afghanistan, and Pakistan. For Islamabad the high-level negotiations with Riyadh and the long-term promises amount to Saudi recognition of the Taliban reign over Afghanistan.

Russian sources tracked both the money transfers and the arms purchases that the Taliban had acquired with the money. "These weapons played a crucial role in the Taliban's swift offensive in early August 1998 that consolidated their hold over all of Afghanistan," Bodansky wrote.[6]

Four years after 9/11, when the Saudi ambassador to the United States retired, the royal family appointed Prince Turki al-Faisal—bin Laden's friend, college classmate, intelligence case officer, and financial patron—to replace the former ambassador, who was a close friend of the Bush family.[7]

Why *Him*?

When the Saudis, nonetheless named the prince ambassador to the United States, Steven Weisman of *The New York Times* reported that an American official, speaking off the record, confirmed that Prince Turki knew members of al Qaeda and the Taliban.

"'At times he delivered messages to us,'" the official said, "'and from us regarding Osama bin Laden and others. Yes, he had links that in this day and age would be considered problematic . . .' The official said that Prince Turki al-Faisal seemed to have 'gotten out of that business' since 9/11. . . ."[8]

II

The United States had not always understood the Saudi role in global terrorism, viewing that country instead as an indispensable ally. Robert Baer wrote in his book, *Sleeping with the Devil,* that when he was a CIA station chief in the Middle East, Saudi allegiance to the United States went unquestioned; critical CIA investigations into the Saudi royals were discouraged and he never witnessed CIA officials seriously discuss a possible Saudi threat in his presence. *Sleeping with the Devil* describes the Bush administration's indifference to the Saudi financing of terrorists and their nuclear sponsors.[9]

Ralph Peters, an early critic of the Saudis, warned of the Saudi menace in his January 4, 2002 *Wall Street Journal* article, "The Saudi

Threat." Later that year in the *New York Post,* Peters elaborated even more forcefully on the Saudis' ability to buy off not mere politicians but entire administrations:

"The Saudis sponsor terror, export hatred, undercut American interests and kill Americans. They are our enemies. Period. History will marvel at this administration's insistence that they remain our friends. . . .

"The sad explanation seems to be that this oilman's administration cannot see beyond the lure of oil deals. . . .

"Reluctantly, one is forced to wonder what the Saudi ruling family knows that might prove embarrassing to our current political leadership, were it to be revealed."[10]

Peters's charges were so uncomfortably prescient that the press— even the Democratic Party—was loathe to discuss them. The facts were indeed painful to ponder.

- Saudi Arabia was one of only three nations that recognized Afghanistan's Taliban.[11]

- Fifteen of the nineteen 9/11 hijackers were Saudis, but the Bush team did not demand instant access to their files in Riyadh or the right to immediately interrogate their friends, family, and associates in the Saudi kingdom. Nor did the Bush administration punish the Saudis for their refusal to cooperate with U.S. agents, for their willful obstruction of U.S. justice.[12]

- Craig Unger documented in *House of Bush, House of Saud* that the two Bush presidents, their close associates, and some of the major institutions they were associated with, both in and out of office, accepted a total of $1.475 billion in Saudi paychecks, donations, and investments. In fact, Unger left out several lucrative payments—since he could not obtain precise figures—so he may have understated the total.[13]

- As we said earlier, the U.S. government had blacked out twenty-eight pages on the Saudis' 9/11 participation in the official congressional report on 9/11. Members of the Senate Intelligence Committee in both parties characterized those deletions as a cover-up.[14] Former senator Bob Graham, chairman of the committee from June 2001 through the Iraqi War buildup, had read the twenty-eight pages that a Saudi support network backed two of the 9/11 hijackers. Their back-up network included Saudi government agents; the Bush administration and the FBI, however, stopped a congressional inquiry into that connection. Despite pleas from senators of both parties, financial facts—which evinced Saudi economic involvement with the 9/11 hijackers—were expunged.[15]

- After leaving the Senate, former senators Bob Graham and Bob Kerrey filed affidavits in court, stating that serious evidence of Saudi involvement in 9/11 had not been pursued. Graham had been chair of the Senate Select Committee on Intelligence and had held that position on 9/11. He'd also chaired the Joint Inquiry into Intelligence Community Activities Before and After the Terrorist Attacks of September 11, 2011. Kerrey had served on the official 9/11 Commission. They both had detailed knowledge about what the Bush team had hidden from the American public.[16]

Senator Graham was especially concerned about evidence that exposed high-level Saudi involvement in 9/11, which the FBI had concealed from the 9/11 Commission. In one instance, a rich Saudi couple in an affluent gated Sarasota, Florida, community had walked away from their lavishly appointed home. They abandoned their opulent furnishings as well: three expensive automobiles, dirty diapers in a bathroom, the running toy-filled pool, food in the refrigerator, mail on the table, and clothes in the closet. They fled to Riyadh, Saudi Arabia . . . two weeks before 9/11.[17]

The friends they left behind included three of the 9/11 pilots. Mohammed Atta, who had lived nearby, was one of them. Phone records, photographic evidence, which the security guards had gathered when their car went through the gate, and the guards' questioning of the passengers—all of it established the Saudi family's personal relationship with the three 9/11 pilots, who had phoned and visited the couple on a number of occasions. Furthermore, the house's owner was a wealthy Saudi financier closely connected to the ruling Saudi family, *but Bush's FBI had concealed all this information from the 9/11 Committee.*[18]

As we said earlier, two days after 9/11 the White House ordered 160 important Saudis—including two dozen relatives of bin Laden—flown out of the United States before the FBI's counterterrorism experts could debrief them, even though many of them had clear connections to the bin Laden family. They flew out of Washington, New York, Los Angeles, Chicago, Houston, Boston, Detroit, Atlanta, Dallas, Denver, San Francisco, Cincinnati, Newark, and Tampa. The Tampa flight—at the White House's request—was airborne at a time when all other private flights in the United States were grounded due to 9/11. Fifteen of the Saudis, who flew out of Lexington, Kentucky, left the United States in style. Craig Unger reported that their Boeing 727 came equipped with "a master bedroom suite furnished with a large upholstered double bed, a couch, a nightstand, and a credenza. Its master bathroom had a gold-plated sink, double illuminated mirrors, and a bidet. There were brass, gold, and crystal fixtures. The main lounge had a fifty-two-inch projection TV. The plane boasted a six-place conference room and dining room with a mahogany table that had controls for up and down movement."[19]

Dan Grossi, a former Tampa police officer, and Manuel Perez, a retired FBI agent, accompanied the passengers on the flight. Perez now says, "The White House, the FAA, and the FBI all said the flight didn't happen." Grossi confirmed that Craig Unger's account of the Tampa flight in his book, *House of Bush, House of Saud*, was accurate. However, when *The St. Petersburg Times* attempted to cover the story thirty-three months later, they reported, "The FAA is still not talking about the flights, referring all questions to the FBI, which isn't answering anything either. Nor is the 9/11 Commission."[20]

The 9/11 Commission ignored the Tampa flight, which was authorized by the White House when all U.S. private flights were still grounded.[21]

Furthermore, the Tampa International Airport said "its records indicated that no member of its [security] force screened the Lear [jet's] passengers."[22]

Two days after 9/11, they were flying out of the country.[23]

The contrast between the Bush administration's treatment of Saudi suspects and those of other Middle East countries was extreme. Unlike those Saudis, who were sneaked out of the United States after 9/11, other Middle Easterners—clearly unconnected to bin Laden and al Qaeda—were herded up and incarcerated in Guantanamo and in INS (Immigration and Naturalization Service) facilities, often for years on end. Colonel Douglas Macgregor, who retired from the U.S. Army in June 2004, reports, "We ended up incarcerating over 46,000 people, less than 10 percent of whom deserved to be incarcerated."[24]

Steven Brill, in *After: How America Confronted the September 12 Era*, reported:

> In the hours and days immediately following [the September 11] attacks, Attorney General John Ashcroft ... directed that FBI and INS agents question anyone they could find with a Muslim-sounding name ... in some areas ... they simply looked for names in the phone book ... Anyone who could be held, even on a minor violation of law or immigration rules, was held under a three-pronged strategy, fashioned by Ashcroft and a close circle of Justice Department deputies including criminal division chief Michael Chertoff, that was intended to exert maximum pressure on these detainees.[25]

Years After 9/11, al Qaeda Funders Still Operated with Impunity

Douglas Farah reported in *The Washington Post* that a full twenty-seven months after 9/11, Saudi charities backing bin Laden—supposedly shut down—still operated world-wide with impunity. Governments around the globe ignored sanctions designed to halt the flood of cash to al Qaeda, "allowing the terrorist network to retain formidable financial resources."[26]

Businessmen and charities labeled by the UN as al Qaeda funders were allowed to run huge global operations and traveled unchecked. The General Accounting Office (now called the Government Accountability Office) reported U.S. law enforcement was equally in the dark and that the FBI still did not "systematically collect or analyze" data on al Qaeda's fund-raisers. "The Justice and Treasury departments had fallen more than a year behind in developing plans to attack terrorist financial mechanisms, such as the use of diamonds and gold to hide assets." The Council on Foreign Relations reported that over six months after 9/11 "Saudi Arabia . . . ha[d] yet to demand personal accountability" from its more prominent financiers of terrorism.[27]

- Crown Prince Abdullah, meanwhile, told the Saudi people on national television that "Zionism is behind [9/11]," and Saudi interior minister Prince Nayef blamed the rash of al Qaeda attacks—beginning with the May 12, 2003, Riyadh bombing—on the Israelis, explaining that "Al-Qaida is backed by Israel and Zionism."[28]

- Saudi antipathy toward America forced the U.S. government to urge U.S. citizens to leave Saudi Arabia thirty-two months after 9/11. The largest Western contractor in Saudi

Arabia, BAE Systems, had to offer substantial bonuses to its Western employees to stem their exodus from Saudi Arabia, and *The Washington Post* reported that "97 percent of Saudis view[ed] the United States in a negative light."[29]

Monuments to Saddam Hussein

Had Saddam Hussein adopted the Saudis' financial tactics, some critics believed, had he deployed and bankrolled a free-spending ambassador comparable to the Saudis' Prince Bandar—"Bandar Bush" as the Bush family referred to him—an ambassador who would have bestowed emoluments on Washington's political elite, the United States would have erected monuments to the Iraqi tyrant rather than executing him.

4

DONALD RUMSFELD

Rummy . . . is a ruthless little bastard.
—RICHARD NIXON[1]

George W. Bush's defense secretary during his tenure with that administration, Donald Rumsfeld condemned rogue nations that sought to obtain nuclear weaponry. Yet, as we have previously stated, when Rumsfeld was a board director at the Swiss nuclear contractor, Asea Brown Boveri (ABB), that firm offered nuclear reactors to North Korea.[2]

That Rumsfeld was a harsh Bush administration critic of North Korea and a fierce opponent of constructive engagement—even coercive engagement—with North Korea is well documented. He viewed engagement of any kind—whether constructive, aggressive, or coercive—with North Korea as tantamount to rewarding dictators.[3] Moreover, Rumsfeld didn't think North Korea could use a nuclear power plant effectively. "'They don't need a nuclear power plant. Their power grid couldn't even absorb that,' Rumsfeld said."[4]

In late 2002, North Korea expelled the UN's nuclear monitors. In response, the Bush administration in late 2002 publicly rescinded the Clinton administration's "red line" in North Korea, which stated that if North Korea attempted to unlock its spent-fuel rods—which were being monitored by international inspectors—the United States would bomb them and North Korea's reactors. When North Korea unlocked the spent-fuel boxes, the Bush people looked the other way. Senator John McCain (R-AZ) excoriated the Bush administration for this reversal of the "red line" policy, saying that "force could eventually prove to be the only means to prevent North Korea from acquiring a nuclear arsenal." McCain then charged that the Bush administration's revocation of Clinton's "red line" was "a dangerously shortsighted precedent that even the Clinton administration did not publicly suggest."[5] I can find no record of Rumsfeld challenging Bush's inaction.

Rumsfeld's actions suggested an indifference to nuclear proliferation, and in 1998—while he was working in the private sector—he chaired the Commission to Assess the Ballistic Missile Threat to the United States, which issued its report to Congress. In that report, he argued that nonproliferation programs were ultimately ineffective.[6]

Despite the 1991 collapse of the Soviet Union, Rumsfeld had argued in that report the need for the Cold War Strategic Defense Initiative, known as Star Wars. To continue to justify Star Wars, he had to claim that Third World countries with very primitive ballistic missile programs could eventually threaten the United States with intercontinental ballistic missiles (ICBMs). Rumsfeld had not focused on the more likely menace of terrorist nukes made from smuggled nuclear bomb-fuel, which America's enemies could surreptitiously deliver with far greater accuracy than nuclear-tipped ICBMs. Such bombs would also leave no return addresses and would be impervious to missile

defenses. Unlike astronomically expensive nuclear-tipped ballistic missiles, which are almost prohibitively difficult to build, terrorist nukes
are relatively cheap and easy to produce and much harder to retaliate
against—if the strikes are done anonymously or pseudonymously.[7]

It was all part of the same picture. Rumsfeld and the other Bush
people were not overly concerned with the nuclear terrorist threat.
Although the Bush administration had justified its Iraq invasion under the pretext that Saddam Hussein was developing nuclear weapons,
that argument would seem, in retrospect, to have been empty rhetoric.
Rumsfeld and the other Bush people did not appear to be particularly
anxious over the nuclear terrorist threat. After all, when North Korea
crossed Clinton's red line and began reprocessing its spent-fuel rods,
Rumsfeld and Bush had the chance to bomb those spent-fuel rods into
radioactive dust. North Korea could not hit the United States with
nuclear-tipped ICBMs—Rumsfeld's Commission to Assess the Ballistic Missile Threat report notwithstanding—but they could certainly
have sold their nukes to skillful, well-financed terrorists. The two men
had found a real nuclear terrorist threat, and they could have killed
that nuclear program in its cradle. Instead they let North Korea build
its own nuclear weapons and continued its war with non-nuclear Iraq.[8]

5

U.S.–INDIAN NUCLEAR POLICY:
HOW TO FOMENT A NUCLEAR ARMS RACE
FOR FUN AND PROFIT

I
---

ndia's nuclear expansionism encouraged her rivals and neighbors—China, North Korea, and most notably Pakistan—to expand their nuclear programs. However, rather than reining India in, the Bush team—like the Obama team after them—rewarded India with nuclear reactor deals.

Moreover the Bush team did not play nuclear favorites. They offered China the financing for $5 billion worth of cutting-edge nuclear reactors.[1] Rumsfeld also offered to help Pakistan buy state-of-the-art aircraft—some of them low-flying radar-resistant stealth aircraft—which with minor modifications could be converted into nuclear delivery systems. Rumsfeld made his presentation while India and Pakistan were in the middle of Indian–Pakistani disarmament negotiations, and the Indian defense minister Pranab Mukherjee warned Rumsfeld that he could wreck the delicate peace negotiations between the two nuclear enemies. Rumsfeld was undeterred, however, and the Bush team, through its actions, encouraged a nuclear arms race in Asia.[2]

Nor did India stop buying the Bush team's high-tech weaponry. After all, she had already fought a war with China and wars with Pakistan in 1947–48, 1965, 1971, and 1999. Plus, its 1999 war had almost gone nuclear.[3]

Despite all the Bush team's public praise for India's growth as a democracy and its rapid economic progress, Indian demographics called into question its long-term stability and its ability to manage nuclear arms. Racked by a proliferating birthrate, its population will surpass China's by 2025.[4]

Will the Indian State Survive the Twenty-First Century?

"Given that in 2025 India's population could be close to 1.5 billion," Robert D. Kaplan noted in *The Coming Anarchy*, "that much of its economy rests on a shrinking natural-resource base, including dramatically declining water levels, and that communal violence and urbanization are spiraling upward, it is difficult to imagine that the Indian state will survive the [21st] century. India's oft-trumpeted Green Revolution has been achieved by overworking its croplands and depleting its watershed. Norman Myers, a British development consultant, worries that Indians have 'been feeding themselves today by borrowing against their children's food sources.'"[5]

Was India mature and stable enough to handle the nuclear reactors and potential nuclear delivery systems the Bush and Obama administrations were selling them? The way their laws treated women and children suggested that their culture was neither responsible nor reliable.

India was not doing nearly enough to protect its exploding child population from gross exploitation—sexual or economic. India had no practicable laws forbidding the retailing and wholesaling of child brides, and one out of four Indian brides was married before the age of sixteen.[6] According to the World Bank, the country's child malnutrition rate doubled sub-Saharan Africa's. Even worse, India—as of the writing of this book—had no serious laws against child molestation.[7] India also refused to protect its children from exploitive labor. In fact, that country boasted the highest number of child workers in the world; responsible estimates ranged as high as 100 million. *Forbes* described India as "a giant backyard sweatshop to the world, staffed by underage boys and girls." Many of America's biggest firms, which manufactured their products in India, covertly employed child laborers.[8]

While the Indian government spent huge sums on U.S. weapons, India's ability to handle those acquisitions was questionable—at least in the long term. A land rife with terrorist movements, India's ransom kidnappings and political murders were everyday events. Plagued by abject poverty, its people continually succumbed to disease and malnutrition. Its hospitals overrun, Indian medical care was abysmal for most of the billion-plus population. Health care centers are devoid of clean toilets, running water, and proper sanitation, the segregation and disposal of waste, and an adequate emergency transportation system. In addition, financial thievery by government officials habitually sabotaged India's health care system. It was not for nothing that the term "baksheesh" (bribe) originated in India.[9]

Public Defecation in India

India has 60 million people who, on average, enjoy a standard of living superior to Britain's and France's middle class. India also has 900 million people who live in dire poverty. Mani Shankar Ayar, a former government minister, is highly critical of India's class society. He told journalist Tim Sebastian: "We have a tiny elite that is obsessed with itself. If democracy doesn't deliver for the rest—we could be heading for violence. We're seeing a failure to bring 900 million people inside the system of entitlements. Without entitlements, you pick up the gun."[10]

Those 900 million people live in almost indescribable misery. According to UN figures, 638 million of them still defecate in public, out in the open. Indian women, who universally abhor the practice, are consequently plagued with severe excretory diseases and disorders. In Delhi, where school dropout rates are especially high among girls, teachers blame this absenteeism on the students' lack of private toilets.[11]

One could only shudder at the potential fate of India's plutonium canisters and weapons detonators en route to their weapons factories. Yet the Bush and the Obama administrations were selling them the reactors necessary to fabricate nuclear bomb-fuel and the planes, which, with minor modifications, could serve as delivery systems.

II

Henry Sokolski, a senior Defense Department nonproliferation official under George H. W. Bush, had argued that in India new U.S.-built nuclear facilities—which the George W. Bush team had proposed—would allow India to fuel an additional twelve Hiroshima-style bombs per year and up to seventy-five Nagasaki-style bombs. Furthermore, the George W. Bush administration had promised to help India develop its satellite launch vehicles. Unfortunately, satellite launch vehicles can be converted into ICBMs. As John Kennedy once said, the only difference between the two was "altitude." Through the Bush administration's space aid, India could have the opportunity to upgrade its ICBM guidance systems, similar to the way American space aid to China did for Chinese ICBMs in the 1990s.[12]

India had announced that it intended to "double its nuclear fuel production in anticipation of operating new power plants" during the last year of Bush's second term, the Indonesian News Service reported.[13]

As we have discussed, scientists had proven repeatedly that the technology of nuclear reactors and nuclear bomb-fuel production were, in the words of the 1946 Acheson-Lilienthal Report, largely "interchangeable and interdependent," or as Mohamed ElBaradei, the UN's former International Atomic Energy Agency chief phrased it, "too close for comfort."[14]

India's first nuclear test inspired the Treaty on the Non-Proliferation of Nuclear Weapons, or the Non-Proliferation Treaty (NPT) of 1970. In signing the NPT, the United States pledged not to transfer such materials and technology to states where those items could be used for weapons production—India in particular. Since India would not allow "full-scope safeguards," the United States was obligated to honor that pledge. Still, the Bush administration forged ahead with its proposed sales.[15]

India's ability to protect its nuclear facilities from terrorist attacks—or perhaps even more frightening, from terrorist infiltration of its facilities—was highly problematic. The United States and Russia were notoriously inept at such nuclear safeguarding, and their security challenges were trivial compared to India's. Halfway through Bush's second term—even as he was offering India all these weapons and reactor deals—the country was plagued with massive Islamist bombing attacks on its rush-hour Mumbai trains, its sacred shrines in its holiest Hindu city, Varanasi, and in its New Delhi shopping malls. The police responded so brutally to these attacks that Prime Minister Manmohan Singh feared that police reprisals might radicalize India's 140 million Muslims. Instead of an extremist Muslim minority terrorizing cities, the great mass of the Muslim population might rise up against the Indian people.[16]

Terrorists had established a powerful network in India's major cities. "Intelligence agencies," Singh had said, "warn of further intensification of violent activities on their part; use of suicide bombers; attacks on economic and religious targets; targeting vital installations, including nuclear establishments, army camps, and the like." Singh had even warned the United States that India's nuclear facilities were under siege. The terrorists were targeting army units in their own bases. Even so, the Bush coterie had determined to sell nuclear bomb-fuel technology to India.[17]

Did Bush always plan on abandoning the war against nuclear proliferators, who are the illicit progenitors of the nuclear terrorist? Bush's actions in India—not his elusive rhetoric—answered that question and defined his nuclear purposes. By procrastinating U.S. nuclear talks with Iran and North Korea; by doing far too little about Russia's loose nukes; by offering China billions of dollars in subsidies for its nuclear power industry as well as nuclear technology and engineering expertise; by diverting finances and military resources into Iraq's nuclear-poor but oil-rich regime—which was too shattered, impotent, and above all devoid of nukes to menace the United States—the Bush administration extravagantly encouraged the world's nuclear proliferators to escalate their lethal labors.

Lawless India: Legislatures that Teem with Killers and Extortionists

Nor was there any evidence that the Indian government was responsible enough to secure the Bush administration's nuclear facilities. India's parliament seldom passed bills that didn't line its legislators' pockets. Road and building construction bills, which were popular profit centers for Indian politicians, passed the legislature easily. However, health care and education bills—which generated little in the way of kickbacks—were routinely rejected. Consequently, India was embarrassingly behind in almost all social indices. According to India's Ministry of Health and Family Welfare—as we pointed out earlier—the prevalence of malnourished children in India was nearly twice that of sub-Saharan Africa. Poor immunization programs had reinvigorated diseases such as polio among India's children in record numbers. Its birthrate was a living, waking nightmare.[18]

The corruption of India's legislature, however, went beyond kickbacks and baksheesh. Its parliament had been so
lawless that at times nearly 25 percent of India's 535 elected
representatives had been up on criminal indictments or
had charges pending against them. Half of those pending
charges carried prison sentences of five years of more. In
India's most populous state, Uttar Pradesh, half of its 403
assembly members faced criminal charges.

India's criminal justice system had charged many legislators with murder and the political assassination of rivals.
Tales of these legislators and their crimes were filled with
bullet-riddled corpses, orphaned children, and grieving
widows—even as India's legislatures were overrun with hard-
ened killers and brutal extortionists. One legislator reportedly paid murderers to fire on another legislator's motorcade
with assault rifles, killing the legislator and five associates.[19]

By rewarding India—a violator of the nuclear Non-Proliferation
Treaty—with nuclear aid, Henry Sokolski warned that the United
States would move a severely wounded patient from the emergency
room into the morgue. In other words, the United States would render the Non-Proliferation Treaty irrelevant and ineffectual.[20]

Nor was India innocent of nuclear trafficking. David Albright, a
former UN nuclear inspector and Institute for Science and International Security (ISIS) president, said that "Indian procurement
methods . . . leak sensitive nuclear technology." The ISIS reported
that it had "uncovered a well-developed, active, and secret Indian
program to outfit its uranium enrichment program and circumvent
other countries' export control efforts."[21]

The Nuclear Proliferator's Creed: "No Foes . . . Just Customers"

Abdul Qadeer (A. Q.) Khan is a nuclear scientist. The father of Pakistan's atom bomb program, he was also the biggest proliferator of nuclear weapons technology in history. Providing Iran, Libya, and North Korea with nuclear technology, his assistance was critical to the development of their fledgling programs. Among other things, he helped these countries build centrifuges with enough enriched uranium until it was bomb-grade.[22]

Khan was such a prolific purveyor of nuclear technology that he seemed willing to sell it to almost anyone. Nuclear India—Pakistan's most feared and hated enemy—had apparently benefited from Khan's nuclear proliferations. There is highly cogent evidence that some of Khan's key nuclear proliferators supplied India with parts for its gas centrifuge program.[23]

Like A. Q. Khan, the Bush people also wanted to proliferate nuclear technology to India. So problematic was the Bush administration's proposed reactor sales to India that the Bush White House refused to consult with Congress prior to its agreement in principal, pursuing their deal covertly and unilaterally. Bush-Cheney-Rice conferred with no one save a few members of their inner circle. Michael Krepon, an arms-control expert and president emeritus of the Stimson Center, argued that Bush's unilateral preparations for the Indian nuclear proliferation pact mirrored—in both method and approach—Bush's buildup for the Iraq War. Skeptics and dissenters were shunned. The potential proliferation risks and deadly nuclear hazards were treated with willful disregard. The portentous consequences of their actions never received an exhaustive public hearing.[24]

Congress was excluded from the decision-making process, and the pact was presented to them as a fait accompli. Secretary of State Condoleezza Rice told Congress they should rush through a U.S.–India civilian nuclear cooperation agreement at breakneck speed, not with due diligence. Moreover, Bush's nuclear proliferation to India might very well have encouraged other nations to proliferate as well. William Potter—director for the Center for Nonproliferation Studies at the Monterey Institute—argued that Rice's policies seriously threatened global control of nuclear materials, particularly the Non-Proliferation Treaty. He worried about nations that had obeyed the NPT. "[A] Brazil, a South Africa, a Kazakhstan, a Ukraine, they have to ask themselves, did we do the right thing when we gave up our nuclear weapons?"[25]

Ending Thirty Years of Non-Proliferation in One Fell Swoop

Ironically, the Non-Proliferation Treaty was enacted to counter India's nuclear proliferation threat, after that country hot-tested a nuclear weapon in 1974. The passage of the NPT mandated that any U.S. nuclear customer from that day forth had to comply with full-scale International Atomic Energy Agency (IAEA) safeguards. The treaty required the United States to halt nuclear shipments to any future nuclear customer who detonated a nuclear device. The United States then organized the Nuclear Suppliers Group (NSG), made up of forty leading nuclear nations—including Russia, the UK, France, and China—dedicated to implementing and enforcing the NPT. When Bush proposed this pact with India, he not only did not consult with legislative leaders in the United States and nuclear proliferation experts in the government, he ignored the NSG. That body had been created to monitor precisely these kinds of deals, and Bush's pact ran contrary to their guidelines.[26]

NSG guidelines required that the nuclear technology in every one of the nation's nuclear facilities be subject to NSG guidelines and submit to "full-scope" IAEA safeguards. Condoleezza Rice's proposal violated both those mandates and was prohibited by law in the United States. When the U.S. Congress eventually enacted legislation permitting nuclear shipments to India, it ordered that all Indian nuclear technology must fall under NSG guidelines and that all of India's nuclear facilities must submit to "full-scope" IAEA safeguards—all of which India rejected. George W. Bush rescued Rice's deal. Signing the legislation, he then rescinded its restrictive caveats with a "signing statement," which in one fell swoop revoked Congress's two iron-clad conditions for India's nuclear-technology exports as well as nullifying the NSG guidelines, the NPT's international mandate, and the imposition of "full-scope" IAEA safeguards.[27]

Bush, Cheney, and Rice had blown open the nuclear proliferator's global floodgates. If these Bush players succeeded in spreading the gospel of unrestricted nuclear trade—including the free trade of nuclear bomb-fuel technology—nothing would stop China from trafficking its reverse-engineered Westinghouse reactors to Pakistan. Pakistan might, in turn, sell this new technology to Iran and North Korea. It had made these kinds of sales to them in the past.

One year before Condoleezza Rice's sales offer was proposed, the Bush team had convinced Russia to terminate a nuclear agreement to build four 1,000-megawatt electrical (MWe) nuclear power plants in India. Russia agreed to back out of the contract precisely because all of India's nuclear facilities did not fall under NSG guidelines and submit to "full-scope" IAEA safeguards. However, after Russia stood down, the Bush coterie made its offer of four AP1000 "canned" Westinghouse-designed, 1,100-megawatt reactors to India.[28]

Ten bipartisan U.S. nonproliferation experts and former U.S. officials wrote Congress arguing that the Rice agreement had not only violated and jeopardized the Non-Proliferation Treaty, it would also expand India's nuclear weapons program because it "free[d] up India's limited domestic nuclear fuel-making capacity to produce highly enriched uranium and plutonium for weapons."[29]

Rice's State Department conceded that the agreement might help India to expand its nuclear arsenal but argued that her agreement did not violate the NPT. Nonproliferation experts Henry Sokolski and Christopher Paine argued in response that Rice's State Department had defined the NPT so narrowly as to nullify it. Sokolski and Paine also argued that since the United States, unlike India, was a signatory of the NPT, the U.S. was obligated not to assist "other states' nuclear weapons programs in any way."[30]

Henry Hyde (R-IL), former chairman of the House Committee on

International Relations, complained that Congress would have to change national law to pass the legislation. He also criticized Bush and Rice for giving the Congress "little if any information" regarding the agreement's key provisions.[31]

Bush and Rice sought to expand India's nuclear weapons program even though India was a close economic ally of Iran. That country was a notorious nuclear rogue, and the United States had economic sanctions against her. Nonetheless, India was entering into energy alliances with Iran. For instance, India had offered to assist Iran in a natural gas pipeline venture. When questioned about that Iranian pipeline at a joint press conference with Condoleezza Rice, Indian Foreign Minister Natwar Singh announced, "We have no problems of any kind with Iran."[32]

Pakistan and India, moreover, had a long history of nuclear tensions. In fact, they had unending military conflicts in Kashmir, and during their 1999 war had come terrifyingly close to a nuclear exchange.[33] Nonetheless, former defense secretary Rumsfeld had gone on junkets to both countries, promoting sales for aircraft which could serve as nuclear delivery systems after minor modifications . . . even as the two countries were engaged in extremely sensitive military discussions to reduce nuclear tensions. The Indian foreign minister Natwar Singh was quick to express his displeasure at Rumsfeld's retailing of aircraft with nuclear-delivery potential to Pakistan. He told the Indian parliament that Rumsfeld's sale of these delivery systems to Pakistan came "at a time when the India–Pakistan dialogue is at a sensitive stage [and] would have a negative impact."[34] Other Indian officials as well, the Associated Press (AP) reported, "cautioned Defense Secretary Donald Rumsfeld . . . that [his sales] could damage a fragile peace process between the nuclear-armed neighbors and harm India–U.S. relations."[35]

Indian officials were also shocked by Rumsfeld's assistance in the sale of upgraded P-3C Orion aircraft to Pakistan—aircraft he'd also promoted to India. The P-3C Orion is a long-range, land-based, low-flying aircraft perfectly designed for evading radar. With a few alterations, it could deliver nuclear bombs.[36]

Ironically, Rumsfeld also offered India and Pakistan a new generation of radar systems.[37]

Pakistan was not pleased with Rumsfeld's visit to India, saluting his trip with a ballistic-missile greeting, test-firing "a nuclear capable, surface-to-surface ballistic missile, capable of hitting targets deep inside arch-rival India," Reuters reported.[38]

Why Would India Build a Nuclear Missile Capable of Hitting the U.S.?

India is also working on a 15,000-km missile—almost halfway around the world. A missile with such enormous range would overshoot India's traditional foes but would be capable of hitting the United States. Why India would want the ability to nuke the United States is a very strange conundrum.[39]

Rumsfeld's Pentagon eventually offered to sell F-16s to both countries. "Preliminary plans call for India to receive as many as 125 jets, while Pakistan would buy about 24," the Global Security Newswire reported.[40]

One thing was clear: The Bush administration was perfectly willing to sell arms to countries which hated each other and had a long history of warring against one another. Even if these arms sales heightened tensions and accelerated an arms race, the Bush people would not hesitate to encourage the sales. Arms sales trumped peace in the region.

The Bush Team Bankrolls a New Nuclear Arms Race

Pakistan, in particular, was deeply concerned about India's new reactors. With the Bush administration's new reactor sales, India could raise its uranium production to five hundred tons a year. It only needed 380 tons for its civilian programs. The Bush reactor deal would allow India to divert an additional 120 tons of uranium into weapons production. Prior to the Bush reactor proposal, India's annual nuclear weapons production rate had been six to ten weapons per year.[41]

Pakistan's fear of India's accelerated nuclear bomb-fuel production would no doubt fuel many more mega-arms deal over the next decade.

When Rumsfeld was at Asea Brown Boveri (ABB), the firm's attempted sale of nuclear reactors to North Korea probably made other Asian states consider upgrading their nuclear technology.[42]

Cheney, meanwhile, planned a trip to China. He was to talk to the Chinese leadership about North Korea, but he was also there to discuss the U.S. nuclear power industry. It could help China with their energy plans and be a source for future technology. Henry Sokolski, a leading nonproliferation expert, told the House Committee on International Relations that the Cheney trip to China was especially ill-advised. China was already planning to help Pakistan fabricate two large plutonium-producing reactors. If the goal was to avoid worldwide proliferation of nuclear weaponry, it was a mistake to reward China with nuclear technology after they made plans to disseminate nuclear technology to other countries.[43]

China was asking for bids on the construction of four nuclear power plants, and Cheney wanted them to consider U.S. firms. Ironically, the U.S. firm which was interested was merely based in the United States. At that time, the Westinghouse firm was owned by the British; the company was subsequently sold to Japan's Toshiba. The sale price for the company was only $5.4 billion. The loan guarantees by the U.S. government's Export-Import Bank of the United States (Ex-Im) were for $5 billion—almost as much as the amount Toshiba paid for the British-owned Westinghouse. The U.S. taxpayer-financed Ex-Im loan guarantees were especially controversial since they benefitted the UK and China at the expense of U.S. taxpayers. Moreover, NBC News stated that the total cost of the four reactors could be as low as $6 billion. Thus, the U.S. taxpayers' loan guarantees were expected to cover over 83 percent of the UK company's tab.[44]

Even worse, China had said openly that it planned to replicate and recycle the Westinghouse technology in these cutting-edge state-of-the-art reactors. *The New York Times* reported that Chinese officials "demanded that the bidders share advanced nuclear technology as part of Beijing's efforts to develop its domestic nuclear power industry."[45]

> **"I don't think [nuclear proliferation]**
> **is any of our business."**
> **—Ronald Reagan**

Republicans had long opposed nonproliferation sanctions in India and Pakistan—even though India, like Pakistan, refused to sign the nuclear Non-Proliferation Treaty—and in 1983, President Ronald Reagan sought to lift those sanctions. By 1984, his administration was authorizing the sale of nuclear technology to India. In the case of Pakistan, Reagan had used Pakistan's opposition to the USSR in the Soviet-Afghan War as an excuse to waive nuclear restrictions. In India's case, however, Reagan had no excuse for attempting to lift that country's nuclear sanctions.[46]

Reagan was never concerned about Third World nuclear proliferation. On the campaign trail in Jacksonville, Florida, on January 31, 1980, when asked about Pakistan's nuclear program, he replied: "I just don't think it's any of our business."[47]

Nuclear Bomb Technology for Saddam Hussein?

At one point, the Reagan administration even looked favorably on letting Saddam Hussein purchase American-made dual-use nuclear technology which had not previously been available to him. (Dual-use nuclear technology can have both power plant and weapons applications.) The construction company, Bechtel Corporation, was attempting to sell Saddam Hussein a pipeline, and in 1983–84 Reagan sent Donald Rumsfeld, Gerald Ford's former defense secretary, to Iraq as a presidential envoy to meet with Saddam. Among other things, Rumsfeld reportedly told Saddam that President Reagan felt such a pipeline was a good idea since the Syrians had closed one of Iraq's major pipelines and the Iranians had shut down Saddam's Persian Gulf oil facilities.[48]

Saddam never commissioned the Bechtel pipeline, and the possible offer of dual-use nuclear technology may never have been discussed. Nor do we know whether Rumsfeld knew of that possible offer. However, at one time the administration had looked approvingly on it. As Joyce Battle wrote in *Shaking Hands with Saddam Hussein: The U.S. Tilts Toward Iraq 1980–1984:* "During the spring of 1984, the United States reconsidered policy for the sale of dual-use equipment to Iraq's nuclear program, and its 'preliminary results favor[ed] expanding such trade to include Iraqi nuclear entities.'"

That the Reagan people even considered making such an offer indicated their indifference to nuclear proliferation. Moreover, shortly before those meetings Saddam Hussein had been publicly vilified for using poison gas against his own people. While we do know that Rumsfeld discussed Iraq's need for an alternate pipeline, we have no evidence that Rumsfeld discussed Saddam's poison gas war crimes or chastised him for it, and we do have notes detailing the discussions at that Saddam Hussein–Donald Rumsfeld meeting.[49]

While George Shultz denies having personally promoted the Bechtel pipeline to either Ronald Reagan or Saddam Hussein, he had been Bechtel's CEO before taking the secretary of state post under Reagan. Rumsfeld, of course, helped to organize the George W. Bush invasion of Iraq when he was defense secretary.

Reagan's waiving of nuclear sanctions in the case of India and Pakistan was especially hazardous since the two states were mortal enemies, having fought two bloody wars and having expressed their mutual antipathy in the starkest possible terms. He was, in effect, encouraging their nuclear-arms buildups; and by 1986, Pakistan had the atom bomb.[50]

When in May 1998—approximately a month after Pakistan's first nuclear test—India tested five nuclear devices, those nuclear trade sanctions were stiffened. Sanctions were also imposed on Pakistan. After 9/11, those sanctions on Pakistan were eased in exchange for help with the War on Terrorism. Even after A. Q. Khan's nuclear black market was exposed in early 2004, Bush did not reinstate the Clinton nuclear sanctions.[51]

6

NUCLEAR LUNATICS

Some national leaders—both in the United States and abroad—have viewed nuclear weapons . . . in near-religious terms. Robert Jay Lifton has written several influential books on the psychological impact of nuclear weapons on people and nations, and he has described these nuclear cultists as identifying with what they perceive to be the divine power of these diabolic instruments. If nothing else, the language these people employ to describe nuclear blasts has too often been filled with religious awe instead of horror and revulsion. The "father of the atom bomb," Robert Oppenheimer—on witnessing the first nuclear test at Trinity Site, New Mexico—cited the Bhagavad Gita. In that verse he later said he saw himself as the Vedic god of destruction and said: "I am become Death, the destroyer of worlds."[1]

Nations have felt this religious impulse, too. The Buddha, who carried his divine enlightenment from India to China, became, in the eyes of many, the potential savior of all humanity, and after India's first nuclear detonation, the people at the test site told their prime minister, Indira Gandhi, "The Buddha smiles," as if the blazing nuclear fireball was the Buddha's grinning incarnation.[2] Lifton tells us that some nuclear cult leaders view atomic weapons as "near deities, possessing a capacity not only for unlimited destruction but also for godlike creation." The truly psychopathic leader believes he can foment, control, and prevail in a nuclear Armageddon of his creation. As an example, Lifton wrote of Shoko Asahara, the head of Aum Shinrikyo, a violent apocalyptic cult now infamous for dispersing sarin nerve gas in a Tokyo subway. Ashara believed that the Vedic lord of salvation-through-destruction, Shiva, appeared to him. Shiva told him he had to destroy the world to save it. Asahara had quested after Armageddon ever since.[3]

Nor is Asahara the only nuclear apostle out there. A. Q. Khan, the Pakistani Oppenheimer, is revered in his native land, and the people there are frequently said to "deify him." In 2005, in *The Atlantic* William Langewiesche described in "The Wrath of Khan" how the Pakistani people view "the Father of their A-bomb":

> Though he worked in the realm of state secrets, Khan had become something of a demigod in Pakistan, with a public reputation second only to that of the nation's founder, Muhammad Ali Jinnah ... Accompanied by his security detail, he would go around Pakistan accepting awards and words of praise, passing out pictures of himself, and holding forth on diverse subjects—science, education, health, history, world politics, poetry, and (his favorite) the magnitude of his achievements. ... Word filtered through the streets until even ordinary people knew of this grand man, and some recognized him as he whisked by in his cavalcades, surrounded

by loyalists and guards. Medals and awards were showered upon him, and every one of them he counted, and every one, he felt, was justified. Ultimately he received six honorary doctoral degrees, forty-five gold medals, three gold crowns, and, twice, the Nishan-i-Imtiaz, Pakistan's highest civilian award.[4]

We too have known nuclear ecstasy. William Laurence was a noted science writer, and when he was allowed to witness Nagasaki, he wrote, "One felt as though he had been privileged to witness the Birth of the World . . . to be present at the moment of Creation when God said, 'Let there be Light.'"[5]

He once compared the creation of the atom bomb to the second coming of Christ, and after Laurence witnessed an airborne hydrogen bomb test in the Pacific in 1956, he described the burgeoning mushroom cloud as a "world-covering, protective umbrella . . . shielding us everywhere . . . harnessing the vast power of the hydrogen in the world's oceans to bring in an era of prosperity such as the world has never dared dream about."[6]

Brigadier General Thomas F. Farrell, stationed at the control shelter, wrote of what he witnessed at the first nuclear test at Trinity Site, New Mexico, in 1945: "The effects could be called unprecedented, magnificent, beautiful, stupendous and terrifying. . . . It lighted every peak, crevasse and ridge of the nearby mountain range with a clarity and beauty that cannot be described but must be seen to be imagined. It was that beauty the great poets dream about but describe most poorly and inadequately."[7]

President Truman did not apotheosize the bomb but called it "the greatest thing in history."[8]

Perhaps no one will ever surpass General Curtis LeMay of the

A Very, Very Small Club

The head of Saddam Hussein's nuclear weapons program, Dr. Khidhir Hamza, was possessed by the same hubris. He writes in his book (with Jeff Stein), *Saddam's Bombmaker: The Terrifying Inside Story of the Iraqi Nuclear and Biological Weapons Agenda*:

"I mean, how many people get to make a nuclear bomb, just to see if it will work . . . just to see it go off—the double flash, the instant darkness, the roar of the wind and dust . . . the mushroom cloud rising over the desert. Everything they had seen at Los Alamos at the dawn of the nuclear age in 1945.

"It was a thrill. I was knocking on the door of membership in a very, very small club, with names like Fermi, Hans Bethe, and Oppenheimer."[9]

United States Air Force (USAF) for sheer transcendent ecstasy in his description of a nuclear-armed bomber:

"That beautiful devilish pod underneath, the baby of the fuselage . . . clinging as a fierce child against its mother's belly—the [bomber] carries all the conventional bomb explosive force of World War II and everything which came before. A single [bomber] can do that.

"It lugs the flame and misery of attacks on London . . . the rubble of Coventry and the rubble of Plymouth. . . . Blow up or burn up fifty-three per cent of Hamburg's buildings. . . . and kill fifty thousand people into the bargain. Shatter and fry Essen and Dortmund and Gelsenkirchen, and every other town in the Ruhr. Shatter the city of Berlin. Do what the Japanese did to us at Pearl, and what we did to the Japanese at Osaka and Yokohama and Nagoya. Do Tokyo over again.

"The force of these, in a single pod.

"One [bomber] can load that comprehensive concentrated fire-power, and convey it to any place on the globe, and let it sink down, and let it go off, and bruise the stars and planets and satellites listening in.

"... Big Bertha bombarding Paris ... musketry of the American Revolutionary battles or the Napoleonic ones. Spotsylvania and Shiloh and the battles for Atlanta.

"Firepower. All the firepower ever heard or experienced upon this earth. All in one bomb, all in one [plane]."[10]

As far as nuclear energy's ability to generate electricity—as we have demonstrated—it is preposterously expensive and apocalyptically dangerous. However, in his famous 1953 UN "Atoms for Peace" speech, President Eisenhower put the United States in the forefront of the nuclear proliferation business—retailing nuclear reactors to over forty nations. In 1953 alone, the United States exported twenty-two tons of bomb-grade uranium and plutonium to nations world-wide. The nuclear nations would eventually ship their "Atoms for Peace" nuclear exports to such unlikely recipients as Iran, Pakistan, India, Vietnam, North Korea, the Congo, Bangladesh, and the former Yugoslavia.[11]

Hoping to convert warring states to the path of nuclear peace, the United States provided them with U.S.-subsidized nuclear reactors. The research reactors were the bomb builder's training wheels, and the power plant reactors would provide the bomb-fuel fabricators. The claim that after these sales the new owners would turn their reactors into peaceful plowshares was fatuous at best, cynically deceptive at worst.[12]

A Nuclear Bomb-Fuel Reactor for . . . the Congo?

In 1958, when the Belgians still ran the Congo, they received an "Atoms for Peace" nuclear reactor. Since then the Congo has suffered multiple, stupefyingly brutal civil wars, and since the mid-1990s, the nation has also endured repeated incursions by neighboring Rwanda. After two decades, over four million people have perished there, mostly from starvation and pestilence.

The history of the Congo illustrates the problem with selling nuclear reactors abroad. The seller never ultimately knows what will happen to them.

In fact, at least two fuel rods were stolen out of them. One is believed to have been found en route to a Middle Eastern country. Some think it was sent via the Mafia. The other fuel rod is still missing.[13]

As was the promiscuously quoted claim that nuclear-powered electricity would be "too cheap to meter."

The net effect of "Atoms for Peace" is that today we live in a world with hundreds of reactors, which, with a few, completely manageable modifications, can be converted into nuclear bomb-fuel factories.

When Eisenhower presented his vision to the UN in 1953 and gave his famous "Atoms for Peace" speech, Vyacheslav Molotov—the USSR's second-in-command—approached U.S. Secretary of State John Foster Dulles and told him he did not think Eisenhower understood that nuclear power reactors could easily be converted to nuclear bomb-fuel reactors. Molotov told Dulles the United States would proliferate nuclear weaponry worldwide.

Dulles stared back at him, incredulous. Gerard C. Smith, a Dulles aide, was present, took notes on the meeting, and later wrote: "[W]hen Molotov protested to a dubious John Foster Dulles that the proposal would result in the spread worldwide of stockpiles of weapons-grade materials, I had to explain to Dulles that Molotov had been better informed technically than he. Subsequently, the Soviets asked how we proposed to stop this spread. The best we could reply was 'ways could be found.' We are still searching for these ways."[14]

The Purpose Was Not "Peace"

On December 8, 1953, President Eisenhower gave his famous "Atoms for Peace" address before the United Nations, saying, "The United States knows that peaceful power from atomic energy is no dream of the future. That capability, already proved, is here now—today."

That capability, in fact, would not exist for another decade and the statement was flagrantly untrue.

President Eisenhower continued: "Who can doubt, if the entire body of the world's scientists and engineers had adequate amounts of fissionable material with which to test and develop their ideas, that this capability would be rapidly transformed into universal, efficient and economic usage?"

In other words, Eisenhower said, if the USSR and the U.S. proliferated nuclear bomb-fuel worldwide, the nations of Earth would undoubtedly use it for exclusively peaceful means.[15]

Had Eisenhower gone mad? What in the hell had happened since 1945 to make global nuclear proliferation safe and secure? Had human nature changed? Did Eisenhower believe that the world leaders had miraculously turned into saints and angels? What is the hold nuclear power has over policymakers?

The latest claim is that nuclear power doesn't release carbon into the atmosphere. The people who make that claim, however, ignore nuclear power's dangers and costs. In fact, they act as if nuclear waste were not a pollutant. As we have discussed, the nuclear industry is racked by waste disposal problems—which will encumber and endanger over ten thousand generations to come. Nuclear power has also proven itself to be a financially invalid, insupportable method without government-financed feeding tubes. Even worse, in test after test it has also proven itself embarrassingly vulnerable to terrorist attack.

Armageddon on a Barge, the Apocalypse on Pontoons

George W. Bush agreed in writing to help Russia develop "floating nuclear reactors." (A link to that agreement is listed in the source note to this paragraph.) Shipped up rivers and canals, these pontooned power plants could be moored in inland lakes, off the country's coasts, anywhere, including Third World countries, which lacked the infrastructure and expertise to build and maintain such reactors on land. Russia wanted to sell them to China (one of the world's leading nuclear proliferators), Algeria, Egypt, and the other Arab nations; Thailand, Indonesia, Malaysia, the Philippines; Namibia and the other countries of Africa as well as Asia and Latin America. Argentina, Chile, and Brazil have shown interest. Indonesia has the largest Islamic population in the world, and Malaysia was one of A. Q. Khan's most helpful trading partners in his global nuclear black-market network. At times, the Philippines had been an al Qaeda training ground. Several of those nations resided in the "Ring of Fire," that notoriously seismic zone in the Pacific, which had produced periodic mega-quakes along with their subsequent tsunamis, including the one that—with its tsunami—melted down Fukushima.[16]

The Russian firm Rosenergoatom has built floating nuclear reactors, and by one report has one assembled. Based on Russian naval designs, the reactors were initially designed to operate on weapons-usuable uranium—which runs between 20 percent and 60 percent. A Greenpeace official has suggested it might be slightly less that 20 percent; whether that is true is unclear. Weapons-usable uranium fuel can be detonated in a bomb but will produce a lower yield. The Russian government admitted the reactor's HEU was well above the 20 percent typically required for civilian uranium-fueled nuclear power reactors.[17]

Russia wanted the United States to help them build and market these floating bomb-fuel reactors because Chernobyl had tarnished Russia's reputation as a nuclear exporter. America's reputation as the world's premier nuclear contractor—indeed, the creator of the world's nuclear industry—would add indispensable credibility to Russia's effort.[18]

George W. Bush concluded an agreement with Russia expressing U.S. intentions to cooperate with that country in these endeavors— even though Russia had offered these waterborne reactors to some of the most problematic countries and regions on Earth.[19]

Nor did the agreement Bush signed explain who would secure these reactors once they were delivered, how they would be protected, or how the nuclear fuel and waste would be stored and secured. Bush agreed to help develop these plants even though no one ever spelled out how the plants could be protected against terrorist attacks or catastrophic natural disasters such as the Fukushima tsunami, to say nothing of who would be financially responsible and who would handle the cleanup if such a disaster befell a developing nation.[20]

Nor was the deployment of these floating reactors in Russia's northern seas without peril. In fact, environmentalists were up in arms over the prospect. Russia's Greenpeace and Norway's Bellona argued that accidents were likely that could poison water, sea life, people, and the air. "The weather in these [northern] areas is extraordinarily unpredictable, in the winters waves can go up to 10 or 20 meters," Bellona's Charles Digges said in an interview. Environmentalists also pointed out that wave and wind energy were cheaper and safer means of generating energy in coast regions.[21]

Or as the nuclear-energy analyst Mycle Schneider said, "You can't promise an inherently safe nuclear reactor . . . and by floating these things and towing them off to remote locations you multiply the risks. It's entirely ridiculous."[22]

It's the Dirt That Does It

Over the decades many of our nuclear pundits have been desperate to pretend that nuclear war is not that bad. Henry Kissinger rose to fame in the 1950s advocating the viability of limited nuclear strikes.

Curtis LeMay believed fear of nuclear weapons was unwarranted: They were no scarier than conventional bombs. He said in his memoir, "[The atom bomb's] unmitigated terror has . . . no basis in fact."[23]

Robert Scheer, in his book, *With Enough Shovels: Reagan, Bush and Nuclear War*, gives an example of this seeming withdrawal from reality.

Thomas K. Jones, the man Ronald Reagan had appointed Deputy Under Secretary of Defense for Research and Engineering, Strategic and Theater Nuclear Forces, told me that the United States could fully recover from an all-out nuclear war with the Soviet Union in just two to four years. T. K., as he prefers to be known, added that nuclear war was not nearly as devastating as we had been led to believe. He said, if there are enough shovels to go around, everybody's going to make it. The shovels were for digging holes in the ground, which would be covered somehow or other with a couple of doors and with three feet of dirt thrown on top, thereby providing adequate fallout shelters for millions who had been evacuated from America's cities to the countryside. It's the dirt that does it, he said.[24]

John McPhee, in interviews with professional scientists and engineers, assembled the following statements:

"[Nuclear] Bomb damage is vastly exaggerated."

"The largest bomb that has ever been exploded anywhere was sixty megatons, and that is one-thousandth the force of an earthquake, one-thousandth the force of a hurricane. We have lived with earthquakes and hurricanes for a long time."

"After the bomb goes off, and the fire ends, quiet descends again, and life continues."

"At the start of the First World War, the high-explosive shell was described as 'the ultimate weapon.' It was said that the war could not last more than two weeks. Then they discovered dirt. They found they could get away from the high-explosive shell in trenches. When hijackers start holding up whole nations and exploding nuclear bombs, we must again discover dirt. We can live with these bombs. The power of dirt will be re-exploited."[25]

Presidential candidate Barry Goldwater, and in the following election presidential candidate George Wallace's running mate, General Curtis LeMay—in their respective presidential campaigns—threatened to use nuclear weapons in Vietnam. Although the two respective candidates were defeated, the two men received a substantial number of votes. Goldwater received 40 percent of the vote. LeMay—along with his presidential running mate, George Wallace—received one-third of Richard Nixon's total vote in the 1968 presidential election when Nixon won.[26]

The Nuclear Bazooka

"Goldwater's [presidential campaign] troubles began," Peter Kuznick wrote in the *Bulletin of the Atomic Scientists,* "with an October 1963 press conference at which he said that NATO's six divisions could 'probably' be cut by one-third or more if NATO commanders had the power to decide to use tactical nuclear weapons." In 1960, in his book *The Conscience of a Conservative,* Goldwater supported the deployment of small battlefield nukes.

Goldwater disparaged disarmament accords—particularly

the nuclear test ban treaty—and the Arms Control and Disarmament Agency. [27]

Goldwater supported the deployment of all sorts of small, portable, tactical nukes. One weapon, developed by the Pentagon, which Goldwater might have considered was the Davy Crockett "nuclear bazooka." It could be packed into battle by two to three men in knapsacks and assembled on the spot. The nuclear weapon was then fired from its tripod-mounted bazooka. Whether the bazooka team would have survived the launch is a matter of some dispute.[28]

The Communist World Would Cease to Exist

The grossest example of the kind of overpowering nuclear zealotry, which Goldwater espoused, was embodied in Curtis LeMay's 1960 "Single Integrated and Operational Plan" (SIOP). It even scared the hell out of President Eisenhower," Tom Engelhardt wrote. "It was to hit 1,060 targets in the USSR and China in at least 130 cities, which would then . . . vanish. Casualty estimates ran 285 million dead, 40 million injured, plus radiation ailments. Marine Corps Commandant David Shoup asked how China would fare if they stayed neutral. The director of Strategic Target Planning, General Thomas Power, said he hoped no one else thought of that. Shoup suggested: "[A]ny plan that kills millions of Chinese when it isn't even their war is not a good plan."[29]

William F. Buckley Jr.—the intellectual father of the conservative movement—recommended using nuclear bombs in 1964 against China's fledgling nuclear reactors.[30]

In 2003, Charles Krauthammer—the *Washington Post*'s Pulitzer Prize–winning neo-conservative columnist—saw nuclear weapons as a powerful diplomatic weapon. Frustrated that China had not sufficiently pressured North Korea to shut down her nuclear program, he wrote in his column that the United States should offer Japan a trade deal on nuclear-tipped ballistic missiles, capable of hitting both China and North Korea.

"Play the trump . . ." the neo-con columnist wrote. "If our nightmare is a nuclear North Korea, China's [is] a nuclear Japan. It's time to share the nightmares."[31]

Krauthammer ignored the probability that a nuclear Japan would more likely accelerate—not freeze—a regional nuclear arms race. Few nations disarm in the face of mounting military threats.

And while we're speaking of nuclear lunacy, as previously discussed, Joe Biden wanted to sell nuclear power reactors to Iraq, even though they did not have and, as of the writing of this book, still do not have a stable and fully functional government.[32]

In fact, the U.S. special inspector-general for Iraq reconstruction, Stuart Bowen, said that after a decade and $60 billion in U.S. taxpayer dollars, Iraq is still so unstable and broken that even its leaders argue that the Washington reconstruction program wasn't worth the cost.[33]

Nuking the Moon

One of the supreme nuclear fallacies is that U.S. policymakers hate and fear nuclear weapons. As we have seen, quite a few of them did not appear to. Over the years some U.S. leaders have too often seemed to glorify them. Dr. Edward Teller—the scientific father of the hydrogen bomb and the Star Wars missile defense—pleaded with Congress and President Eisenhower to reject even the idea of a nuclear test ban treaty. He also argued that the United States could use nuclear devices to explore for oil, excavate mineral deposits, forge diamonds, dig canals, change the course of rivers, and even control the weather. He thought it would be fun to hammer the moon with nukes and watch the fireworks. In part to circumvent a prospective nuclear test ban treaty, Teller advocated testing nuclear arms in deep caves and on the far side of the moon.

At a time when American citizens worried about the fallout generated by nuclear tests, Teller argued that, on the contrary, fallout was inconsequential and might in fact be beneficial.

Teller's position was of course preposterous.[34]

Ten Times Hotter than the Sun's Core

Many advanced nations, including the United States, South Korea, and those countries in the European Union (EU), are working hard to develop fusion power, which would, in principle, fuse hydrogen isotopes together, thereby duplicating the energy-generating processes of the sun. To achieve this goal, the reactor must squeeze and heat the fusion fuel's plasma to over 150 million degrees centigrade—ten times hotter than the sun's core. Fusion power's proponents plan on using particle beams, radio waves, lasers, and ultra-powerful magnets to make their invention work. So far, the amount of energy required to reach these temperatures has been more than that which the fusion power reactor is capable of producing.[35]

The world isn't anywhere close to creating a successful fusion power reactor. Still the nations of Earth are obsessed with building one. The United States, the European Union, China, Japan, Russia, India, and South Korea are all working hard and coughing up colossal amounts of money in that effort.[36]

The world's most ambitious and expensive foray into fusion power is the International Thermonuclear Experimental Reactor (ITER), which is to be based in Cadarache, France. Its charter, the European Fusion Development Agreement (EFDA), describes some of the obstacles to ITER's successful completion. Its main problem is containing the reaction's 150 million degrees of heat and then expelling it at the proper time. No one knows how or with what material to create and then line the power plant's plasma vessel. Fusion produces enough energy to destabilize the vessel wall's molecules and turn the structure radioactive. Scientists don't even have an energy source powerful enough to test the vessel's containment walls or the materials out of which they would eventually be constructed. Moreover, ITER would only be a reactor. Those developing the power plant itself would face even far more overwhelming difficulties.[37]

Nonetheless, nations around the world are trying to make fusion power a reality. Their attempts go back almost seventy years and will require well over $100 billion. As for ITER, it has been stalled repeatedly by delays and cost overruns. The total bill is now expected to run over $21 billion, triple the first cost estimates in 2006. Some critics wonder if it will ever work. Thomas Cochran, an expert with the Natural Resources Defense Council in Washington, D.C., has questioned ITER's financial feasibility: "It is already obvious that future commercial-size machines will be too large and costly, and too expensive to operate, to generate competitive energy." Some serious scientists estimate that the creation of viable fusion power could well take another century, and even then they do not guarantee success.[38]

In other words, if you enjoyed the financial excesses of the nuclear power industry, you'll love the economic extravagances of the fusion power experimenters. (We have to call them "experimenters"; after almost seventy years there is no evidence that fusion power will ever be more than an experiment, that it will work or be cost-effective enough to become an industry.)

Fusion power's advocates are, nonetheless, fanatical on the subject. South Korea is a prime example. It is so desperate to develop fusion power that it plans to spend one trillion won on the project, or $941 billion.[39]

The Iranian government announced that they too will build a fusion reactor. They plan on finishing theirs by 2020.[40]

One can only imagine what the world would be like if the planet had spent the last seventy years and hundreds of billions of dollars developing sensible alternate energy industries instead of throwing money down the nuclear power abyss.

After Goldwater's resounding defeat, politicians learned the danger of praising nuclear weapons in public. Unlike Edward Teller, the U.S. public knows nuclear weapons are not useful and that no one profits from a nuclear exchange. After Chernobyl, Three Mile Island, and the Fukushima disasters, the U.S. public learned the downside of nuclear power. Hence, over the decades, policymakers have learned to disguise their nuclear chauvinism and have planned and arranged for the financing of their nuclear programs behind closed doors.

And he opened up the bottomless pit.

—Revelation 9:2

PART III

1

THE FATAL FALLACY OF
NUCLEAR HOMELAND SECURITY

The most likely target for a nuclear terrorist attack is New York, the country's largest city and the world's financial nerve center.

What would a powerful but relatively simple-to-construct Hiroshima-style nuke do to a major urban center, such as New York City? One study demonstrated that in Manhattan, such a weapon detonated in Times Square at rush hour could kill 500,000 people. A large part of Manhattan might well be rendered uninhabitable, depending upon the wind-driven firestorms and the fallout dispersal.[1]

Since this blast would be a ground-level detonation—something never seriously attempted before—the fallout would be exponentially greater than that of air bursts. Over the years its fallout-generated radiation poisoning could kill many hundreds of thousands more than that of air bursts. The consequent radioactive particles would continue to murder tristate inhabitants for decades to come.

The immediate costs would be incalculable—well into the trillions of dollars.

The nation's GDP would plummet.

Fear of subsequent attacks would be paralyzingly pandemic.

In its final phase, radiation sickness would replicate the terminal stages of such horrible hemorrhagic killers as AIDS and Ebola-Zaire.

The strike's victims would overwhelm New York's hospitals.

The New York survivors would endure horrific levels of traumatic shock. Robert Jay Lifton described the mental condition of many of the Hiroshima survivors as death-in-life, with many of their emotional scars—particularly the fear of recurring strikes and the gnawing death guilt—as permanent conditions.[2]

For over fifty years, the United States government has seriously understated the destructive effects of nuclear weapons by not including firestorm damage in its nuclear war assessments—arguably the most catastrophic of the effects. Given that for Hiroshima's survivors the firestorms were among their worst nightmares, the Pentagon's concealment of firestorm destruction was almost pathologically perverse.[3]

What happens when a nuclear weapon is detonated in a metropolis? Its thermal pulse generates temperatures that rival those of the sun. The air within and surrounding the incipient fireball is squeezed into a ball of superheated, superpressurized air, which becomes a stupendously powerful blast wave. It shatters everything in its path, reducing buildings to slivers and shards—supremely flammable tinder. Due to the fireball's astronomical heat, it swells with lightning speed. Innumerable fires would immediately ignite everywhere, quickly merging into huge firestorms. The immense quantities of superheated air levitate, their convective action creating hurricane-force winds on the Earth below, which act on the city's fires as a billow. The firestorms would grow in heat and amplitude, coalescing into a massive conflagration of inconceivable power, producing tornado-force winds over an enormous area.[4]

Russia is believed to have deployed two thousand tactical nuclear weapons and to also have more in storage. These are small, highly mobile nuclear weapons. Russia's tactical nukes are not covered by our Strategic Arms Reduction Treaty (START), and many experts fear they are not accurately inventoried or secured. Many of those— particularly the nuclear landmines and artillery shells—are frighteningly portable. Their kilotons would typically range anywhere from a fraction of a kiloton to ten kilotons or more.[5]

2

THE FATAL FALLACY OF
FORTIFYING A NUCLEAR FIRETRAP

Throughout the Bush administration, at the country's nuclear weapons labs and power plants, security was ill planned, under-funded, and woefully inadequate. The Bush team's apathy toward U.S. nuclear security continued even after 9/11 and after intelli-gence agencies uncovered terrorist threats against nuclear weapons sites and power-generating facilities.

Mohammed Atta, for instance, actively considered melting down a nuclear reactor rather than striking the World Trade Center. *The Wall Street Journal* reported a "credible" terrorist plot to melt down Three Mile Island for a second time shortly after 9/11. Khalid Sheikh Mo-hammed, the 9/11 mastermind, said he'd initially planned to take out a nuclear power plant—probably Indian Point, since he was focusing on New York City. A London terror suspect was captured with a ter-ror manual listing high-value global targets, including nuclear power plants.[1]

As we reported earlier, reputed Al Qaeda associate Sharif Mobley worked and trained at five U.S. nuclear power plants.[2]

As we have also discussed in some detail, not only nuclear power plants, but U.S. nuclear bomb-fuel sites are deplorably protected. Instead of upgrading security, however, the NRC and DOE under the Bush administration classified all test results so the public would not learn how badly the facility defenders had failed, how ridiculously many of the tests had been rigged, and how vulnerable U.S. nuclear plants were.[3]

The Fatal Fallacy of the Impatient Terrorist

The best of the al Qaeda/Taliban–style terrorists are tenacious and meticulously organized. If they attacked the Indian Point nuclear facility just outside of New York City, for instance, or the DOE nuclear weapons facility near San Francisco, they would not employ half-measures. *The New York Times* has reported on just how thorough al Qaeda terrorists were before the U.S. embassy bombing in Kenya.[4]

"[Al Qaeda] scouted the streets. They took photographs. They wrote detailed surveillance reports. And then, after five years of patiently waiting, Al Qaeda operatives carried out the devastating suicide truck bombing at the American embassy in Nairobi, Kenya, in August, 1998, killing more than two hundred people and injuring thousands." Al Qaeda is notorious for "studying targets and fine-tuning strategies for years before an attack. . . ." Former al Qaeda member

L'Houssaine Kherchtou recalled that "[i]f they were to learn about a specific room, they were to scout 'the walls, the colors, how big are the walls, and which color are they, and how high they are, the lights, the doors, the floor, everything that you can see, all information about that room.' Operatives were trained to file these detailed surveillance reports on disks so they could carry them around."[5]

Al Qaeda spent two to four years planning the USS *Cole* attack, five years for the assault on Kenyan and Tanzanian embassies, and five to six years preparing for 9/11.[6]

The more recent al Qaeda/Taliban assaults on Pakistan's nuclear facilities and army headquarters were even more complex and sophisticated than their attacks on the USS *Cole* and the U.S. African embassies.[7] The United States should assume a more potent and complex attack—such as simultaneous assaults on multiple nuclear facilities—would be painstakingly planned, meticulously executed, and requiring perhaps a decade of preparation.

On the other hand, for such trained professionals, melting down Indian Point might not be that difficult. In the case of a nuclear power plant—as opposed to a nuclear bomb-fuel facility—the terrorists wouldn't be looking to steal anything or even occupy it long-term.

Their Only Goal Is to Incinerate a Firetrap

According to Danielle Brian, executive director of the Project on Government Oversight, the nuclear industry's anti-terrorist defenses do not reflect "what intelligence experts say is realistic, but what the industry is willing to pay for." Ms. Brian also said that activating a police SWAT team would take ninety minutes while the terrorists would win or lose in less than eight minutes. In other words, the cavalry would be an hour and half late.

The difficulty in defending nuclear facilities is exacerbated by the explosively combustible materials the defenders are protecting and the single-minded simplicity of the terrorists' goal: They only want to incinerate a firetrap.[8]

Neither the Bush nor the Obama administrations provided U.S. nuclear power plants with adequate protection. In *Time* magazine, Mark Thompson dramatized how a skilled, well-equipped cadre of two dozen terrorists could assault a nuclear power plant. They would first break through the fences with bolt cutters and pipe-shaped explosives developed by the British in India a hundred years ago. They would then breach the outer walls with World War II–vintage platter charges and head straight for the control room. Blinding the plant's surveillance cameras and electronic jammers with lasers, they would neutralize the opposition's communications. Thanks to their "active violent insider," they would have hand-sketched schematics of the layout, the best routes to the control room, drawings of and instructions for the control panels, and holes in security.[9] One of the terrorists might have worked in a U.S. nuclear power plant, as Sharif Mobley—who associated with terrorists—did, or he could have been trained by such a person. The U.S. nuclear industry might have trained the individual at one of their foreign nuclear power plants.

We learned from Fukushima that to melt down a nuclear power plant, terrorists need only to blow up the cooling pumps and intake pipes.[10] After effecting a loss-of-coolant meltdown, a radioactive plume would soar high into the sky. Depending on wind direction, the radioactivity could ultimately kill hundreds of thousands of people. By inflicting so many casualties and poisoning nearby property areas, some estimates put the dollar cost to taxpayers as high as $11 trillion.[11]

One study at Indian Point—thirty miles from downtown New York City—found that only 19 percent of its guards said they could "adequately defend the plant." One guard claimed that if subjected to a 9/11-style attack by, say, nineteen heavily armed, well-organized terrorists, he might very well use his 9mm pistol to fight his way out of the plant, then run home to evacuate his family. When 20 to 25 percent of Indian Point guards said they couldn't get up from the ground by themselves, Al Franken (before he was a U.S. senator) quipped that bin Laden's guys could, no doubt, rise unassisted from the prone position.[12]

Many guards at Indian Point complained that hundreds of keys and electronic key cards had disappeared. Guards complained that it sometimes took years to get the locks changed.[13]

Nor are U.S. nuclear power plants equipped to fight the nuclear fires which terrorists would ignite.

A Nursing Home Has More Fire Protection
Than This Nuclear Power Plant

Most assault scenarios result in plant fires—whether in the reactor or the cooling pools—yet nuclear power plants for the most part have refused to install the fire-safety systems that automatically shut the reactors down in case of fire. Instead of penalizing the power plant owners, the Nuclear Regulatory Commission eliminated the regulations requiring nuclear power plants to automatically shut down in the event of fire. Failure to shut down the reactor can of course subject plants to meltdown similar to the disaster at Three Mile Island, and the fictional meltdown made famous in the film *The China Syndrome*—which preceded and predicted the Three Mile Island catastrophe.

Journalist Anne-Marie Cusac published a shocking report on the lack of fire-safety equipment in U.S. nuclear facilities, including nuclear power plants located near or in major U.S. cities. In "Fire Hazard: Bush Leaves Nuclear Plants at Risk," Cusac demonstrated that a major safety problem at nuclear facilities was the NRC's failure to force the installation of proper fire-safety equipment. Consequently, nuclear plant employees found it extraordinarily difficult to prevent and put out fires . . . to say nothing of extinguishing genuine conflagrations. These power plant fires could cost the United States far more lives and far more tax dollars than the terrorist assault itself.

Cusac points out that in order to shut down some nuclear

power plants, workers had to perform over one hundred physical shutdown operations. In order to prevent a meltdown, plant employees would have to battle lethal radiation, high temperatures, armed suicide terrorists, blazing flames, and blinding smoke, get to those stations, and then perform those hundred operations. Since some of those operations required shutting down hot electrical boxes filled with poorly labeled cables in small smoke-filled rooms and cabinets, the work itself could be lethal.

Jerry Brown, a former nuclear industry consultant, said, "There are more fire barriers in a nursing home than in a nuclear power plant."[14]

3

A TERRORIST ARMAGEDDON

n 2003, Dan Verton published the frightening and prophetic book *Black Ice: The Invisible Threat of Cyber-Terrorism,* in which he described how cyber attacks could knock out electrical, telecommunications, medical, and Internet systems. The cyber terrorist could then disrupt the services of fire and police departments, national guard units, health facilities, and major hospitals, preventing them all from assisting survivors of the earlier strikes. Verton also explained how multi-city physical assaults combined with nationwide cyber strikes could inflict unparalleled devastation on the United States.[1]

An all-out cyber attack on our energy, financial, military, and communications sectors could be coupled with well-coordinated nuclear terrorist strikes against our major cities. The recovery from those strikes would have to be accomplished without power and without electronically interdependent communications systems. Such combined assaults would wreak irremediable destruction.

Not only would a major cyber attack be relatively easy to pull off for skilled hackers, Verton wrote that our cyber terrorist might have worked as a computer systems designer in the very U.S. industry or federal department he was obliterating. Prime targets might be the energy, telecommunications, or medical care industries; Wall Street; the Department of Defense or even the Internal Revenue Service (IRS). Since much of that work is outsourced, our cyber terrorist could have worked for these U.S. institutions offshore—in India, Indonesia, or China—and the United States in a sense might very well have paid for his cyber-terrorist education.[2]

In order to prepare for and respond to these attacks, the government designed exercises to simulate them. Operations such as Black Ice and Blue Cascades worked out virtual, coordinated assaults on U.S. power and communications grids with conventional explosives and localized cyber attacks. In the case of Blue Cascades, projected power and telecommunications blackouts spread rapidly from the Pacific Northwest to other western states, and the recovery dragged out with torturous slowness. Critical parts for the damaged electrical power plants, which were manufactured abroad, were not readily obtainable in the United States. Downed power plants kept the telecommunications industries off-line, which further magnified problems.[3]

Black Ice and Blue Cascades proved that a well-planned, easy-to-execute nationwide cyber attack—costing under $100,000—could shut down power grids, telecommunications, the Internet, banking networks, the National Guard in dozens of states, as well as fire, police, and health departments. Black Ice and Blue Cascades revealed that once a chain reaction of interlocking disasters was initiated, among those compromised would be transportation systems, nuclear plants, oil refineries, chemical storage dumps, dams, water treatment facilities, fuel stations, the North American Aerospace Defense Command (NORAD), Congress, the Pentagon, and even the Pentagon's communications systems. Ships at sea would have little or no contact with command centers such as the Commander in Chief Pacific Command (CINCPAC).[4]

Cyber terrorists could contaminate online computer systems with exponentiating viruses or "denial-of-service worms." One infamous denial-of-service worm was capable of shutting off phone calls to a critical facility—such as 911.[5]

As discussed earlier, the United States and Israel reportedly created a nuclear reactor–killing worm and then used it primarily on Iran. Stuxnet attacked one of the computerized controlling systems. Known as Supervisory, Control and Data Acquisition (SCADA), these systems monitor and control industry, power, communications, Internet, and defense networks. Nuclear power plants have already been targeted.[6]

Nor does the cyber attack have to be exclusively electronic. Cyber terrorists could coordinate systematic hacking with terrorist bombing assaults on Internet communications nodes and regional switching stations. These switching centers service the major Internet providers, which connect there in order to share data. Millions of Internet transmissions per second can pass through a switching center. One well-known "regional Internet switching center" handles up to 40 percent of the nation's Internet activity.[7] A successful attack would bring that activity to a halt.

The cyber terrorist could also set off an electromagnetic device, an EMP bomb (or e-bomb) in a major city. The simplest e-bomb consists of a large copper tube, densely wrapped in copper wire and packed with conventional explosive. The wire is charged by a battery. This powerful electromagnet—short-circuited by the blast—compresses, transmitting a devastating electromagnetic pulse, the so-called EMP. The two most common types of e-bombs are the flux compression generator (FCG) and the high-power microwave (HPM). The FCG can reportedly be built in a garage with low-tech materials. The device's efficacy is controversial, but some experts believe its pulse could conceivably fry all electronic transmissions, radio communications, and electrical and computer linkages within a two-mile radius. Everything from pacemakers, car ignitions, traffic or train signals, industrial controls, and radio-TV-telephone communications might well be gone. If there are strategic routing transmission facilities within that two-mile radius, the cascade of rolling power outages would spread rapidly for hundreds, even thousands of miles.[8]

And the terrorist's crudely built e-bomb costs only $1,500.[9]

If a functioning e-bomb was detonated near the New York Stock Exchange or a major nuclear power plant such as New York's Indian Point, the destruction would be incalculable.

A nuclear weapon detonated in a low orbit can electromagnetically disable entire states, arguably whole countries.[10]

All the studies, all the exercises in cyber-terrorist prevention pointed to one dramatic fact: U.S. national security was increasingly in the hands of private enterprise. Federal reluctance to impose cyber-security standards on these firms has led to a national cyber-security disaster-in-the-making. Lack of federal regulation has left the United States defenseless against cyber warfare.[11]

As I said, Verton's book was prophetic. On October 11, 2012, then defense secretary Leon Panetta warned that cyber attacks on the United States had become increasingly dangerous. He envisioned assaults that could dismantle America's energy grid as well as its water, transportation, and financial systems. He described such a series of strikes as "a Cyber Pearl Harbor."[12]

As Verton had warned, the United States was increasingly vulnerable to these cyber threats in part because U.S. businesses would not seriously secure their computer systems. In fact, the U.S. Chamber of Commerce fought and defeated one very aggressive cyber-security bill just two months before Panetta spoke. The lobbying group argued that such cyber-security laws would be too onerous for American businesses, and a coalition of Republican legislators, led by Senator John McCain (R-AZ), blocked the bill. Ironically, McCain—a noted defense hawk—turned out to be soft on national cyber security.[13]

Then four months later, *The New York Times* reported that a global cyber war had begun in earnest. The evidence was overwhelming that a People's Liberation Army (PLA) base for China's cyberwarrior corps was housed on the edge of Shanghai. This headquarters was known as PLA Unit 61398. Its U.S. victims referred to it as the "Comment Crew" or the "Shanghai Group." As part of their economic espionage operations, the Comment Crew stole terrabytes of data from major U.S. firms, including U.S. financial institutions. Increasingly, however, the Crew was focusing on the U.S. infrastructure—its water system, gas lines, and electrical grid. One firm which they had targeted had electronic access to more than 60 percent of the gas and oil pipelines in North America. The Comment Crew had penetrated twenty U.S. industries, including chemical plants, defense contractors, and satellite and telecommunications firms. One of the companies they hit was Lockheed Martin Corporation, America's largest military contractor.[14]

Their most worrisome assault, experts said, was on a software company whose product gave gas and oil firms and electrical-grid operations electronic access to the valves, switches, and security systems that run those operations. The company, Telvent DMS, *The New York Times* reported, "keeps detailed blueprints on more than half of all the oil and gas pipelines in North and South America, and has access to their systems." When Telvent found out, they cut that access so intruders couldn't commandeer the systems. One expert described this kind of attack as "the holy grail" of cyber warfare.[15]

End of Days

Nor are a half-dozen simultaneous cyber-nuclear strikes our worst-case scenario. Herman Kahn wrote over fifty years ago that one day nuclear bomb-fuel and nuclear delivery systems could proliferate so promiscuously that small vengeful powers could obtain them. If they also obtained the delivery systems of enemy states and were such rogue states crafty, skillful, and evil enough, they might hit the great nuclear powers with a series of disguised strikes, all the while convincing their victims that other nations were the perpetrators. Through such methods, Kahn's small vengeful powers could pit the great powers against each other in a global nuclear apocalypse. Kahn called this scenario "catalytic nuclear warfare."[16]

This book argues that the nuclear bomb-fuel and delivery systems—including cruise missiles—are so widely available today that a small vengeful power could nuke a country but create the impression that a different nation did it. One could imagine Iran stealing enough bomb-fuel to set off a nuclear device in Pakistan, then finding some way to blame Israel. Pakistan is so fearful of India, one could imagine that country nuking China, then trying to blame India. China and India also have conflicts going back fifty years, fighting a war in 1962.[17]

I dramatized such a worldwide nuclear conflagration at great length in my novel *End of Days*.

Quis Custodiet Ipsos Custodes? (Who Shall Guard the Guards Themselves?)
—Decimus Iunius Iuvenalis (c. 60–c. 140)

1

NUCLEAR CONFLICTS-OF-INTEREST

I

_____

The Iraq War reminded the world of many painful truths. One of those truths is as tragic as it is timeless: Too many powerful leaders have waged too many catastrophic wars for too long. A brief glance at several such conflicts will corroborate that dictum: Britain's two wars against the Thirteen Colonies; Napoleon Bonaparte's assaults on Europe, Egypt, and Russia; the American South's firing on Fort Sumter and the subsequent Civil War; Kaiser Wilhelm's invasions of France and Russia; Hitler's and Hirohito's wars; the French in Vietnam and Algeria; India and Pakistan in Kashmir; the USSR in Afghanistan and Chechnya; Saddam's war against Iran; the United States' wars in Vietnam and Iraq—to say nothing of those eternal "brushfire wars" that blaze by the hundreds through the undeveloped world each year.

The U.S. leaders misjudging and mishandling the Iraq War is a critique generally accepted by experts on the right and the left—even by those Bush generals and officials who launched the war. That the Bush and Obama administrations did no better against the nuclear terrorist is less appreciated. Neglecting to stem the spread of nuclear bomb-fuel, they also failed to cut the nuclear terrorist's funding—in part because they and their business partners trafficked financially with too many of the nuclear terrorist's paymasters and proliferators. Controlling the terrorist's access to nuclear bomb-fuel—particularly highly enriched uranium (HEU)—is perhaps the most important job that Bush and Obama had, yet their efforts were embarrassingly feeble. In the end, too many people simply did not, and do not care.

The Bush coterie's ineptitude in Iraq, its misguided war against the nuclear terrorist, and Bush and Obama's failure to cut the nuclear terrorists' supply lines did not exist in a vacuum. History is littered with thousands of mistaken wars, and when the Iraq debacle is viewed in that context, nuclear weapons are even more unacceptable. Nothing in the Bush team's or in Barack Obama's track record, or in the long dismal fiasco-ridden march of military history, suggests that the world's leaders are qualified to oversee—let alone employ—apocalyptic weapons. How can citizens safely entrust political leaders with nuclear weapons? Too many leaders have proven themselves unfit. As a species, we are too incompetent to manage Armageddon's arms.

Nobody Hates the Swedes

One time I was having lunch with a friend of mine, who had been an expert on U.S.-Soviet nuclear strategy. We were discussing how it had become increasingly easy for rogue states who wanted, say, a half-dozen crude-but-powerful terrorist nukes to surreptitiously acquire the bomb-fuel and the components on the black market, then assemble the weapon. I asked him what sort of nuclear strategy the United States should follow in an age in which it could not be certain whether its enemies had terrorist nukes.

"You learn to be a good neighbor," the former Cold Warrior said. "You learn not to meddle. You help other nations where and when you can, and you earn their trust. Primarily, however, you leave others alone; you focus on your problems and opportunities at home."

"What about deterrence?" I asked.

"In an age," he said, "in which almost any irresponsible state that wants a nuke can get a nuke, you stay strong, but you also find a lot of your deterrence in not pissing people off, in not having implacable enemies. The price for meddling in other people's problems—the resultant nuclear blowback—will be too painful. You will learn there is a lot of deterrence in getting along with other countries and cultures. After all, when was the last time someone bombed a Swedish embassy or skyjacked a Swedish airliner?"

"Probably never," I said.

"Know why? Nobody hates the Swedes. So in our brave new world, you want to get along with everyone. You want to stop pissing people off. You want to become like . . . the Swedes."

I am not the only nuclear skeptic. Former Defense Secretary Admiral William Perry, former chairman of the Senate Committee on Armed Services Sam Nunn, and former secretaries of state Henry Kissinger and George Shultz have written in a *Wall Street Journal* joint op-ed piece that they, too, have joined the ranks of the nuclear skeptics.

Throughout their careers all four men were Cold War warriors and nuclear hawks. They believed the United States and the nations of Earth needed formidable nuclear arsenals to deter nuclear antagonists. Now, however, they argue these positions are passé, that "[t]he end of the Cold War made . . . deterrence obsolete." Because of the rise of nuclear terrorists, these elder statesmen argued we could no longer control nuclear arms. They recommended we abolish not only nuclear weapons but highly enriched uranium (HEU) itself. Only then, they maintained, could we create "a world free of nuclear weapons," which is their article's title.[2]

Why did they not advocate abolishing nuclear weapons in 1991 after the Cold War's end when the Soviet economy was in free fall, and Russia's leaders were infinitely more malleable than today? Iran's nuclear reactor program was in its infancy, and al Qaeda had barely begun to stir. North Korea had yet to fabricate its first bomb. Pakistan had a crude bomb, but it had barely commenced its black-market nuclear proliferations. The thirteen Middle Eastern states that currently seek nuclear power programs—including Egypt, Syria, Jordan, and the Saudis—eschewed the nuclear ambitions they harbor now. Oil prices were low, which made Russia and the Middle East's rogue regimes poorer and therefore more pliant. With some economic assistance, the United States could have convinced Russia to secure their own nuclear stockpiles quicker and easier than today. Russia and Iran were also exceedingly susceptible to financial pressure and coercive engagement back then. Plus, the U.S., Russia, and the EU had a better chance of successfully outlawing the production of HEU—which the four former officials had advocated—back then rather than today.

All the proposals these four elder statesmen outlined in their *Wall Street Journal* op-ed piece were far more feasible in the early 1990s than in the twenty-first century. Had these ex-officials advocated nuclear weapons abolition, they might have succeeded—in which case the world would have honored them as heroes rather than as Cold War anachronisms who had outlived their time. Why did it take them sixteen years to come to these conclusions anyway? These men's inability to comprehend a new reality for years confirms that powerful leaders are too inept to manage our nuclear arsenals and storage facilities.

Nuclear Conflicts-of-Interest?

Ironically, when out of office, at least three of the four "wise men" worked for the nuclear industry. Sam Nunn has just stepped down from the board of directors at General Electric, which is a nuclear contractor among other things.[3]

George Shultz is a former president and board director of Bechtel, part of whose business is and was nuclear contracting. He only retired from Bechtel's board of directors nine months before joining Perry, Nunn, and Kissinger to write the January 2007 *Wall Street Journal* op-ed piece.[4]

William Perry is a board director of Los Alamos National Security, LLC, which is the private corporation that manages the Los Alamos National Laboratory. Los Alamos develops both nuclear weapons and nuclear power technology.[5]

Henry Kissinger's firm, Kissinger Associates Inc., refuses to divulge its client list. Consequently, no one knows what financial affiliations he has or might have had with the nuclear industry.[6]

II

Many Washington insiders reject conflict-of-interest charges out of hand. One journalist wrote in *The New York Times,* of an interview with a former high-ranking official, "if the fact that he was an advocate of the Iraq war while sitting on the board of a company that would benefit from it left him concerned about the appearance of a conflict of interest.

"[H]e said . . . 'nobody looks at it as something you benefit from.' "[7]

Most Washington powerbrokers are reluctant to make conflict-of-interest charges against colleagues because such accusations can reach back and bite them, threatening their earning power on leaving office. They intend to use their political contacts for financial gain. The taxpayers, however, favor generals and top officials with lavish retirement and medical packages, which are far more generous than those most taxpayers receive or provide for themselves. These leaders have no financial need to make money off their political or military connections in the service of defense/energy contractors and lobbyists. If the United States wants to stop the nuclear terrorist, however, former officials must not be allowed to transact business with nuclear proliferators, their oil-rich paymasters, and the middle men they employ. The penalties for convicted officials should include prison time.

Future scholars may well argue that the most significant datum in U.S. history was that—for the sake of personal avarice—our politicians, flag officers, and high-ranking officials directly or indirectly traded with America's nuclear enemies and helped bankroll the nation's financial ruin and its nuclear destruction.

A Detonating Debt Bubble of Apocalyptic Proportions

This overspending on defense contractors does not exist in a financial void. It is part of an American spending-borrowing spree, which, if unchecked, will bankrupt the United States. A number of America's principal creditors—China and Saudi Arabia, for instance—are uncertain friends. Were they to redeem the debt they have purchased from the United States, they would bankrupt the nation overnight.

U.S. firms are heavily invested in global derivative debt, which as of this book's writing tops $1.2 quadrillion. Scholars, such as Kevin Phillips, argue that this monstrous debt load, combined with the profligacy of America's defense/energy sector and its debt-finance industry—

particularly its notoriously ill-regulated derivative industry—portend a detonating debt bubble of apocalyptic proportions. Phillips argues that the collapse of great powers is often fueled by indebtedness.[8]

The history of this period might well record that the U.S. government during the Ronald Reagan and George W. Bush administrations even borrowed trillions of dollars, which were dispensed on their wealthy backers in the form of tax cuts and government subsidies. As David Stockman, Reagan's budget director, explained in a 1981 *Atlantic* interview with William Greider, supply-side economics never had anything to do with sound economics but was always "a Trojan horse for upper-bracket tax cuts."[9]

That two of the country's biggest lenders—Saudi Arabia and China—are among the nuclear terrorists' most prominent financiers and/or proliferators in no way deterred American officials' avarice or prevented them from trafficking with these countries financially once out of office, or from placing the United States in their financial debt.

III

As we have discussed, bomb-grade, highly enriched uranium (HEU) is the most dangerous, destabilizing substance in world history. While the trafficking of HEU and bomb-grade plutonium is hard to control, the manufacturing of HEU and nuclear reactors is costly and inconceivably complex. The world could—with a little luck—secure and control HEU production. Only a small number of nations can build and fuel reactors unilaterally.

Then, as those four elder statesmen have belatedly advocated, the world could abolish HEU's production.

And the world could then be weaned from HEU.

However, to outlaw HEU, the nuclear reactors it fuels, and ultimately plutonium production, the United States would first have to join with Russia, the EU, Japan, and China in controlling and securing the world's HEU's production. Those nations that reject intrusive inspections, tight controls, and a subsequent ban would have to face crippling, painful sanctions, culminating in the mandatory dismantlement of their nuclear facilities—by military force, if necessary.

After HEU and plutonium were outlawed and eliminated, the detection of nuclear rogues would be more straightforward. Any nation or group that sought HEU technology would have to go on the black market, and they would have only one motive—nuclear weaponry. They could no longer run the nuclear power confidence game, and the world could then deal with those states and individuals as nuclear outlaws.

Nuclear Weapons Can Go the Way of the Dinosaur

The manufacturing of nuclear reactors and bomb-fuel centrifuges is extortionately expensive and forbiddingly complex. Terrorists cannot cobble nuclear reactors together in their basement machine shops.

> If the penalties for violating the global nuclear ban were unacceptably severe, the world would have a realistic shot at abolishing nuclear reactors, plutonium, and HEU. Nuclear weapons could eventually go the way of the dinosaur.

To cut off the nuclear terrorist's cash flow, the United States must reduce its own dependence on the Middle East's oil-rich states, which have historically funded both the nuclear terrorists and their nuclear suppliers—particularly those operating through Pakistan's black market. As we have discussed, the Saudis still finance much of Pakistan's nuclear weapons program. Obama offered to help the Saudis acquire nuclear bomb-fuel reactors as well as place a massive high-tech arms order even though for years the Saudis have been al Qaeda's major contributors. Fifteen out of the nineteen 9/11 terrorists were Saudis.

Iran still underwrites the Hezbollah.

To counter the threats these states pose, the United States must reduce its own excessive oil consumption, which has supplied the petrodollar funding of nuclear proliferators and their illicit spawn, the nuclear terrorist.

With only 5 percent of the planet's population, the United States still consumes 25 percent of the world's available oil—much of it from the Middle East—even though the world is rife with alternate fuel opportunities. Nonetheless, the United States continues to hold the title as the biggest, least-efficient energy glutton on Earth.

The world has viable alternatives for creating clean, economical energy. Most people, however, think the only valid energy choices are the hydrocarbon and nuclear power industries. In fact, public ignorance of the alternate energy industries is the biggest hurdle to building a clean, green, economical energy system. Somehow the public must be convinced that such industries are financially feasible and technologically practicable.

Most Americans do not understand that a nationwide, economically competitive solar power industry is achievable in less than forty years. *Scientific American* made the case for such a large-scale U.S. solar power system in an extraordinary study entitled "A Solar Grand Plan: By 2050 solar power could end U.S. dependence on foreign oil and slash greenhouse gas emissions." Written by three solar energy researchers—Ken Zweibel, James Mason, and Vasilis Fthenakis—it carefully demonstrated how such an industry would work, pointing out that most of the systems were already proven and operating around the world.

According to the study, to make solar power work on a national scale, a parcel of barren southwestern desert, 175 miles by 175 miles, would have to be blanketed with photovoltaic panels and solar heating troughs. Several technological breakthroughs have made these "photovoltaic farms" possible. The solar cells covering the desert would be made out of thin cadmium telluride film, which is much more cost-effective than other kinds of cells. They would absorb solar energy during the daylight hours.[10]

During the sunless hours, high-voltage direct-current (HVDC) lines would transmit the electricity from the photovoltaic farms to compressed-air underground storage facilities, located in aquifers, subterranean caverns, vacant mine shafts, and abandoned natural gas wells. (Compressed air storage is not new or untested. Germany has successfully employed the system for thirty-five years, and in the United States, Alabama has had an effective, functional operation for over twenty years.) Then, along the major interstate highways, HVDC transmission towers and lines would have to be constructed. Direct current transmission is far more efficient than our present alternating current (AC) system, and the new HVDC lines would do a better job of delivering solar-produced electricity to our major cities than the transmission lines we already have.[11]

"Concentrated solar power" would provide one-fifth of America's solar energy. That system is comprised of long metallic mirrors, which concentrate solar energy onto fluid-filled pipes, heating the liquid with the magnified sunlight. The hot fluid passes through a heat exchanger, creating steam that powers a turbine. The United States has nine such plants, which have been producing electricity for years.[12]

Again, concentrated solar power is not blue-sky technology.

Solar Energy—Already Cheaper Than You Think!

The cost of solar energy production dropped precipitously between 2009 and 2013—around 50 percent. In certain regions of the United States, including the Southwest, building a solar energy plant costs as little as building a gas-turbine power plant, which is relatively inexpensive to construct. Consequently, in Kern and Los Angeles counties, the world's biggest solar power installation—the Antelope Valley Solar Project—is being built. It will generate enough electricity to power the homes of two million people and will cut 775,000 tons of CO^2 emissions each year. Ironically, the introduction of new, more efficient solar energy technology has also bankrupted older, less sophisticated solar energy plants, which could not compete with the newer plants' lower costs per watt.[13]

Hybrid plants, which combine both solar and wind power, have also become more efficient. At certain times and in certain areas solar panels receive more sunlight than wind turbines receive wind, and other times, wind is more plentiful. Since hybrid plants can exploit either energy sources, hybrid-generated electricity flows more evenly and more continuously into the grids during the entire year than electricity from plants which are exclusively solar or wind. The energy flow isn't subject to as many peaks and valleys, which is desirable. Also, the fear that turbine shadows on the solar panels would undermine energy production seems to have been overstated.[14]

Solar-generated electricity is already less expensive than nuclear, and those nuclear expenses doesn't include nuclear's loan, insurance, and catastrophe bills, to say nothing of the astronomical amounts of red ink that decommissioning nuclear plants, shipping their toxic waste, and storing it will generate.[15]

There are some challenges ahead, but for the most part the technology is available. By 2050, according to the study, solar power could supply 69 percent of American electricity and 35 percent of all U.S. energy. It could also provide electricity for the hundreds of millions of hybrid cars, which the United States will need, if it is to liberate itself from Middle East oil and greenhouse gas emissions.

Over the last decade, wind power production has increased 25 percent a year. In the United States alone, it produces enough energy to electrify 17.5 million homes. U.S. turbines are up to twenty stories high. Powered by three 200-foot-long wind-spun blades, the turbine rotates a shaft, which is attached to a generator, which pumps out the electricity.[16]

Germany gets 10 percent of its electricity from wind power, and Denmark gets 10 percent. While no experts argue that wind power should generate 100 percent of a nation's energy, studies of the German and Danish wind power industries indicate that wind power can successfully and economically handle 20 percent of a nation's electrical needs.[17]

Perhaps the most exciting of all the alternate energy projects is Japan's plan for an orbiting solar power industry. The Japan Aerospace Exploration Agency (JAXA) believes that by 2030, it will have a working solar power generator in geosynchronous orbit, which will be sending back to the planet one gigawatt of energy. In a geo-synch orbit, the sun shines 24-7, and the amount of electricity that lone power station could propagate would be comparable to the energy yielded by a very large power plant.[18]

The orbiting solar power station will consist of a vast structure of solar panels, condenser mirrors, and microwave transmitters as well as the ten-kilometer 100-unit laser array. The energy will be delivered to the Earth in microwave or laser form. Japan plans to deploy and cordon off an enormous receiving station at sea.[19]

The genius of orbiting solar generators is not only that it will produce cheap, clean, abundant electricity from the sun, it gets humanity back into space in a profitable, productive way. Many scientists, from Stephen Hawking to Neil deGrasse Tyson, have argued that the human race is doomed to extinction unless it has an aggressive, expansionistic space program. As Robert Heinlein once said, "The Earth is too small and fragile a basket for humanity to keep all its eggs in."

Walmart believes alternate energies are both clean and cost-effective.

The global leader in big box stores plans to use clean, renewable energy systems to power all of its stores worldwide. In a press announcement Walmart pledged:

"In the U.S. alone, Walmart hopes to install solar power on at least 1,000 rooftops and facilities by 2020, a significant increase from just over 200 solar projects in operation or under development currently. In addition to onsite solar, the company will continue to develop projects in wind, fuel cells, and other technologies. It will also procure offsite renewable energy from utility-scale projects, such as large wind projects, micro-hydro projects, and geothermal."

Walmart believes green energy and increased energy efficiency will seriously reduce their energy expenses. The press announcement predicted:

"Based on external estimates of projected energy costs and other factors, the two new commitments are anticipated to generate more than $1 billion annually in energy savings once fully implemented."

The oil industry staffed, dominated, and financed the Bush administration as it had no other administration in history. Oil firms benefited profusely from the Bush team's policies, setting world records for corporate profitability, and afterward they benefited from the policies of the Obama team.

Even so, the United States does not have to continue down this road. Middle East oil dependency and nuclear power addiction are curable diseases.

We still have choices.

New sources of power are needed if we are to pull ourselves out of the fossil-fuel abyss. Orbiting solar generators would provide cheap, clean, limitless energy for a billion years to come. The NASA scientists I've spoken to believe the costs and difficulty of building and orbiting a viable prototype are overstated and the potential profitability of such operations underestimated.

The hydro-electric power of the Gulf Stream and Humboldt Current is still untapped.

Electric vehicles and hybrid cars could radically cut gasoline consumption.

The resources would be there . . . if the nuclear power cabal and Big Oil weren't cannibalizing the subsidies these infant industries so desperately need.

As Major General Sid Shachnow, former head of all U.S. Special Forces worldwide, has observed, the government alone cannot stop terrorist acts against its citizens. American citizens must mobilize and join in the effort. In this case, the citizens themselves must shine the harsh light of publicity on the aspiring nuclear terrorist's financiers, proliferators, and their political backers—particularly in the United States. A determined look at their business careers—how they've made their personal wealth and how their policies advance their personal aggrandizement and that of their financial confreres—will expose these financial conflicts.[20]

Instead of combating the nuclear terrorist and his patrons, the United States rejected the Kyoto Protocol and the Comprehensive Test-Ban Treaty; refused to back and enforce the Non-Proliferation

Treaty; promoted the expansion of arms, nuclear energy, and oil markets . . . even as we enriched nuclear terrorists, patrons, and proliferators.

And Bush and Obama have sought to expand the nuclear power industry.

We cannot allow this nuclear zealotry to continue . . . unless we want the nuclear terrorist to win. The officials who back and traffic with the nuclear terrorist's paymasters must be identified and exposed. If they are not expelled from high office—and their dirty finances exposed—they will continue to undermine all future efforts to defeat the nuclear proliferators, paymasters, and their misbegotten progeny, the nuclear terrorist.

2

THE DOOR OF DEATH

s it comforting or discomfiting to know that our dilemma is not new? Sir Arnold J. Toynbee argued in his *A Study of History* that it has all happened before: Fifteen civilizations faced terminal crises comparable to America's, but he argued their fall was in no way inevitable. Their leaders had choices. They could have changed course. Thus, when other cultures and civilizations overran them, they found that the fallen nation had laid the groundwork for its destruction. Even before its conquest, it had already killed itself through "suicidal statecraft."[1]

Toynbee was especially obsessed with the world's first democracy, ancient Athens. He wrote that "[Athenian] society was a suicide who . . . when his life was past saving . . . received a coup de grace from his own mishandled and alienated children at a time when . . . the patient was manifestly dying from the after-effects of his old self-inflicted wounds." Toynbee came to see himself as "a historian-coroner" whose task was "to determine exactly when and how the suicide had first laid violent hands upon himself."[2]

Losing sight of its vital center through foreign entanglements, each dominating power deliberately chose its path to perdition. Fifteen civilizations, Toynbee reminds us, traveled down the same road as ours . . . only to disappear through "the door of death." He feared nuclear weapons would hasten America's demise.[3]

Toynbee predicted that the United States' martial mentality and budget-breaking weapons systems would also contribute to America's final fatal collapse. The tendency to overtax the populace and to exploit client states economically—in order to line the coffers of the rich and powerful—also undermined every past civilization that Toynbee studied.[4]

Toynbee argued that such financially aggressive, expansionistic policies eventually frightened and angered other countries—in the same way Athens had terrified her neighbors—inciting them to unite against their common enemy. But when the dominating power fell, Toynbee believed it was not hostile alliances that did it in. Economic exploitation at home and the monetary demands of aggression abroad crippled their infrastructure and drained both their fiscal and spiritual resources."[5]

The invaders found they had sacked a hollow shell propped up by mountains of debt.

In *The Decline of the West*, Oswald Spengler prophesied that Western democracy would devolve into "a dictatorship of money" and go the way of both democratic Athens and republican Rome. Nor did he believe "the dictatorship of money" would go gentle. At the close of his book, Spengler wrote, "Money is overthrown and abolished only by blood."[6]

While Spengler believed America was doomed to die by violence, Toynbee believed that dominating powers have choices. This book sides with Toynbee. Our children and grandchildren need not curse our memory. We still have choices.

> *Why must we give our bounty to the dead? . . .*
> *Shall our blood fail? Or shall it come to be*
> *The blood of paradise?*
> —Adapted from Wallace Stevens's "Sunday Morning"

Epilogue

Hell is truth seen too late.
—THOMAS HOBBES

uppose the gods—on the day before the nuclear terrorists' Armageddon—extended to each of us the gift of prophesy. Suppose we knew that a dozen nuclear terrorists were secreted in seven major U.S. cities, utterly undetectable and untouchable. Lacking the time and the means to locate and neutralize the terrorists, we could only wait for them to bring America to her knees.

Suppose we had twenty-four hours to ponder our country's nuclear history of avarice and negligence. How many sins of omission and commission would we list? This book has catalogued more than a few:

- Our government's refusal to seriously secure its own nuclear bomb-fuel and its nuclear power plants.

- America's inept efforts to assist other nations in securing their nuclear bomb-fuel.

- America's backing of the nuclear proliferator's principal promoter, the nuclear power industry—particularly that industry's purveying of nuclear reactors in the developing world . . . that cynical rapacity we would recognize as a sin beyond forgiveness.

Our proliferation of dual-use nuclear technology—de facto nuclear weapons technology—to some of the most unpredictable and potentially unstable regimes on Earth would make our list.

So would our financial support of rogue states that spurn the Nuclear Nonproliferation Treaty.

And so would our aggrandizement of the nuclear terrorist's proliferators and oil-rich paymasters.

Most of all, we would appreciate—now that it was too late—that nuclear power had been the Trojan horse inside of which nuclear rogues had always skulked and planned, waited and hated. We would realize—now that they had reprocessed their waste into nuclear bomb-fuel or acquired the centrifuges necessary to process bomb-grade uranium or simply purchased it on the black market—that they were coming out of hiding and wreaking their bloody hell.

If we documented every single crime, our tally would spiral off into . . .

. . . the howling pit of hell.

Which is where we would dwell.

As Thomas Hobbes told us, hell is nothing but truth seen too late.

On that day before Armageddon, we would know the truth, and there would be no place to hide. We would see what we had wrought. Macbeth had warned us once about those bloody instructions, which we had so arrogantly taught. Now at last they would return to plague the inventor.

During that last dreary twilight, we might also reflect on the wisdom of Aeschylus's *Agamemnon,* which he had set down two thousand five hundred years ago. Looking back on the ten-year siege at Troy and his own twenty-eight-year Peloponnesian War, he wrote:

> *We learn nothing save through suffering.*
> *The pain of memory falls drop by drop*
> *Upon the heart in sleep.*
> *Against our will comes wisdom.*
> *The grace of the gods is forced on us.*

But in this world here, nothing is inevitable. Today does not have to be the day before Armageddon. We still have time to do . . . something.

If nothing else, we can hope and pray that Aeschylus is wrong.

Appendixes

APPENDIX 1
Why I Wrote *The Nuclear Terrorist*

Thirty years ago, I read Herman Kahn's *Thinking About the Unthinkable,* in which he described a doomsday scenario called "Catalytic Nuclear War." Kahn explained that one day nuclear bomb-fuel, weapons technology, and delivery systems could very well proliferate to the extent that "a small vengeful power" could acquire and use this weaponry to nuke the major powers. Even worse, if the perpetrator successfully created the impression that the strikes were coming from rival nuclear nations, the victim nations would probably respond by nuking their falsely blamed foes for reasons of vengeance and self-defense. The wrongfully accused nations might then hit their attackers with nuclear weapons. They might very well go at each other until their nuclear arsenals were spent.[1]

The small vengeful power? It would wait in the wings and watch. At the end of the nuclear inferno, that nation or terrorist group would benefit from the chaos and destruction. Its position in the world would be improved relative to those great powers, which were now covered with soot, ashes, charred rubble, and radioactive dust.

In 1982, I began work on an enormous nuclear apocalyptic novel, *End of Days*, using Kahn's scenario as its premise and plot. At that point in time, however, Kahn's scenario wasn't feasible. Nuclear bomb-fuel and delivery systems hadn't progressed and proliferated sufficiently for "a small vengeful power" to pull off such an apocalyptic scam. I did a few hundred pages, but then put the novel away.

I never stopped pondering the subject, however, even as I went on to writing other books.

A decade later, something happened. Catalytic Nuclear War became possible almost overnight. The Soviet Union had over five hundred national, regional, and local storage sites for both nuclear weapons and nuclear bomb-fuel. They were well protected . . . until 1991, when the USSR disintegrated.[2]

Its storage sites were scattered across a country so massive it covered one-sixth of the globe and was comparable in size to all of North America.[3] Unfortunately, when the Kremlin collapsed, the centralized nuclear security system controlling these far-flung nuclear sites collapsed along with it. The government stopped paying its nuclear security guards, and the guards at these sites walked off the job. People could enter these storage facilities and steal nuclear bomb-fuel at will. No one was there to stop them.[4]

If nuclear terrorists wanted nuclear bomb-fuel, it was no longer prohibitively difficult to obtain it.

I now had enough material to begin work on *End of Days*.

I'm a book editor by trade, and over the years I've bought and edited a lot of military fiction and nonfiction by smart, knowledgeable, retired military men, including two generals and a number of Special Forces officers. I needed more research materials on nuclear terrorism, and so I began asking military authors about unclassified Pentagon studies on nuclear terrorism. To a man, they said there weren't any. I asked one of them, who was closely involved with the Defense Department, why this was the case, and he said that the Pentagon analysts were too frightened of the subject to study it in any depth.

The Pentagon's reluctance to study nuclear terrorism was not unique. Surprisingly little has been written about it anywhere, and that was a problem for me. Here I was, writing a novel about how shrewd nuclear terrorists could parlay their skillfully executed strikes into global Armageddon, and I could find almost nothing on the subject.

I did locate some books and articles here and there with nuclear terrorism in the titles, but invariably I found that the text contained almost nothing on the subject. Mostly they were histories of Cold War nuclear weapons proliferation among nation-states. They really didn't focus on how a nuclear terrorist would acquire his weapons, how he would employ them, or what his motivation would be or who his patrons were.

Then came the 1993 World Trade Center attack, in which violent Islamist radicals attempted to topple one of the towers by blowing up its foundation. They believed if they planted their bomb precisely enough, the skyscraper would fall like a tree, crash into its twin tower, and take that one down with it. They placed their 1,336-pound urea nitrate-hydrogen gas-enhanced device in the wrong spot, and neither tower went down. The 1996 trial of the World Trade Center bombers detailed intelligence about Sunni terrorist groups, and the world was starting to learn about Islamist terrorism.[5]

The world learned more in 1998 when al Qaeda blew up the U.S. embassies in Tanzania and Kenya. The 2001 African trial of those bombings also produced a surprising amount of intelligence on the al Qaeda perpetrators.

Next came the 9/11 attacks, and al Qaeda was in the spotlight, front and center—public threat number one. By this time, I had learned a fair amount about global terrorists.

My vision of the book's villains and their motivation was coming together, but would they be smart and resourceful enough to build a nuke? It turned out they didn't have to be brilliant. Through my research I learned that it was relatively easy to build a crude, primitive, but devastatingly powerful version of the Hiroshima bomb if you had the nuclear bomb-fuel. You simply cut off a small piece of cannon barrel—a Civil War cannon barrel would do. (They are scattered around the United States by the thousands and are easily obtainable.) You weld a tampion into one end of the truncated barrel. You then place two chunks of bomb-grade, highly enriched uranium (HEU) in it, with the first piece against the tampion and the second piece very close to the first piece, but you have to make sure that they do not touch.[6]

You back the second chunk with extra high explosive and tightly secure an immovable tampion in the open end of the barrel. When you're ready to detonate it, the suicide bomber throws the ignition switch.[7]

"Even a High School Kid Could Do It"

Dr. Luis Alvarez, the creator of the Hiroshima bomb's trigger, wrote that one of the hardest things about assembling a Hiroshima-style weapon is making sure that the two chunks of bomb-grade HEU do *not* touch. They will start to chain-react if they do. He wrote in his memoir: "With modern

---

weapons-grade uranium, the background neutron rate is so low that terrorists . . . would have a good chance of setting off a high-yield explosion simply by dropping one half of the material onto the other half. Most people seem unaware that if separated U-235 is at hand it's a trivial job to set off a nuclear explosion . . . [E]ven a high school kid could make a bomb in short order."[8]

If the bomb is in a panel truck, parked in front of the New York Stock Exchange, it's good-bye global economy.

Now I had sufficient research materials to complete my novel, *End of Days*.

My investigations did not stop there, however. I was still mystified that no one was writing about nuclear terrorism. I had accumulated thousands of facts and suppositions, assembled them like pieces in a jigsaw puzzle, and felt, after I'd finished writing *End of Days*, that I had some original insights into the subject. I could feel the beginnings of a nonfiction book on nuclear terrorism. I decided to start it, believing it might be unique.

However, I still had to learn more about the subject. There was so little out there on nuclear terrorism that I had to comb the Internet, subscribe to every magazine imaginable, and pore over all the newspapers I could get my hands on. I had to glean what I could from one article, one minuscule datum at a time, then piece all these unrelated items together into a coherent narrative.

One word-puzzle piece came from a nuclear whistler blower in the United States. He headed "mock-intrusion teams." These teams would disguise themselves as workers; they would then see if they could enter these nuclear bomb-fuel storage sites and walk out the gate with nuclear bomb-fuel. They succeeded 50 percent of the time. At one site they even had success 80 percent of the time. Up to that point, I had thought the main source of contraband bomb-fuel would be Russia. But that whistle blower taught me Russia wasn't the only country whose nuclear sites were vulnerable to theft. The United States was vulnerable as well, and if the U.S. couldn't secure its nuclear bomb-fuel, how could we expect India, Pakistan, and Russia to protect theirs? Those nations were corrupt to the core.[9]

A big breakthrough for the book came when I discovered an Oak Ridge National Laboratory study from 1977, which proved that if low-tech terrorists had the equipment from an old winery or dairy and had access to a nuclear power plant's spent-fuel rods, they could build a nuclear bomb-fuel reprocessor in six months. In one month they could reprocess enough nuclear plutonium to build the Nagasaki bomb.[10]

In other words, any terrorist group or rogue state with access to a nuclear power reactor could fabricate nuclear bomb-fuel in a matter of months.

I began to see that nuclear power plants had the potential to proliferate nuclear bomb-fuel globally.

I was soon fixated on the relationship between nuclear power proliferation and nuclear bomb-fuel proliferation, what the military analyst, Ralph Peters, would later describe as "the infernal no-man's-land between nuclear power and the nuclear bomb." The 1977 Oak Ridge study had proven that if a nation had a nuclear power reactor, it could build a bomb. Through nuclear power reactors, these nations would also acquire the knowledge, skill, and sometimes even the nuclear bomb-fuel itself to build nuclear weapons.[11]

I began to see nuclear power as the Trojan horse, and those nations and leaders—who wished to secretly build nuclear weapons—hiding in it. Through their clandestine nuclear reprocessing, they could get so close to completing their bomb that by the time other nations learned of their activities and tried to stop them, they would have one or more assembled weapons. It was occasionally said that certain nuclear-power nations—Japan was sometimes cited as an example— could be as few as two screwdriver twists and three wrench turns away from creating an atomic bomb.

I found nuclear power perplexing. Everything in the world seemed to be wrong with the industry. A veritable Pandora's box of human woe, it was also disastrously expensive. As this book has demonstrated, the construction costs alone run as much as a dozen times those of a gas-turbine power plant. Moreover, those expenses don't include the decommissioning of the reactors, waste transportation, and storage—to say nothing of possible meltdowns, which are potentially a financial apocalypse. Cost estimates for a truly catastrophic meltdown run anywhere from $1.5 trillion to $11 trillion, depending on how close the disasters are to major urban areas. Insurance companies think the risk is too great, and won't issue nuclear power plants full, comprehensive liability coverage. Consequently, nuclear power plants are only required to buy enough insurance to cover a tiny fraction of those bills.[12]

I learned that banks will not finance a nuclear power plant's construction, because the building expenses are too exorbitant and the ultimate costs too unpredictable. Consequently, governments have to step in and underwrite the costs. Nuclear power is so dependent on government subsidies that its advocates often come across as corporate socialists.[13]

"Let the government pay for it" seems to be nuclear power's battle cry.

The waste would remain toxic for up to 250,000 years, and experts agreed that the best means of storing it was in "deep geologic repositories." This meant boring forty miles of tunnels into a mountain, each shaft twenty-five feet in diameter. The United States already had approximately seventy-five tons of nuclear waste, which would completely fill those tunnels. The transportation of the waste—by truck and by train—would require 100,000 separate trips. Someone called the enterprise, "a Chernobyl on Wheels." The potential cost of shipping accidents and terrorist attacks against these shipments was monumental.[14]

And that would only be the beginning. By the time those tunnels were bored and filled, the United States would have another comparable amount of spent-fuel rods packed into cooling pools. We would have to bore out another forty miles of twenty-five-foot-in-diameter shafts in mountain tunnels, commence another 100,000 shipments, and load them into that labyrinth just as we had filled up its predecessor. We would continue ad infinitum, ad aeternum until we ran out of mountains to ravage.[15]

Yet nations are self-destructively drawn to nuclear power, like moths to a hideously hot, eternally toxic flame. They want it no matter how psychotically expensive and ludicrously lethal it is. More bizarre, they also want most of the world's other nations to own it as well. The United States continually peddles nuclear power plants to some of the most dubious regimes on earth. I describe in this book how the Obama administration was attempting to negotiate nuclear agreements with India and Saudi Arabia, whereby the United States could eventually supply those nations with nuclear power plants. India is a notoriously violent and corrupt land, and Saudi Arabia is the number one financier of Islamist Sunni terrorism in the world. Fifteen out of nineteen hijackers on 9/11 were Saudis.[16]

Yet America feels both countries should have nuclear power.

Vice President Joe Biden has told war-torn Iraq that they should have nuclear power reactors, too, when they could barely keep conventional power plants functioning.[17]

So why are nations so suicidally in love with this self-willed cataclysm?

It all comes down to the individuals running these nations and their nuclear industries, and I began a long search to find out who these people were. Some of the answers shocked me. I found a hawkish, hard-nosed defense secretary who, while out of office, worked for a firm that tried to sell nuclear reactors to North Korea.[18] I found a militantly conservative politician, who, before he became vice president, ran a firm which had helped to build up Iran's natural gas industry, the profits of which could be used to bankroll Iran's nuclear weapons program. His firm had also profited off Iraq's oil industry. Once he joined the Bush administration, however, he would lead the political charge to invade his former business client, Iraq, and demolish much of its infrastructure.[19] I read of an ex-president who, after he left office, worked for a firm that profited off the Saudi royals—even as they were bankrolling al Qaeda. In fact, that firm also did business with the bin Laden family.[20] I read of that man's father; he had been the Third Reich's U.S. banker. Sleeping with the enemy seemed to be in their DNA.[21]

Who were these people? What motivated them? They could have made their fortunes in other ways. Their business dealings did not have to cause such potentially catastrophic consequences.

What was their motive?

What was this longing for the Luciferian flame?

Where did the insanity come from?

These were the questions that inspired my search, and that odyssey became this book.

It is not inaccurate to call it an odyssey. An odyssey, by definition, is never over. At the close of that legendary epic, Odysseus reaches Ithaca only to learn he must set out on another voyage. The eternal wanderer will never be free of war and of the sea.

Unfortunately, it's now the same with me. Like Odysseus, I, too, am on a journey with no terminus, an odyssey, which, I fear, will never end and will never set me free.

Well, that's the way it happens sometimes.

So, at least, I hope you got something out of our trip. I expect to be plying these waters and beating these oars for some time to come.

APPENDIX 2
The Fatal Fallacy of Serving Two Gods

We noted in the opening that too many Bush team members treated their nuclear opponents and the financial backers of those opponents as trading partners. By what moral code did they justify their actions?

Since many of the Bush entourage—and George W. Bush in particular—prided themselves on their faith in Christ, we shall examine their financial ethics in light of that faith. After all, in viewing them through the prism of their religious beliefs, we only hold them to their own self-proclaimed ethical standards.

Religionists have condemned greed for millennia, and Christ ultimately views self-aggrandizement as apocalyptic. In fact, Christ's condemnation of greed is arguably His primary message. In Matthew's earliest scrolls, the Lord's Prayer, literally translated, there is a serious assault on avarice. In the original Greek, Christ says in Matthew 6:12 (English Standard Version) that we should implore God to "forgive us our debts, as we also have forgiven our debtors"—not "our trespasses" or "trespassers."[1] Hence, in the Lord's Prayer we beseech God to treat us the way we treat our debtors and the financial debts they owe us. In other words, if we do not willingly forgive debts owed to us by other people, God will not forgive us when we fail in our obligations to Him. In a sense, the Lord's Prayer begs God to free and forgive us of cupidity.

Moreover, the Lord's Prayer, in the earliest scrolls, nowhere contains the doxology, "For thine is the kingdom and the power and the glory forever." If you accept that the doxology was added for liturgical reasons—as many scholars do—the Lord's Prayer culminates in an even more powerful attack on rapacity.

Covetous greed is also the sin by which Judas betrays Christ, and by which Adam and Eve plunder God's Edenic apples. In fact, the betrayal of friends and protectors—the sin of disloyalty, which dominates the nethermost sin in Dante's *Inferno*—is frequently associated with profiteering.

In Revelation, God's war on greed culminates in the Armageddon. To make money people must sell out to the Antichrist. In John's vision, an authentic angel—God's unmistakable emissary—comes down and explains that humanity will suffer eternally in hellfire and brimstone if humankind doesn't reject the Antichrist, who controls all financial transactions. In other words, humanity must reject its lust for money—the worship "of the works of their hands . . . of gold and of silver and of bronze and of stone and wood." The angel lays these choices out before humanity with unmistakable clarity.[2]

The Antichrist, however, rises up, pretending to be a Christ-like messiah. His power over humanity is the irresistible power of mammon. To buy, sell, and grow rich, people must traffic with the Antichrist and take their profit in the Antichrist's name. The Antichrist provides, as John of Revelation writes, "that no one can buy or sell unless he has the mark [of the beast], that is, the name of the beast or the number of its name." Choosing avarice over Christ's love, one-third of humanity clings to its false financial god—and dwells in perpetuity in lakes of fire.[3]

In short, the Antichrist is an apocalyptic financier.

Faith Without Deeds Is Dead
—James 2:26

Apologists for avaricious officials argue that since we cannot read the officials' minds and hearts, we must grant them the benefit of the doubt. This book argues that rapacious actions speak louder than words and that consistent, financially motivated actions speak clearly and unmistakably. The actions of greedy officials are infinitely more revealing than their self-serving rhetoric.

In the words of James 2:26, "Faith without deeds is dead."

APPENDIX 3
Special Acknowledgments

Since so little had been published on nuclear terrorism, writing this book was a protracted and circuitous ordeal. Along the way, however, I did stumble onto authors whose books and articles kept me going. They were, to me, beacons in the darkness. (I hasten to add that they were not consultants, and they cannot be blamed for errors, omissions, or my intemperate opinions.) They include Graham Allison, Robert Jay Lifton, Harvey Wasserman, Karl Grossman, Robert Alvarez, Matthew L. Wald, Edwin Lyman, David Sanger, Jonathan Schell, Naomi Klein, Robert Baer, Craig Unger, and of course the late, great Sir Arnold Toynbee.

NOTES

Preface

1. T. S. Eliot, *The Waste Land.*

2. Shaun Gregory, "Terrorist Tactics in Pakistan Threaten Nuclear Weapons Safety," Combating Terrorism Center at West Point, June 1, 2011, http://www.ctc.usma.edu/posts/terrorist-tactics-in-pakistan-threaten -nuclear-weapons-safety.

3. Jeffrey Goldberg and Marc Aminder, "The Ally from Hell," *The Atlantic,* December 2011.

4. Peter Goodspeed, "Pakistan's Nuclear Arsenal May Be 'Compromised,'" National Post, August 25, 2011; Goldberg and Aminder, "The Ally from Hell."

5. Gregory, "Terrorist Tactics in Pakistan Threaten Nuclear Weapons Safety."

6. "Wah Cantonment Ordnance Complex," Global Security Newswire, March 1, 2011, www.nti.org/facilities/121/.

7. Gregory, "Terrorist Tactics in Pakistan Threaten Nuclear Weapons Safety"; Jeffrey Goldberg and Marc Aminder, "The Pentagon's Secret Plans to Secure Pakistan's Nuclear Arenal," Global Security Newswire, November 9, 2011.

8. Saeed Shah, "Terrorist Attack in Pakistan Shows How Vulnerable It Is," McClatchy Newpapers, October 11, 2009, http://www.mcclatchydc.com/2009 /10/11/76954/terrorist-attack-in-pakistan-shows.html#storylink=cpy; Reza Sayah, "Hostages at Pakistani Army HQ released," *CNN Asia,* October 11,

2009, http://www.cnn.com/2009/WORLD/asiapcf/10/10/pakistan.shootings/index.html.

9. BBC News, "Militants kill Pakistani soldiers in attack on base," March 31, 2010, http://news.bbc.co.uk/2/hi/south_asia/8596226.stm.

10. Global Bearings, "[Pakistan Primer Pt. 2] From Kashmir to the FATA: The ISI Loses Control," October 28, 2011; Mayed Ali, "The Close Combat at PNS Mehran," The News International, May 25, 2011, http://www.thenews.com.pk/Todays-News-13-6219-The-close-combat-at-PNS-Mehran; Gregory, "Terrorist Tactics in Pakistan Threaten Nuclear Weapons Safety."

11. *International Herald Tribune,* "Gunmen Attack Army Camp, Kill Seven," July 9, 2012, http://tribune.com.pk/story/405717/attack-on-army-camp-in-gujrat-kills-six-soldiers/.

12. BBC News, "Waziristan raid: Taliban 'kill eight Pakistan soldiers,'" August 29, 2012, http://www.bbc.co.uk/news/world-asia-19407661.

13. Salman Masood and Ismail Khan, "Taliban Militants Attack Pakistani Base," *New York Times,* February 2, 2013.

14. Global Security Newswire, "Terror Strikes Hint at Pakistani Nuke Security Gaps," June 14, 2011, http://www.nti.org/gsn/article/terror-strikes-hint-at-pakistani-nuke-security-gaps-expert/.

15. Gregory D. Johnsen, *The Last Refuge: Yemen, al-Qaeda, and America's War in Arabia* (New York: Norton, 2013), p. 235; Gregory D. Johnsen, "The Wrong Man for the C.I.A." *New York Times,* November 19, 2012.

16. Gregory D. Johnsen, "The Wrong Man for the C.I.A."

17. Gregory D. Johnsen, "The Wrong Man for the C.I.A."

18. "March 2013 Update: US covert actions in Pakistan, Yemen and Somalia," The Bureau of Investigative Journalism, http://www.thebureauinvestigates.com/2013/04/02/march-2013-update-us-covert-actions-in-pakistan-yemen-and-somalia/, April 2, 13.

19. Goldberg and Aminder, "The Ally from Hell."

20. Goldberg and Aminder, "The Ally from Hell."

21. United Press International, "Cleric Says American 'Devils" Must Die," November 8, 2010, http://www.upi.com/Top_News/World-News/2010/11/08/Cleric-says-American-devils-must-die/UPI-61991289245343; Ragha-

van Sudarasan, "U.S.-Aided Attack in Yemen Thought to Have Killed Aulaqi, 2 al-Qaeda leaders," *Washington Post,* December 24, 2009, http://www.washingtonpost.com/wp-dyn/content/article/2009/12/24/AR2009122400536.html; Peter Finn, "The Post-9/11 Life of an American Charged with Murder," *Washington Post,* September 4, 2010, http://www.washingtonpost.com/wp-dyn/content/article/2010/09/04/AR2010090403328.html; Scott Shane, "Worker Spoke of Jihad, Agency Says," *New York Times,* October 4, 2010, http://www.nytimes.com/2010/10/05/us/05mobley.html; Mark Mazzetti, Charlie Savage, and Scott Shane, "How a U.S. Citizen Came to Be in America's Cross Hairs," *New York Times,* March 9, 2013, http://www.nytimes.com/2013/03/10/world/middleeast/anwar-al-awlaki-a-us-citizen-in-americas-cross-hairs.html.

22. Finn, "The Post-9/11 Life of an American Charged With Murder."

23. Shane, "Worker Spoke of Jihad, Agency Says."

24. Mark Holt and Anthony Andrews, "Nuclear Power Plant Security and Vulnerabilities," Congressional Research Service, August 28, 2010, http://www.fas.org/sgp/crs/homesec/RL34331.pdf.

25. Keith Bradsher and Hiroko Tabuchi, "Greater Danger Lies in Spent Fuel Than in Reactors," *New York Times,* March 7, 2011, http://www.nytimes.com/2011/03/18/world/asia/18spent.html.

26. Karl Grossman, "The Big Lie: One Year After Fukushima, Nuclear Cover Up Revealed," *CommonDreams.org,* March 5, 2012, https://www.commondreams.org/view/2012/03/05.

27. Juergen Baetz, "Insurance Cost vs. Nuclear Power Risk," Associated Press, May 1, 2011.

28. Pavel Podvig, "Consolidating Fissile Materials in Russia's Nuclear Complex, May 2009, *www.fissilematerials.org.*

29. Eric Pianin and Bill Miller, "Nuclear Arms Plants' Security Lax, Report Says," *Washington Post,* January 23, 2002, http://www.washingtonpost.com/wp-dyn/articles/A22106-2002Jan22.html; Mark Hertsgaard, "Nuclear Insecurity," *Vanity Fair,* November 2003.

30. Mark Hertsgaard, "Mushroom Cloud Over Denver?" *Salon,* April 12, 1999, http://www.salon.com/1999/04/12/whistleblower/; United States

Environmental Protection Agency, "Rocky Flats Plant," www.epa.gov /region8/superfund/co/rkyflatsplant/.

31. Matthew Wald, "Security Questions Are Raised by Break-In at Nuclear Site," *New York Times,* August 7, 2012.

32. Fran Quigley, "How the US Turned Three Pacifists into Violent Terrorists," *CounterPunch,* http://www.counterpunch.org/2013/05/15/how-the -us-turned-three-pacifists-into-violent-terrorists/, May 15, 2013; Matthew Wald, "Security Questions Are Raised by Break-In at Nuclear Site."

33. Matthew Wald, "Security Questions Are Raised by Break-In at Nuclear Site."

34. Frank Munger, "Y-12 protesters arraigned for federal trespassing; more charges could follow," knoxvillenews.com, http://www.knoxnews .com/news/2012/jul/30/y-12-protesters-arraigned-for-federal-more-could/, July 30, 2012.

35. Matthew Wald, "Security Questions Are Raised by Break-In at Nuclear Site."

36. Fran Quigley, "How the US Turned Three Pacifists into Violent Terrorists." "The Untouchables," *Frontline,* PBS.org, http://www.pbs.org/wgbh /pages/frontline/untouchables/.

37. Luis Alvarez, *Adventures of a Physicist* (New York: Basic Books, 1989), 125; Matthew L. Wald, "A Nation Challenged: Nuclear Security; Suicidal Nuclear Threat Is Seen at Weapons Plants," *New York Times,* January 23, 2002, http://www.nytimes.com/2002/01/23/us/nation-challenged-nuclear -security-suicidal-nuclear-threat-seen-weapons-plants.html.

38. Graham T. Allison, Owen R. Coté, Jr., Richard A. Falkenrath, and Steven E. Miller, *Avoiding Nuclear Anarchy: Containing the Threat of Loose Russian Nuclear Weapons and Fissile Material* (Cambridge, MA: MIT Press, 1996), 44–45.

39. U.S. General Accounting Office, "Quick and Secret Construction of Plutonium Reprocessing Plants: A Way to Nuclear Weapons Proliferation?" Report by the Comptroller General of the United States, October 6, 1978, http://archive.gao.gov/f0902c/107377.pdf.

40. Global Security Newswire, "U.S. Nuclear Marketers Visited Saudi

Arabia, As Trade Talks Underway," February 1, 2013, http://www.nti.org /gsn/article/us-nuclear-marketers-visited-saudi-arabia-trade-talks-under -way/; Tim Lister, "WikiLeaks Cables Assess Terrorism Funding in Saudi Arabia, Gulf States," *CNNWorld,* December 6, 2010, www.cnn.com.

41. Associated Press, "Cheney Once Pressed for Halliburton-Iran Trade," October 9, 2004; *60 Minutes,* "Doing Business with the Enemy," January 25, 2004, CBSNews.com; "Business As Usual?" *Newsweek,* msnbc.msn.com, February 16, 2005; Colum Lynch, "Halliburton's Iraq Deals Greater Than Cheney Has Said, Affiliates Had $73 Million in Contracts," *Washington Post,* June 23, 2001. See http://www.globalpolicy.org/component/content /article/170/42166.html; Richard Behar, "Rummy's North Korea Connection," *Fortune,* May 12, 2003, vol. 147, issue 9, http://money.cnn.com/maga zines/fortune/fortune_archive/2003/05/12/342316/; Randeep Ramesh, "The Two Faces of Rumsfeld," *The Guardian,* May 9, 2003, http://www.guardian .co.uk/world/2003/may/09/nuclear.northkorea; Robert Baer, *Sleeping with the Devil: How Washington Sold Our Soul for Saudi Crude* (New York: Three Rivers Press, 2003), 34–35.

PART I   Barack Obama: A Study in Nuclear Denial

1. Over 100,000 Nuclear Shipments—A Chernobyl on Wheels

1. Pierre Sadik, "Radioactive Roads and Rails: Hauling Nuclear Waste Through Our Neighborhoods," U.S. PIRG Education Fund and Penn Environment Research and Policy Center, https://pincdn.s3.amazonaws.com/assets /5F7uHwbKhTsl_oc6mfPtfg/RadioactiveRoadsandRails.pdf, June 2002, p. 12.

2. Belfer Center for Science and International Affairs, "Nuclear Terrorism Fact Sheet," April 2010, http://belfercenter.ksg.harvard.edu/publication /20057/nuclear_terrorism_fact_sheet.html.

3. Karl Grossman, "Nuclear Disaster and Obama's Disastrous Response," *CommonDreams.org,* March 31, 2011, https://www.commondreams.org /view/2011/03/31-1.

4. Global Security Newswire, "U.S. Nuclear Marketers Visited Saudi Arabia, As Trade Talks Underway," February 1, 2013, http://www.nti.org

/gsn/article/us-nuclear-marketes-visited-saudi-arabia-trade-talks-under -way/; Dean Nelson, "Hillary Clinton: US to build nuclear plants in India," *The Telegraph,* July 20, 2009, http://www.telegraph.co.uk/news/worldnews /asia/india/5872836/Hillary-Clinton-US-to-build-nuclear-plants-in-India .html; United Press International, "Emirates, Saudis Drive for Nuclear Power," September 21, 2012, http://www.upi.com/Business_News/Energy -Resources/2012/09/21/Emirates-Saudis-drive-for-nuclear-power/UPI -30481348241422/; Louis Charonneau, "Iraq gets U.N. green light for civil nuclear program," Reuters, December 15, 2010, http://www.reuters.com /article/2010/12/15/us-iraq-un-idUSTRE6BD63620101215.

5. Amena Bakr, "Egypt will issue a tender for its nuclear power plants," Reuters, January 16, 2011.

6. World Nuclear Association, "Radioactive Wastes: Myths and Realities," http://www.world-nuclear.org/info/Nuclear-Fuel-Cycle/Nuclear-Wastes /Radioactive-Wastes—Myths-and-Realities/#.UZZ_bb7D_IU; Juliet Lapidos, "Atomic Priesthoods, Thorn Landscapes and Munchian Pictograms, *Slate.com,* November 16, 2009, http://www.slate.com/articles/health_and _science/green_room/2009/11/atomic_priesthoods_thorn_landscapes _and_munchian_pictograms.html.

7. David Biello, "Spent Nuclear Fuel: A Trash Heap Deadly for 250,000 Years or a Renewable Energy Source?" *Scientific American,* January 28, 2009, http://www.scientificamerican.com/article.cfm?id=nuclear-waste -lethal-trash-or-renewable-energy-source.

8. S. E. Hasan, "International Practice in High-Level Nuclear Waste Management," in *Concepts and Applications in Environmental Geochemistry,* ed. D. Sarkar, R. Datta, and R. Hannigan (Oxford: Elsevier, 2007); Biello, "Spent Nuclear Fuel: A Trash Heap Deadly for 250,000 Years or a Renewable Energy Source?"

9. Biello, "Spent Nuclear Fuel: A Trash Heap Deadly for 250,000 Years or a Renewable Energy Source?"

10. Andrew Sowder, "Used Nuclear Fuel Management: The Back End of the Fuel Cycle," *Health Physics News,* January 2010, http://hps.org/; Ralph Anderson, chief health physicist at the Nuclear Energy Institute (NEI), quoted

in Biello's "Spent Nuclear Fuel: A Trash Heap Deadly for 250,000 Years or a Renewable Energy Source?"

11. Michael Winter, "NRC Clears Way for Scrapping Yucca Mt. Nuke Dump," *USA Today,* September 11, 2011, http://content.usatoday.com/communities/ondeadline/post/2011/09/nrc-clears-way-for-scrapping-yucca-mt-nuke-dump-/1.

12. Leung, "Yucca Mountain," *60 Minutes,* February 11, 2009, http://www.cbsnews.com/8301-18560_162-579696.html.

13. Robert Alvarez, "Five Reasons NOT to Invest in Nuclear Power," *HuffingtonPost.com,* February 17, 2010, http://www.huffingtonpost.com/robert-alvarez/five-reasons-not-to-invest_b_465585.html.

14. Alvarez, "Five Reasons NOT to Invest in Nuclear Power."

15. Biello, "Spent Nuclear Fuel."

16. Biello, "Spent Nuclear Fuel"; Rory Kennedy, "Indian Point: Imagining the Unimaginable," HBO documentary, September 8, 2004; Anita Gates, "Seeing a Mushroom Cloud in New York," *New York Times,* September 9, 2004, http://tv.nytimes.com/2004/09/09/arts/television/09gate.html.

17. Pierre Sadik, "Radioactive Roads and Rails: Hauling Nuclear Waste Through Our Neighborhoods."

18. Tom Parry, "We Plant 'Bomb' on Nuke Train," *Daily Mirror,* July 21, 2006, http://www.mng.org.uk/gh/re/daily_mirror_nukes2.htm.; Pierre Sadik, "Radioactive Roads and Rails."

19. Matthew L. Wald, "Quarrels Continue Over Repository for Nuclear Waste," *New York Times,* June 27, 2013; "Dry Cask Storage Project Underway at Fermi 2," DTE Energy, http://dteenergy.com/nuclear/dryCaskStorageProject.html; Biello, "Spent Nuclear Fuel"; Pierre Sadik, "Radioactive Roads and Rails: Hauling Nuclear Waste Through Neighborhoods."

20. Matthew L. Wald, "Quarrels Continue Over Repository for Nuclear Waste."

21. Matthew L. Wald, "Court Forces a Rethinking of Nuclear Fuel Storage," *New York Times,* June 8, 2012, http://www.nytimes.com/2012/06/09/science/earth/court-says-nuclear-agency-must-rethink-fuel-storage.html.

2. Safe, Easy-to-Handle Nuclear . . . Plutonium

1. Frank N. von Hippel, "Plutonium and Reprocessing of Spent Fuel," *Science*, vol. 293, no. 5539, September 28, 2001: 2397–2398. See online at http://www.sciencemag.org/content/293/5539/2397.summary; A. David Rossin, "U.S. Policy on Spent Fuel Reprocessing: The Issues," *Frontline*, http://www.pbs.org/wgbh/pages/frontline/shows/reaction/readings/rossin.html.

2. Union of Concerned Scientists, "Nuclear Reprocessing: Dangerous, Dirty and Expensive: Nuclear Reprocessing Fact Sheet," April 5, 2011, www.ucsusa.org.

3. Julio Godoy, "Energy: Nuclear Does Not Make Economic Sense Say Studies," Inter Press Service, February 12, 2010, http://www.ipsnews.net/2010/02/energy-nuclear-does-not-make-economic-sense-say-studies/; The Keystone Center, "Nuclear Power Joint Fact-Finding," June 2007, https://www.keystone.org/images/keystone-center/spp-documents/2011/Nuclear-Power-Joint-Fact-Finding-Dialogue/finalreport_nuclearfactfinding6_2007.pdf.

4. Mary Olson, "Reprocessing Is Not the 'Solution' to the Nuclear Waste Problem," Nuclear Information and Resource Service, January 2006, http://www.nirs.org/factsheets/reprocessisnotsolution.pdf; Andrew Sowder, "Used Nuclear Fuel Management: The Back End of the Fuel Cycle," *Health Physics News*, January 2010, http://hps.org/.

5. Union of Concerned Scientists, "Nuclear Reprocessing: Dangerous, Dirty and Expensive: Nuclear Reprocessing Fact Sheet."

6. Reactor Watchdog Project, "Plutonium Proliferation and MOX Fuel," Nuclear Information and Resource Service, www.nirs.org/factsheets/moxproliferation.htm; Testimony of Dr. Charles D. Ferguson, Philip D. Reed, Senior Fellow for Science and Technology, Council on Foreign Relations, in Hearing before Committee on Science and Technology, U.S. House of Representatives on "Advancing Technology for Nuclear Fuel Recycling: What Should Our Research, Development, and Demonstration Strategy Be?" June 17, 2009, http://www.gpo.gov/fdsys/pkg/CHRG-111hhrg50172/pdf/CHRG-111hhrg50172.pdf; Union of Concerned Scientists, "Nuclear Reprocessing: Dangerous, Dirty and Expensive: Nuclear Reprocessing Fact Sheet"; Union

of Concerned Scientists, "UCS Statement on 50th Anniversary of Eisenhower's 'Atoms for Peace' Speech," December 8, 2003, www.ucsusa.org.

7. Union of Concerned Scientists, "A Brief History of Reprocessing and Cleanup in West Valley, NY," December 2007, www.ucsusa.org.

8. Reactor Watchdog Project, "Plutonium Proliferation and MOX Fuel," Nuclear Information and Resource Service, www.nirs.org/factsheets/moxp roliferation.htm; "Nuclear Reprocessing: Dangerous, Dirty and Expensive," Union of Concerned Scientists, "Nuclear Reprocessing Fact Sheet."

3. A Financial Apocalypse

1. Matthew L. Wald, "Nuclear Power Gets Strong Push from the White House," New York Times, January 22, 2010, http://www.nytimes.com/2010/01/22/science/earth/30nuke.html.

2. Julio Godoy, "Energy: Nuclear Does Not Make Economic Sense Say Studies," Inter Press Service, February 12, 2010, http://www.ipsnews.net/2010/02/energy-nuclear-does-not-make-economic-sense-say-studies/.

3. Godoy, "Energy: Nuclear Does Not Make Economic Sense Say Studies."

4. Godoy, "Energy: Nuclear Does Not Make Economic Sense Say Studies."

5. Steven Mufson, "Another Push for Nuclear Power," Washington Post, December 18, 2007, http://www.washingtonpost.com/wp-dyn/content/article/2007/12/17/AR2007121701886.html.

6. Keith Bradsher and Hiroko Tabuchi, "Greater Danger Lies in Spent Fuel Than in Reactors," New York Times, March 17, 2011, http://www.nytimes.com/2011/03/18/world/asia/18spent.html.

7. Ellen Vancko, "Room for Debate: A Comeback for Nuclear Power? Better Environmental Options," New York Times, February 16, 2010, http://roomfordebate.blogs.nytimes.com/2010/02/16/a-comeback-for-nuclear-power/#ellen.

8. Robert Alvarez, "Five Reasons NOT to Invest in Nuclear Power," HuffingtonPost.com, February 17, 2010, http://www.huffingtonpost.com/robert-alvarez/five-reasons-not-to-inves_b_465585.html.

9. BBC News Europe, "Finland's Olkiluoto 3 nuclear plant delayed again," July 16, 2012, http://www.bbc.co.uk/news/world-europe-18862422;

World Nuclear News, "Construction of Flamanville EPR Begins," December 4, 2007, http://www.world-nuclear-news.org/newsarticle.aspx?id=14496; Nuclear Power International, "France doubles down on commitment to Flamanville nuclear project," *Power Engineering,* December 6, 2012, http://www.power-eng.com/articles/2012/12/france-doubles-down-on-commitment-to-flamanville-nuclear-project.html; Godoy, "Energy: Nuclear Does Not Make Economic Sense Say Studies."

10. Godoy, "Energy: Nuclear Does Not Make Economic Sense Say Studies."

11. Mufson, "Another Push for Nuclear Power."

12. Godoy, "Energy: Nuclear Does Not Make Economic Sense Say Studies."

13. Godoy, "Energy: Nuclear Does Not Make Economic Sense Say Studies."

14. Godoy, "Energy: Nuclear Does Not Make Economic Sense Say Studies."

15. Erich Pica, "Don't Jump to Conclusions About Nuclear Reactors: Look at the Facts and Say No," *HuffingtonPost.com,* April 3, 2011, http://www.huffingtonpost.com/erich-pica/dont-jump-to-conclusions-_b_842582.html.

16. Pica, "Don't Jump to Conclusions About Nuclear Reactors."

17. Harvey Wasserman, "Los Angeles to San Onofre: 'Not So Fast!'" *HuffingtonPost.com,* http://www.huffingtonpost.com/harvey-wasserman/los-angeles-to-san-onofre_b_3167482.html, April 29, 2013.

18. Abbey Sewell, "Letters Show Rift Over San Onofre Nuclear Repairs," *Los Angeles Times,* http://articles.latimes.com/2013/may/19/local/la-me-san-onofre-20130520, May 19, 2013; "Southern California Edison Announces Plans to Retire San Onofre Nuclear Generating Station," http://www.songscommunity.com/news2013/news060713.asp.

19. "Thanks to Cheap Natural Gas, America's Nuclear Renaissance Is on Hold," *The Economist,* June 1, 2013.

20. Jim Green, "Nuclear Weapons and 'Fourth Generation' Nuclear Power," *Energy Bulletin,* August 25, 2009, www.energybulletin.net/49949.

21. Reuters, "Arab Countries Look to Nukes," November 5, 2006. See online at http://www.nbcnews.com/id/15557289/; William J. Broad and David

E. Sanger, "With Eye on Iran, Rivals Also Want Nuclear Power," *New York Times,* April 15, 2007, http://www.nytimes.com/2007/04/15/world/middlee ast/15sunnis.html; Richard Beeston, "Nuclear Steps Put Region on Brink of Most Fearful Era Yet," *The Times,* November 4, 2006, http://www.thetimes .co.uk/tto/news/world/middleeast/article2604752.ece.

22. Juergen Baetz, "Insurance Cost vs. Nuclear Power Risk," Associated Press, May 1, 2001.

4. The Nuclear Regulatory Commission (NRC): The Fox in the Nuclear Chicken Coop

1. Union of Concerned Scientists, "Nuclear Reactor Security," March 30, 2005, www.ucsusa.org.

2. Union of Concerned Scientists, "Nuclear Reactor Security"; Union of Concerned Scientists, "Aircraft Threats to Nuclear Plants," March 25, 2005, http://www.ucsusa.org/nuclear_power/nuclear_power_risk/sabotage_and _attacks_on_reactors/nuclear-reactor-air-defenses.html.

3. Edwin S. Lyman, "Testimony to the Subcommittee on Clean Air, Climate Change and Nuclear Security Committee on Environment and Public Works, United States Senate," Union of Concerned Scientists, March 26, 2005, www.ucsusa.org; Mark Holt and Anthony Andrews, "Nuclear Power Plant Security and Vulnerabilities," Congressional Research Service, August 28, 2010, http://www.fas.org/sgp/crs/homesec/RL34331.pdf.

4. Union of Concerned Scientists, "Nuclear Reactor Security"; Lyman, "Testimony to the Subcommittee on Clean Air, Climate Change and Nuclear Security Committee on Environment and Public Works, United States Senate."

5. Lyman, "Testimony to the Subcommittee on Clean Air, Climate Change and Nuclear Security Committee on Environment and Public Works, United States Senate."

6. Lyman, "Testimony to the Subcommittee on Clean Air, Climate Change and Nuclear Security Committee on Environment and Public Works, United States Senate."

7. Mark Thompson, with reporting by Bruce Crumley, "Are These Towers

Safe?", *Time*, June 20, 2005, http://www.time.com/time/magazine/article
/0,9171,1071249,00.html.

8. Keith Bradsher and Hiroko Tabuchi, "Greater Danger Lies in Spent
Fuel Than in Reactors," *New York Times,* March 17, 2011, http://www.nytimes
.com/2011/03/18/world/asia/18spent.html; James M. Acton and Mark
Hibbs, "Why Fukushima Was Preventable," Carnegie Endowment for International Peace," March 6, 2012, http://carnegieendowment.org/2012/03
/06/why-fukushima-was-preventable.

9. Union of Concerned Scientists, "Aircraft Threats to Nuclear Plants."

10. Bradsher and Tabuchi, "Greater Danger Lies in Spent Fuel Than in
Reactors."

11. Harvey Wasserman, "America's Eggshell Nukes," *HuffingtonPost.
com,* November 15, 2010, http://www.huffingtonpost.com/harvey-wasser
man/americas-eggshell-nukes_b_783424.html.

12. Union of Concerned Scientists, "A Decade Later: NRC Reactor Oversight Process Has Failed to Improve Reactor Safety, New Report Finds,"
February 4, 2011, http://www.ucsusa.org/news/press_release/nrc-over
sight-failing-0498.html.

13. Wasserman, "America's Eggshell Nukes."

14. Robert Mueller, Senate Intelligence Committee testimony, February
16, 2005.

15. Alisa Gravitz, "The Top Ten Reasons We Don't Need More Nukes,"
CommonDreams.org, March 1, 2010, http://www.commondreams.org/view
/2010/03/01-8.

16. George Jahn, "Stuxnet Virus Penetrates Nuclear Plant, May Cause
Chernobyl-like Disaster," Associated Press, January 31, 2011. See http://
www.csmonitor.com/World/Latest-News-Wires/2011/0131/Stuxnet-virus
-penetrates-nuclear-plant-may-cause-Chernobyl-like-disaster; Global Security Newswire, "Stuxnet Could Trigger Atomic Calamity, Intel Report
Warns," February 1, 2011, http://www.nti.org/gsn/.

17. Ralph Nader, "No Nukes," *Common Dreams.org*, March 13, 2010,
http://www.commondreams.org/view/2010/02/13.

5. The Most Significant Source of Funding to Sunni Terrorist Groups Worldwide

1. Eric Lichtblau and Eric Schmitt, "Cash Flow to Terrorists Evades U.S. Efforts," *New York Times,* December 5, 2010, http://www.nytimes.com/2010/12/06/world/middleeast/06wikileaks-financing.html.

2. Associated Press, "Obama Renews Commitment to Nuclear Energy," February 16, 2010. See http://www.nbcnews.com/id/35421517/ns/business-oil_and_energy/t/obama-renews-commitment-nuclear-energy/.

3. Dean Nelson, "Hillary Clinton: US to build nuclear plants in India," *The Telegraph,* July 20, 2009, http://www.telegraph.co.uk/news/worldnews/asia/india/5872836/Hillary-Clinton-US-to-build-nuclear-plants-in-India.html.

4. Global Security Newswire, "U.S. Nuclear Marketers Visited Saudi Arabia, As Trade Talks Underway," February 1, 2013, http://www.nti.org/gsn/article/us-nuclear-marketers-visited-saudi-arabia-trade-talks-under-way/.

5. Corbett B. Daly, "U.S., India Formally Sign Nuclear Reprocessing Pact," Reuters, July 30, 2010, http://www.reuters.com/article/2010/07/31/us-usa-india-nuclear-idUSTRE66U00920100731; Nelson, "Hillary Clinton: US to build nuclear plants in India."

6. David Ruppe, "Govt. Report Critiques Bush Nuclear Deal with India," Global Security Newswire, August 16, 2005, http://www.nti.org/gsn/article/govt-report-critiques-bush-nuclear-deal-with-india/; David Ruppe, "U.S. Deal Would Aid Indian Nuclear Weapons, Expert Says," Global Security Newswire, October 13, 2005, http://www.nti.org/gsn/article/us-deal-would-aid-indian-nuclear-weapons-expert-says/; Global Security Newswire, "India to Ramp Up Nuclear Fuel Production," April 10, 2007, http://www.nti.org/gsn/article/india-to-ramp-up-nuclear-fuel-production/.

7. Christopher Drew and Heather Timmons, "Wealthy and Worried, India Is Rich Arms Market," *New York Times,* November 14, 2010, http://www.nytimes.com/2010/11/05/business/05defense.html.

8. Eric Lichtblau and Eric Schmitt, "Cash Flow to Terrorists Evades U.S. Efforts."

9. Global Security Newswire, "U.S. Nuclear Marketers Visited Saudi Arabia, As Trade Talks Underway."

10. Adam Entous, "Saudi Arms Deal Advances," *Wall Street Journal,* September 12, 2010, http://online.wsj.com/article/SB10001424052748704621 204575488361149625050.html.

11. Entous, "Saudi Arms Deal Advances."

12. Elaine M. Grossman, "Preliminary U.S.-Saudi Nuclear Trade Talks Set for Next Week," Global Security Newswire, July 28, 2011.

13. Amena Bakr, "Egypt to Issue Nuclear Plants Tender by End January," Reuters, January 16, 2011, www.reuters.com.

14. Declan Walsh, "WikiLeaks Cables Portray Saudi Arabia as a Cash Machine for Terrorists," *The Guardian,* December 5, 2010, http://www.guardian .co.uk/world/2010/dec/05/wikileaks-cables-saudi-terrorist-funding.

15. United Press International, "Emirates, Saudis Drive for Nuclear Power," September 21, 2012, http://www.upi.com/Business_News/Energy -Resources/2012/09/21/Emirates-Saudis-drive-for-nuclear-power/UPI -30481348241422/.

16. Louis Charonneau, "Iraq gets U.N. green light for civil nuclear program," Reuters, December 15, 2010, http://www.reuters.com/article/2010/12 /15/us-iraq-un-idUSTRE6BD63620101215.

17. Jim Michaels, "6 Months After U.S. Combat Troops Left, Can Iraq Go It Alone?" *USA Today,* June 6, 2012, http://usatoday30.usatoday.com/news /world/iraq/story/2012-06-06/iraq-stability-US-withdrawal/55430086/1.

6. We but Teach Bloody Instructions

1. Mark Clayton, "Stuxnet Worm: Private Security Experts Want US to Tell Them More," *Christian Science Monitor,* October 3, 2010, http://www .csmonitor.com/USA/2010/1003/Stuxnet-worm-Private-security-experts -want-US-to-tell-them-more.

2. Mark Clayton, "Stuxnet Malware Is 'Weapon' Out to Destroy . . . Iran's Bushehr Nuclear Plant?" *Christian Science Monitor,* September 21, 2010, http://www.csmonitor.com/USA/2010/0921/Stuxnet-malware-is -weapon-out-to-destroy-Iran-s-Bushehr-nuclear-plant.

3. John Markoff, "A Code for Chaos," *New York Times,* October 2, 2010, http://www.nytimes.com/2010/10/03/weekinreview/03markoff.html.

4. Marcus Baum, "Stuxnet Malware Mystery Deepens: Another Hint of Israeli Origins," *HuffingtonPost.com,* October 1, 2010, http://www.huffington post.com/2010/10/01/stuxnet-malware-mystery-d_n_747026.html.

5. Clayton, "Stuxnet Worm: Private Security Experts Want US to Tell Them More."

6. Clayton, "Stuxnet Worm: Private Security Experts Want US to Tell Them More."

7. CNN Wire Staff, "Iran Denies Cyberattack Hurt Nuclear Program—But Expert Isn't Sure," *CNNWorld,* September 29, 2010, http://www.cnn .com/2010/WORLD/meast/09/29/iran.cyberattack/index.html.

8. Clayton, "Stuxnet Malware Is 'Weapon' Out to Destroy . . . Iran's Bushehr Nuclear Plant?"

9. Clayton, "Stuxnet Malware Is 'Weapon' Out to Destroy . . . Iran's Bushehr Nuclear Plant?"

10. Clayton, "Stuxnet Malware Is 'Weapon' Out to Destroy . . . Iran's Bushehr Nuclear Plant?"

11. CNN Wire Staff, "Iran Denies Cyberattack Hurt Nuclear Program—But Expert Isn't Sure."

12. Global Security Newswire, "Stuxnet Could Trigger Atomic Calamity, Intel Report Warns," February 1, 2011, http://www.nti.org/gsn/.

13. William J. Broad, John Markoff, and David E. Sanger, "Israeli Test on Worm Called Crucial in Iran Nuclear Delay," *New York Times,* January 15, 2011, http://www.nytimes.com/2011/01/16/world/middleeast/16stuxnet .html.

14. David E. Sanger, "Obama Order Sped up Wave of Cyberattacks Against Iran," *New York Times,* June 1, 2012, http://www.nytimes.com/2012 /06/01/world/middleeast/obama-ordered-wave-of-cyberattacks-against -iran.html.

15. John Vidal, "Ukraine Raises $785m to Seal Chernobyl Under New 'Shell'," *The Guardian,* April 19, 2011, http://www.guardian.co.uk/environment /2011/apr/19/ukraine-funding-chernobyl-arch.

NOTES

16. Phred Dvorak and Mitsuru Obe, "Japan Plots 40-Year Nuclear Cleanup, *Wall Street Journal,* December 22, 2011, http://online.wsj.com /article/SB10001424052970204552304577111752403941694.html.

17. Robert Lemos, "A Way to Attack Nuclear Plants," *MIT Technology Review,* September 29, 2010, http://www.technologyreview.com/news /420970/a-way-to-attack-nuclear-plants/.

18. CBS News, "Cyber War: Sabotaging the System," November 6, 2009, http://www.cbsnews.com/8301-18560_162-5555565.html.

19. Associated Press, "Researchers: Cyber spies break into government computers," *USA Today,* May 29, 2009, http://usatoday30.usatoday.com/tech /news/computersecurity/2009-03-28-cyber-spy-network_N.htm.

20. Ralph Langner, "Why Attack When We Can't Defend?" *New York Times,* June 4, 2012, http://www.nytimes.com/roomfordebate/2012/06/04 /do-cyberattacks-on-iran-make-us-vulnerable-12/why-attack-when-we -cant-defend.

21. David E. Sanger, "Obama Order Sped up Wave of Cyberattacks Against Iran."

22. Nicole Perlroth and David E. Sanger, "New Computer Attacks Traced to Iran, Officials Say," *New York Times,* May 24, 2013.

23. Nicole Perlroth and David E. Sanger, "New Computer Attacks Traced to Iran, Officials Say."

7. What Japan's Nuclear Catastrophe Teaches Us

1. Eric Talmadge and Mari Yamaguchi, "The First 24 Hours Shaped Japan Nuke Crisis," Associated Press, July 1, 2011, reprinted in *Seattle Times,* http://seattletimes.com/html/businesstechnology/2015487776_apasjapan thefirstday.html; Jarod Hayers, "Fukushima and the Politics of Nuclear Energy," Sam Nunn School of International Affairs, Georgia Institute of Technology, December 13, 2011, gatech.academia.edu.

2. Eliza Strickland, "What Went Wrong in Japan's Nuclear Reactors," IEEE Spectrum, March 16, 2011, http://spectrum.ieee.org/tech-talk/energy/nuclear /explainer-what-went-wrong-in-japans-nuclear-reactors; Harvey Wasserman,

NOTES

"Is Fukushima Now Ten Chernobyls into the Sea," *CommonDreams.org*, May 26, 2011, https://www.commondreams.org/view/2011/05/26-7.

3. Kim Carollo, "Radiation from Japan Disaster Found in Kelp Along California Coast," ABC News, April 10, 2012, http://abcnews.go.com/blogs/health/2012/04/10/radiation-from-japan-disaster-found-along-calif-coast/.

4. Strickland, "What Went Wrong in Japan's Nuclear Reactors." Wasserman, "Is Fukushima Now Ten Chernobyls into the Sea."

5. William Robert Johnston, "Database of Radiological Incidents and Related Events," November 19, 2011, www.johnstonsarchive.net/nuclear/radevents/index.html; David Lochbaum "The NRC and Nuclear Power Plant Safety in 2010: A Brighter Spotlight Is Needed," Union of Concerned Scientists, March 17, 2011, http://www.ucsusa.org/assets/documents/nuclear_power/nrc-2010-full-report.pdf.

6. Lochbaum, "The NRC and Nuclear Plant Safety in 2010."; Erich Pica, "Don't Jump to Conclusions About Nuclear Reactors: Look at the Facts and Say No," *HuffingtonPost.com,* April 3, 2011, http://www.huffingtonpost.com/erich-pica/dont-jump-to-conclusions-_b_842582.html.

7. Norimitsu Onishi and Ken Belson, "Culture of Complicity Tied to Stricken Nuclear Plant," *New York Times,* April 26, 2011, http://www.nytimes.com/2011/04/27/world/asia/27collusion.html.

8. William Saletan, "Nuclear Incest: Did Industry-Government Collusion Contribute to Japan's Nuclear Disaster," April 28, 2011, *Slate.com,* http://www.slate.com/articles/health_and_science/human_nature/2011/04/nuclear_incest.html; Tom Zeller, Jr., "Nuclear Agency Is Criticized as Too Close to Its Industry," *New York Times,* May 7, 2011, http://www.nytimes.com/2011/05/08/business/energy-environment/08nrc.html.

9. Onishi and Belson, "Culture of Complicity Tied to Stricken Nuclear Plant."

10. Onishi and Belson, "Culture of Complicity Tied to Stricken Nuclear Plant."; Juergen Baetz, "Insurance Cost vs. Nuclear Power Risk," Associated Press, May 1, 2011.

11. Onishi and Belson, "Culture of Complicity Tied to Stricken Nuclear Plant."

12. Onishi and Belson, "Culture of Complicity Tied to Stricken Nuclear Plant."; Hiroko Tabuchi, Norimitsu Onishi, and Ken Belson, "Japan Extended Reactor's Life, Despite Warning," *New York Times,* March 21, 2011.

13. Zeller, "Nuclear Agency Is Criticized as Too Close to Its Industry."

14. Karl Grossman, "Nuclear Disaster and Obama's Disastrous Response," *CommonDreams.org,* March 31, 2011.

15. Tom Zeller, Jr., "With US Nuclear Plants Under Scrutiny, Too, a Report Raises Safety Concerns," *New York Times,* March 17, 2011, http://www.nytimes.com/2011/03/18/science/earth/18scientists.html.

16. Lochbaum, "The NRC and Nuclear Plant Safety in 2010: A Brighter Spotlight Needed."; Pica, "Don't Jump to Conclusions About Nuclear Reactors: Look at the Facts and Say No."

17. John Sullivan, "NRC Waives Enforcement of Fire Rules at Nuclear Plants," *Pro Publica,* May 11, 2011, http://www.propublica.org/article/nrc-waives-enforcement-of-fire-rules-at-nuclear-plants.

18. Sullivan, "NRC Waives Enforcement of Fire Rules at Nuclear Plants."

19. Anne-Marie Cusac, "Fire Hazard: Bush Leaves Nuclear Plants at Risk," *Progressive,* vol. 68, no. 8, August 2004.

20. Pica, "Don't Jump to Conclusions About Nuclear Reactors: Look at the Facts and Say No."; Keith Bradsher and Hiroko Tabuchi, "Greater Danger Lies in Spent Fuel Than in Reactors," *New York Times,* March 17, 2011, http://www.nytimes.com/2011/03/18/world/asia/18spent.html.

21. Matthew L. Wald, "Court Forces a Rethinking of Nuclear Fuel Storage," *New York Times,* June 8, 2012, http://www.nytimes.com/2012/06/09/science/earth/court-says-nuclear-agency-must-rethink-fuel-storage.html.

22. Robert Alvarez, "In a Perfect World Fukushima Would Halt Nuclear Renaissance in Its Tracks," Foreign Policy in Focus, March 16, 2011, http://www.fpif.org/blog/in_a_perfect_world_fukushima_would_halt_nuclear_renaissance_in_its_tracks.

23. NRC Fact Sheet, "Fact Sheet on Improvements Resulting from Davis-

Besse Incident," www.nrc.gov/reading-rm/doc-collections/fact-sheets/fs
-davis-besse-improv.html, September, 2009; Union of Concerned Scientists,
"Davis-Besse," http://www.ucsusa.org/assets/documents/nuclear_power
/davis-besse-ii.pdf; Union of Concerned Scientists, "Davis-Besse: The Reactor with a Hole in Its Head," http://www.ucsusa.org/assets/documents
/nuclear_power/acfnx8tzc.pdf.

24. Tom Zeller, Jr., "Nuclear Agency Is Criticized as Too Close to Its Industry."

25. World Nuclear News, "Nuclear Power in the USA," March 2012,
www.world-nuclear.org/info/inf41.html.

26. Wald, "Court Forces a Rethinking of Nuclear Fuel Storage."

27. Zeller, "Nuclear Agency Is Criticized as Too Close to Its Industry.";
Shay Totten, "Nuclear Regulatory Commission: Nuclear Watchdog or Lapdog," New England Center for Investigation, May 6, 2011, http://necir-bu.org
/investigations/the-canary-in-the-nuclear-plant-the-spent-fuel-crisis
/nuclear-regulatory-commission-watchdog-or-lapdog/web-story/.

28. Zeller, "Nuclear Agency Is Criticized as Too Close to Its Industry."

29. Union of Concerned Scientists, "Nuclear Reactor Security," March
30, 2005, www.ucsusa.org; Edwin S. Lyman, "Testimony to the Subcommittee on Clean Air, Climate Change and Nuclear Security Committee on Environment and Public Works, United States Senate," Union of Concerned
Scientists, March 26, 2005, www.ucsusa.org.

30. Totten, "Nuclear Regulatory Commission: Nuclear Watchdog or
Lapdog."

31. Eric Lipton, "Ties to Obama Aided in Access for Big Utility," New
York Times, August 22, 2012, http://www.nytimes.com/2012/08/23/us
/politics/ties-to-obama-aided-in-access-for-exelon-corporation.html; Abdon
M. Pallasch, "Rahm Emanuel's $18.5 Million Paychecks: How Did He Do
It?" Chicago Sun-Times, February 7, 2011.

8. And Hell Followed with Him

1. Sasha Chavkin and Sheri Fink, "US Nuclear-Disaster Preparedness
Hobbled by Uncertain Chain of Command," Pro Publica, April 8, 2011,

http://www.propublica.org/article/u.s.-nuclear-disaster-preparedness-hob
bled-by-uncertain-chain-of-command.

2. Alexander Cockburn, "The Lessons of Fukushima," *The Nation,* March 26, 2012, *thenation.com*; Harvey Wasserman, "People Died at Three Mile Island," *CounterPunch,* March 24, 2009, http://www.counterpunch. org/2009/03/24/people-died-at-three-mile-island/; Michael Parks, "Chernobyl Lies By Soviets Confirmed—Contaminated Meat, Milk Mixed with Other Supplies," *Los Angeles Times,* as reported in *Seattle Times,* April 25, 1992, http://community.seattletimes.nwsource.com/archive/?date=19920425 &slug=1488316; Karl Grossman, "The Big Lies Fly High: Fukushima and the Nuclear Establishment," *CounterPunch,* June 16, 2011, http://www .counterpunch.org/2011/06/16/fukushima-and-the-nuclear-establishment/; Karl Grossman, "The Big Lie: One Year After Fukushima, Nuclear Cover Up Revealed," *CommonDreams.org,* March 5, 2012, https://www.common dreams.org/view/2012/03/05.

3. Edwin S. Lyman, "Impacts of a Terrorist Attack at Indian Point Nuclear Power Plant," Union of Concerned Scientists, September 2004, http://www.ucsusa.org/nuclear_power/nuclear_power_risk/sabotage _and_attacks_on_reactors/im pacts-of-a-terrorist-attack.html.

4. Karl Grossman, "NRC's Pro-Nuke Spin on Evacuation Zone," *Common Dreams.org,* May 5, 2011, http://www.commondreams.org/view/2011/04/05-4.

5. Grossman, "NRC's Pro-Nuke Spin on Evacuation Zone."

6. Helen Caldicott, "How Nuclear Apologists Mislead the World Over Radiation," *The Guardian,* April 11, 2011, http://www.guardian.co.uk /environment/2011/apr/11/nuclear-apologists-radiation.

7. Public Employees for Environmental Responsibility (PEER), "Obama Approves Raising Permissible Levels of Nuclear Radiation in Drinking Water. Civilian Cancer Deaths Expected to Skyrocket," Global Research News, http://www.globalresearch.ca/obama-approves-raising-permissible-levels -of-nuclear-radiation-in-drinking-water-civilian-cancer-deaths-expected -to-skyrocket/5331224, April 14, 2013.

8. Tim Kelly and David Dolan, "Japan Eyes State-Backed Insurer to Save

Tepco," Reuters, April 15, 2011, http://www.reuters.com/article/2011/04
/15/japan-nuclear-insurer-idUSL3E7FF0BV20110415.

9. Phred Dvorak and Mitsuru Obe, "Japan Plots 40-Year Nuclear
Cleanup," *Wall Street Journal,* December 22, 2011, http://online.wsj.com
/article/SB10001424052970204552304577111752403941694.html.

10. Associated Press, "Nuclear Power: Adequate Insurance Too Expensive," April 21, 2011, reprinted by *CommonDreams.org,* https://www.com
mondreams.org/headline/2011/04/21-4.

11. Associated Press, "Nuclear Power"; John Sullivan, "NRC Waives Enforcement of Fire Rules at Nuclear Plants," *Pro Publica,* May 11, 2011, http://
www.propublica.org/article/nrc-waives-enforcement-of-fire-rules-at-nuclear
-plants; Juergen Baetz, "Insurance Cost vs. Nuclear Power Risk," Associated
Press, May 1, 2011.

12. Kyle Rabin, "9/11 Report Reveals Al Qaeda Ringleader Contemplated
a NY-area Nuclear Power Plant as Potential Target," *Energy Bulletin,* July 25,
2004,   http://www.resilience.org/stories/2004-07-25/911-report-reveals-al
-qaeda-ringleader-contemplated-ny-area-nuclear-power-plant-p.

13. Doug Koplow, "Nuclear Power: Still Not Viable Without Subsidies,"
Union of Concerned Scientists, February 2011, http://www.ucsusa.org
/assets/documents/nuclear_power/nuclear_subsidies_report.pdf.

14. Kelly and Dolan, "Japan Eyes State-Backed Insurer to Save Tepco."

15. Martin Fackler, "Leak Found in Steel Tank for Water at Fukushima,"
New York Times, June 5, 2013; Martin Fackler, "Flow of Tainted Water Is
Latest Crisis at Japan Nuclear Plant," *New York Times,* April 29, 2013; Har-
vey Wasserman, "The Fukushima Nightmare Gets Worse," *The Progressive,*
August 9, 2013.

16. Martin Fackler, "Flow of Tainted Water Is Latest Crisis at Japan
Nuclear Plant."

17. Aaron Sheldrick and Antoni Slodkowski, "Insight: After disaster, the
deadliest part of Japan's nuclear clean-up," Reuters, http://www.reuters.com
/article/2013/08/15/us-japan-fukushima-insight-idUSBRE97D00M20130815,
August 13, 2013; Christina Consolo, "Fukushima apocalypse: Years of 'duct

tape fixes' could result in millions of deaths," *RT.com*, http://rt.com/news/fu
kushima-apocalypse-fuel-removal-598/, August 17, 2013.

9. Back from the Abyss

1. Bernie Sanders: U.S. Senator for Vermont Web site, "Senator Seeks
Broad Nuclear Moratorium," March 21, 2011, http://www.sanders.senate
.gov/newsroom/news/?id=02e4b57c-3286-4330-9c60-257ae983a3b0.

PART II   A Habitation of Devils

l. Trading with the Nuclear Devil

1. Associated Press, "Cheney Once Pressed for Halliburton-Iran Trade,"
October 9, 2004; *60 Minutes,* "Doing Business with the Enemy," January 25,
2004, *CBSNews.com*; *Newsweek,* "Business As Usual?" February 16, 2005.

2. Colum Lynch, "Halliburton's Iraq Deals Greater Than Cheney Has Said,
Affiliates Had $73 Million in Contracts," *Washington Post,* June 23, 2001. See
http://www.globalpolicy.org/component/content/article/170/42166.html.

3. Richard Behar, "Rummy's North Korea Connection," *Fortune,* vol. 147,
issue 9, May 12, 2003, http://money.cnn.com/magazines/fortune/fortune_
archive/2003/05/12/342316/; Randeep Ramesh, "The Two Faces of Rumsfeld,"
The Guardian, May 9, 2003, http://www.guardian.co.uk/world/2003/may/09
/nuclear.northkorea.

4. Joyce Battle, ed., "Shaking Hands with Saddam Hussein: The U.S.
Tilts Toward Iraq, 1980–1984," National Security Archive Electronic Briefing Book No. 82, George Washington University, February 25, 2003, http://
www.gwu.edu/~nsarchiv/NSAEBB/NSAEBB82/.

5. Former CIA director George Tenet, "The Worldwide Threat 2004:
Challenges in a Changing Global Context," in testimony before the Senate
Select Committee on Intelligence on February 24, 2004, quoted in Graham
Allison, *Nuclear Terrorism: The Ultimate Preventable Catastrophe,* (New
York: Holt, 2005), 194.

6. Judicial Watch, "Maps and Charts of Iraqi Oil Fields," March 7, 2006,
www.judicialwatch.org/printer_iraqi-oil-maps. shtml; Ron Suskind, *The*

Price of Loyalty: George W. Bush, the White House and the Education of Paul O'Neill (New York: Simon & Schuster, 2004), 96.

7. Wolf Blitzer, "Search for the 'Smoking Gun,'" *CNN.com*, January 10, 2003, http://www.cnn.com/2003/US/01/10/wbr.smoking.gun/. Blitzer is quoting his September 8, 2002 interview with Condoleezza Rice; "Chevron to Pay $30 Million to Settle Kickback Charges," Associated Press/www .nytimes.com, November 15, 2007.

8. Russ W. Baker, "Iraqgate: The Big One That (Almost) Got Away: Who Chased It—and Who Didn't," *Columbia Journalism Review*, March/April 1993, http://www.cjr.org/issues/.

9. Craig Unger, *House of Bush, House of Saud: The Secret Relationship Between the World's Two Most Powerful Dynasties* (New York: Scribner, 2004), 295–98; *Washington Post*, "Two Months Before 9/11, an Urgent Warning to Rice," October 1, 2006, http://www.washingtonpost.com/wp-dyn/content /article/2006/09/30/AR2006093000282.html; Anthony Summers and Robbyn Swan, "The Kingdom and the Towers," *Vanity Fair*, August 2011, http://www .vanityfair.com/politics/features/2011/08/9-11-2011-201108.

10. Josh Meyer, "Report Links Saudi Government to 9/11 Hijackers, Sources Say," *Los Angeles Times*, August 2, 2003.

11. Robert Baer, *Sleeping with the Devil: How Washington Sold Our Soul for Saudi Crude* (New York: Three Rivers Press, 2003), 34–35.

12. John Buchanan and Stacey Michael, "Bush: Nazi Dealings Continued Until 1951," *New Hampshire Gazette*, vol. 248, no. 3, November 3, 2003. See http://www.globalresearch.ca/bush-nazi-dealings-continued-until-1951 -federal-documents/1176.

13. Herbert Parmet, "What Should We Make of the Charge Linking the Bush Family Fortune to Nazism?" History News Network, November 17, 2003, http://hnn.us/node/1811; Ben Aris and Dunean Campbell, "How Bush's Grand-father Helped Hitler's Rise to Power," *The Guardian*, September 25, 2004.

2. The Iraq War: Nuclear Diversions, Petrodollar Dreams

1. Wolf Blitzer, "Search for the 'Smoking Gun,'" *CNN.com*, January 10, 2003, http://www.cnn.com/2003/US/01/10/wbr.smoking.gun/. Blitzer is

quoting his September 8, 2002 interview with Condoleezza Rice; Vice President Dick Cheney on *Meet the Press,* March 16, 2003. See transcript at https://www.mtholyoke.edu/acad/intrel/bush/cheneymeetthepress.htm.

2. Reuters, "Arab Countries Look to Nukes," November 5, 2006, *msnbc. msn.com*; William J. Broad and David E. Sanger, "Eye on Iran, Rivals Pursuing Nuclear Power," *New York Times,* April 15, 2007, http://www .nytimes.com/2007/04/15/world/middleeast/15sunnis.html; Richard Beeston, "Nuclear Steps Put Region on Brink of Most Fearful Era Yet," *The Times,* November 4, 2006, http://www.thetimes.co.uk/tto/news/world /middleeast/article2604752.ece.

3. Broad and Sanger, "Eye on Iran, Rivals Pursuing Nuclear Power."

4. Global Security Newswire, "Saudi Arabia: Nuclear," NTI, http:// www.nti.org/country-profiles/saudi-arabia/nuclear/.

5. Bruce Riedel, "Saudi Arabia: Nervously Watching Pakistan," The Brookings Institution, January 28, 2008. http://www.brookings.edu/research /opinions/2008/01/28-saudi-arabia-riedel.

6. David McGlinchey, "Iran: Russian Nuclear Assistance Motivated by Economic Needs," Global Security Newswire, February 27, 2003.

7. McGlinchey, "Iran: Russian Nuclear Assistance Motivated by Economic Needs."

8. Michael R. Gordon and General Bernard E. Trainor, *COBRA II: The Inside Story of the Invasion and Occupation of Iraq* (New York: Vintage, 2007), 503–4.

9. Gordon and Trainor, *COBRA II,* 503–4.

10. Michael T. Klare, "More Blood, Less Oil: The Failed U.S. Mission to Capture Iraqi Petroleum," *TomDispatch.com,* September 21, 2005, in *Common.Dreams.org,* http://www.commondreams.org/views05/0921-33.htm.

11. Klare, "More Blood, Less Oil."

12. Donald L. Barlett and James B. Steele, "Iraq's Crude Awakening," *Time,* May 19, 2003, http://www.time.com/time/magazine/article/0,9171 ,1004844,00.html.

13. Klare, "More Blood, Less Oil."; Barlett and Steele, "Iraq's Crude Awakening."; Gordon and Trainor, *COBRA II,* 220–25, 513–15.

14. Vice President Richard Cheney, remarks before the Senate Armed Services Committee, September 11, 1990—five weeks after Iraq's invasion of Kuwait; also see Michael T. Klare, "Bush-Cheney Energy Strategy: Procuring the Rest of the World's Oil," Foreign Policy in Focus, January 2004, in *CommonDreams.org*, http://www.commondreams.org/views04/0113-01.htm.

15. Gordon and Trainor, *COBRA II*, 158–62, 545–57; Klare, "More Blood, Less Oil."

16. Stephanie Heinatz, "Eustis Chief: Iraq Post-War Plan Muzzled: Army Brig. Gen. Mark Scheid, an Early Planner of the War, Tells About Challenges of Invasion and Rebuilding," *Daily Press,* September 8, 2006, http://articles.dailypress.com/2006-09-08/news/0609080088_1_central-command-defense-secretary-donald-rumsfeld-iraq.

17. Ron Suskind, *The Price of Loyalty: George W. Bush, the White House and the Education of Paul O'Neill* (New York: Simon & Schuster, 2004), 96.

18. Suskind, *The Price of Loyalty,* 96; Judicial Watch, "Maps and Charts of Iraqi Oil Fields," March 7, 2006, www.judicialwatch.org/printer_iraqi-oil-maps.shtml.

19. A. K. Gupta, "Prize of the Century: Major Oil Companies Ready to Claim Iraqi Resources," *The Independent,* February 27, 2007, http://www.independent.org/2007/02/27/prize-century-major-oil-companies-ready-claim-iraqi-resources.

20. Suskind, *The Price of Loyalty,* 96.

21. Blitzer, "Search for the 'Smoking Gun.'"

3. The Saudi Nuclear Threat

1. "Wolfowitz: US Intelligence Murky," *CNN.com,* July 27, 2003.

2. Yossef Bodansky, *Bin Laden: The Man Who Declared War on America* (Roseville, CA: Prima Lifestyles, 2001), 282–85; Robert Baer, *Sleeping with the Devil: How Washington Sold Our Soul for Saudi Crude* (New York: Three Rivers Press, 2003), 180, 23.

3. BBC News, "Who Is Osama bin Laden?" September 18, 2001, http://news.bbc.co.uk/2/hi/south_asia/155236.stm; Bodansky, *Bin Laden: The Man Who Declared War on America,* 10–20.

4. Bodansky, *Bin Laden*, 282–85.

5. Bodansky, *Bin Laden*, 282–85.

6. Bodansky, *Bin Laden*, 282–85.

7. Steven R. Weisman, "Saudi Arabia Longtime Ambassador to the U.S. Is Resigning," *New York Times,* July 21, 2005, http://www.nytimes.com /2005/07/21/international/middleeast/21bandar.html.

8. Weisman, "Saudi Arabia Longtime Ambassador to the U.S. Is Resigning."

9. Baer, *Sleeping with the Devil,* 35–36.

10. Ralph Peters, "Dubya's Grovel," *New York Post,* August 9, 2002.

11. Josh Meyer, "2 Allies Aided Bin Laden, Say Panel Members," *Los Angeles Times,* June 20, 2004.

12. Baer, *Sleeping with the Devil,* 20, 35–36.

13. Craig Unger, *House of Bush, House of Saud: The Secret Relationship Between the World's Two Most Powerful Dynasties* (New York: Scribner, 2004), 295–98.

14. Josh Meyer, "Report Links Saudi Government to 9/11 Hijackers, Sources Say," *Los Angeles Times,* August 2, 2003.

15. Helen Kennedy, "New Rage Over 9/11 & Saudis Pols Get Censored Report," *New York Daily News,* July 25, 2003.

16. Kennedy, "New Rage Over 9/11 & Saudis Pols Get Censored Report."

17. Eric Lichtblau, "Saudi Arabia May Be Tied to 9/11, 2 Ex-Senators Say," *New York Times,* February 29, 2012, http://www.nytimes.com/2012/03/01 /us/graham-and-kerrey-see-possible-saudi-9-11-link.html.

18. Zac Anderson and Robert Eckhart, "FBI Investigated Another Sarasota Link to 9/11," *Herald-Tribune* (Sarasota, FL), September 8, 2011, http:// www.heraldtribune.com/article/20110908/article/110909586.

19. *Pittsburgh Tribune-Review,* "160 Saudis Flew Home After 9/11," March 30, 2004; Unger, *House of Bush, House of Saud,* 258.

20. *Pittsburgh Tribune-Review,* "160 Saudis Flew Home After 9/11."; Unger, *House of Bush, House of Saud,* 253–59.

21. Craig Unger, "The Great Escape," *New York Times,* June 1, 2004, http://www.nytimes.com/2004/06/01/opinion/the-great-escape.html.

22. Jean Heller, "TIA Now Verifies Flight of Saudis," *St. Petersburg Times*, June 9, 2004, http://www.sptimes.com/2004/06/09/Tampabay/TIA _now_verifies_flig.shtml.

23. *Pittsburgh Tribune-Review*, "160 Saudis Flew Home After 9/11."

24. Nathan Hodge, "Maverick Colonel Blames US Army's 'Sycophantic' Culture and Heavy-Handedness for Failures in Iraq," *Financial Times*, June 9, 2004.

25. Steven Brill in *After: How America Confronted the September 12 Era* (New York: Simon & Schuster, 2003), quoted in Nat Hentoff's "Is Ashcroft Fit for Office?" *Truthout.com*, June 27, 2003, http://archive.truthout.org /article/nat-hentoff-is-ashcroft-fit-for-office; Tom Regan, "Daily Update: Hatfill, While Under Investigation for Anthrax, Trained US Intelligence Agents for Bioweapons Searches," *Christian Science Monitor*, July 3, 2003.

26. Douglas Farah, "Al Qaeda's Finances Ample, Say Probers: Worldwide Failure to Enforce Sanctions Cited," *Washington Post*, December 14, 2003.

27. John Mintz, "Saudi Anti-Terror Efforts Criticized," *Washington Post*, June 15, 2004, http://www.washingtonpost.com/wp-dyn/articles/A41730 -2004Jun14.html.

28. Lisa Myers, "Saudi Prince: Zionism to Blame for Terror Attack," *Nightly News with Tom Brokaw*, NBC News, June 15, 2004, http://www .msnbc.msn.com/id/5218227/.

29. Reuters, "US Embassy Warns U.S. Citizens in Saudi Arabia," *Washington Post*, June 13, 2004.

4. Donald Rumsfeld

1. Watergate Tapes, March 9, 1971, http://whitehousetapes.net/clips/rmn _rumsfeld.htm.

2. Randeep Ramesh, "The Two Faces of Rumsfeld," *The Guardian*, May 9, 2003, http://www.guardian.co.uk/world/2003/may/09/nuclear.northkorea; Randeep Ramesh, "Rumsfeld Link to Sale of Reactors to North Korea," *The Guardian*, May 10, 2003, http://www.smh.com.au/articles/2003/05/09 /1052280441337.html.

3. David Rennie, "Rumsfeld Calls for Regime Change in North Korea,"

Daily Telegraph, April 22, 2003, http://www.telegraph.co.uk/news/world news/asia/northkorea/1428126/Rumsfeld-calls-for-regime-change-in -North-Korea.html.

4. *PBS Online News Hour,* "N. Korea Re-Opens Nuclear Facilities, Agency Says," December 24, 2002, http://www.pbs.org/newshour/updates /nkorea_12-24-02.html.

5. *PBS Online News Hour,* "N. Korea Re-Opens Nuclear Facilities, Agency Says."; John McCain, "Rogue State Rollback," *Weekly Standard,* January 20, 2003, http://www.weeklystandard.com/Content/Public/Articles/000 /000/002/093wsrnmh.asp.

6. Donald Rumsfeld, et al., "Executive Summary of the Report of the Commission to Assess the Ballistic Missile Threat to the United States," July 15, 1998, https://www.fas.org/irp/threat/bm-threat.htm.

7. Rumsfeld, et al., "Executive Summary of the Report of the Commission to Assess the Ballistic Missile Threat to the United States." Central Intelligence Agency, "Global Trends 2015," April 6, 2007, https://www.cia.gov /news-information/cia-the-war-on-terrorism/terrorism-related-excerpts -from-global-trends-2015-a-dialogue-about-the-future-with-nongovern ment-experts.html.

8. Fred Kaplan, "Rolling Blunder: How the Bush Administration Let North Korea Get Nukes," *Washington Monthly,* May 2004, http://www.wash ingtonmonthly.com/features/2004/0405.kaplan.html.

5. U.S.–Indian Nuclear Policy: How to Foment a Nuclear Arms Race for Fun and Profit

1. Matthew L. Wald, "US Loans for Reactors in China Draw Objections," *New York Times,* February 28, 2005, http://www.nytimes.com/2005/02/28 /business/worldbusiness/28westinghouse.html.

2. Shankhadeep Choudhury, "India Warns Rumsfeld Against U.S. Arms Sales to Pakistan," *Los Angeles Times,* December 10, 2004, http://articles. latimes.com/2004/dec/10/world/fg-rumsfeld10.

3. Manoj Joshi, "Could India Have Won the China War?" *Times of In-*

dia, November 24, 2002, http://articles.timesofindia.indiatimes.com/2002
-11-24/india/27306736_1_air-power-tibet-air-operations; Pakistan De-
fence, "India Victory in 65, 71 and 99," http://www.defence.pk/forums
/military-history-strategy/47077-indian-victory-65-71-1999-a.html; Tom
Hundley, "Pakistan and India: Race to the End," Pulitzer Center on Crisis
Reporting, September 5, 2012, http://pulitzercenter.org/reporting/pakistan
-nuclear-weapons-battlefield-india-arms-race-energy-cold-war.

4. Sam Roberts, "In 2025, India to Pass China in Population, U.S. Estimates," *New York Times*, December 15, 2009, http://www.nytimes.com
/2009/12/16/world/asia/16census.html?_r=0.

5. Robert D. Kaplan, *The Coming Anarchy: Shattering the Dreams of the
Post Cold War* (New York: Vintage, 2001), 51.

6. *ScienceDaily*, "Prevalence of Child Marriage in India High Fertility
Risks," March 9, 2009, *www.sciencedaly.com*.

7. Amnesty International, "India: Historic Ruling Against 'Sodomy'
Laws, the First Step to Equality," July 2, 2009, http://www.amnesty.org/en
/for-media/press-releases/india-historic-ruling-against-%E2%80%9Csod-
omy%E2%80%9D-laws-first-step-equality-20090702.

8. Megha Bahree, "Child Labor," *Forbes*, February 28, 2008, http://www
.forbes.com/forbes/2008/0225/072.html.

9. Vishal Arora, "Prescription for Failure: The Need for Addressing Corruption in India," Harvard College Global Health Review, October 19, 2011,
http://www.hcs.harvard.edu/hghr/online/india-corruption; Shubhlakshmi
Shukla, "India probes corruption in flagship health programme," *The Lancet*,
vol. 379, issue 9817:698, February 25, 2012, http://www.thelancet.com/jour
nals/lancet/article/PIIS0140-6739(12)60293-1/fulltext.

10. Malise Ruthven, "Excremental India," *The New York Review of Books*,
May 13, 2010.

11. Malise Ruthven, "Excremental India."

12. David Ruppe, "U.S. Deal Would Aid Indian Nuclear Weapons, Expert Says," Global Security Newswire, October 13, 2005, http://www.nti.org
/gsn/article/us-deal-would-aid-indian-nuclear-weapons-expert-says/;

Richard Speier, "U.S. Space Aid to India: On a 'Glide Path' to ICBM Trouble?" *Arms Control Today*, March 2006, http://www.armscontrol.org/act /2006_03/March-IndiaFeature.

13. Global Security Newswire, "India to Ramp Up Nuclear Fuel Production," April 10, 2007, http://www.nti.org/gsn/article/india-to-ramp-up -nuclear-fuel-production/.

14. David Waller, "Atoms for Peace: A Perspective from the IAEA," International Atomic Energy Agency, December 8, 2003, http://www.iaea.org /newscenter/statements/ddgs/2003/waller08122003.html; Global Security Newswire, "Peaceful Nuclear Technology Can Be Effective 'Deterrent,' IAEA Chief ElBaradei Warns," December 10, 2004, http://www.nti.org/gsn /article/peaceful-nuclear-technology-can-be-effective-deterrent-iaea-chief -elbaradei-warns/; Leonard Weiss, "Atoms for Peace," *Bulletin of the Atomic Scientists*, 59, no. 6 (November–December 2003), *thebulletin.org*.

15. David Ruppe, "Govt. Report Critiques Bush Nuclear Deal with India," Global Security Newswire, August 16, 2005, http://www.nti.org /gsn/article/govt-report-critiques-bush-nuclear-deal-with-india/.

16. Elizabeth Roche, "India Upgraded Security at Nuclear Facilities Amid Terror Warnings," Agence France-Presse (AFP), September 5, 2006, *news.yahoo.com*.

17. Roche, "India Upgraded Security at Nuclear Facilities Amid Terror Warnings."

18. World Bank, "India: Malnutrition Report," *www.web.worldbank.org*.

19. Adapted from Peter Wonacott, "Lawless Legislators Thwart Social Progress in India," *Wall Street Journal*, May 4, 2007, http://online.wsj.com /article/SB117823755304891604.html.

20. David Ruppe, "U.S. Deal Would Aid Indian Nuclear Weapons, Expert Says."

21. Agence France-Press, "India Involved in Illicit Nuclear Activities: US Think Tank," March 11, 2006, *news.yahoo.com*.

22. IISS Reports, "A. Q. Khan and onward proliferation from Pakistan," 2006–2012, The International Institute for Strategic Studies (IISS); Mark

Fitzpatrick, ed., *Nuclear Black Markets: Pakistan, A. Q. Khan and the Rise of Proliferation Networks* (London: IISS, 2007).

23. Joshua Pollack and George Perkovich, "The A. Q. Khan Network and Its Fourth Customer," Carnegie Endowment for International Peace, January 23, 2012, http://carnegieendowment.org/2012/01/23/q-khan-network-and -its-fourth-customer.

24. David Francis, "Expert Warns Risks of India-US Nuclear Pact," Global Security Newswire, March 22, 2006, http://www.nti.org/gsn/article /expert-warns-of-risks-of-india-us-nuclear-pact/.

25. Jocelyn Hanamirian, "Analysis: U.S.-India Nuke Deal Revisited," United Press International, July 18, 2006, http://www.upi.com/Business _News/Security-Industry/2006/07/18/Analysis-US-India-nuke-deal -revisited/UPI-97481153234185/.

26. Gordon Prather, "Condi's Diplomatic Triumph," *Antiwar.com*, December 23, 2006, http://www.antiwar.com/prather/?articleid=10210.

27. Prather, "Condi's Diplomatic Triumph."

28. Prather, "Condi's Diplomatic Triumph."

29. David Ruppe, "U.S.-Indian Deal Would Violate NPT, Critics Say," Global Security Newswire, June 21, 2006, http://www.nti.org/gsn/article/us -indian-deal-would-violate-npt-critics-say/.

30. Ruppe, "U.S.-Indian Deal Would Violate NPT, Critics Say."

31. BBC News, "Congress Mulls India Nuclear Deal," October 27, 2005, http://news.bbc.co.uk/1/hi/world/south_asia/4379850.stm.

32. *Sydney Morning Herald*, "Rice Offers India Nuclear Help, But Objects to Natural Gas Line," March 18, 2006, http://www.smh.com.au/.

33. Hundley, "Pakistan and India: Race to the End."

34. Choudhury, "India Warns Rumsfeld Against U.S. Arms Sales to Pakistan."

35. Rajesh Mahapatra, "Rumsfeld Warned on Arms Sale," Associated Press, December 10, 2004.

36. Sandeep Unnithan, "US Decision to Sell P-3C Orion Strike Aircraft to Pakistan Shocks India," *India Today*, December 6, 2004, http://indiatoday

.intoday.in/story/us-decision-to-sell-p-3c-orion-strike-aircraft-to-pakistan-shocks-india/1/195104.html.

37. Jim Bencivenga, "The Other News Rumsfeld Made," *Christian Science Monitor,* December 9, 2004, *www.csmonitor.com.*

38. Amir Zia, "Pakistan Tests Medium-Range Nuclear-Capable Missile," Reuters, December 8, 2004.

39. Eric Margolis, "The Nuclear New-Boy We Should Be Watching Is India," April 27, 2013, http://ericmargolis.com/2013/04/the-nuclear-new-boy-we-should-be-watching-is-india/.

40. Global Security Newswire, "Pakistan, India Could Receive U.S. F-16s," *nti.org,* March 15, 2005, http://www.nti.org/gsn/article/pakistan-india-could-receive-us-f-16s/.

41. Jon Fox, "Physicists Back Claim that US-Indian Deal Could Allow for 509 New Indian Nuclear Weapons a Year," Global Security Network, August 23, 2006, *www.nti.org.*

42. Randeep Ramesh, "The Two Faces of Rumsfeld," *The Guardian,* May 9, 2003, http://www.guardian.co.uk/world/2003/may/09/nuclear.northkorea; Randeep Ramesh, "Rumsfeld Link to Sale of Reactors to North Korea," *The Guardian,* May 10, 2003, http://www.smh.com.au/articles/2003/05/09/1052280441337.html.

43. Associated Press, "Cheney to Pitch Nuclear Reactors During China Trip," NBC News, April 9, 2004, http://www.nbcnews.com/id/4704302/ns/business-world_business/t/cheney-pitch-nuclear-reactors-during-china-trip/; Matthew L. Wald, "US Loans for Reactors in China Draw Objections."

44. *Pittsburgh Business Times,* "Westinghouse Sold to Toshiba for $5.4B," February 6, 2006, http://www.bizjournals.com/pittsburgh/stories/2006/02/06/daily3.html; David Lague, "Russia Covets China Nuclear Deals," *International Herald Tribune,* April 15, 2006, reprinted in *China Daily,* http://www.chinadaily.com.cn/china/2006-04/14/content_567580_2.htm; Matthew L. Wald, "US Loans for Reactors in China Draw Objections."

45. *Pittsburgh Business Times,* "Westinghouse Sold to Toshiba for $5.4B.";

Lague, "Russia Covets China Nuclear Deals."; Wald, "US Loans for Reactors in China Draw Objections."

46. Paul Leventhal, "Getting Serious About Proliferation," *Bulletin of the Atomic Scientists,* vol. 40, no. 3, March 1984; National Security Archive, "New Documents Spotlight Reagan-era Tensions over Pakistani Nuclear Program," George Washington University, April 27, 2012, http://www.gwu.edu/~nsarchiv/nukevault/ebb377/.

47. Douglas Frantz and Catherine Collins, "Those Nuclear Flashpoints Are Made in Pakistan," *Washington Post,* November 11, 2007, http://www.washingtonpost.com/wp-dyn/content/article/2007/11/07/AR2007110702280.html.

48. Battle, ed., "Shaking Hands with Saddam Hussein: The U.S. Tilts Toward Iraq, 1980–1984," National Security Archive Electronic Briefing Book No. 82, George Washington University, February 25, 2003; Jim Vallette with Steve Kretzmann and Daphne Wysham, "Crude Vision: How Oil Interests Obscured U.S. Government Focus on Chemical Weapons Use by Saddam Hussein," based on documents obtained from the Government's National Archives and the non-profit National Security Archive, Sustainable Energy & Economy Network, Institute for Policy Studies: IPS, page 9, March 2003.

49. Battle, ed., "Shaking Hands with Saddam Hussein: The U.S. Tilts Toward Iraq, 1980–1984."; Jim Vallette with Steve Kretzmann and Daphne Wysham, "Crude Vision: How Oil Interests Obscured U.S. Government Focus on Chemical Weapons Use by Saddam Hussein."

50. Leonard Spector, *Nuclear Proliferation Today* (Cambridge, MA: Ballinger, 1984); Pervez Hoodbhoy, "Myth-Building: The 'Islamic' Bomb," *Bulletin of the Atomic Scientists,* June 1993, thebulletin.org.

51. BBC News, "India and Pakistan: Tense Neighbors," December 16, 2001, http://news.bbc.co.uk/2/hi/south_asia/102201.stm; BBC News, "India—Will Sanctions Bite?" June 1, 1998, http://news.bbc.co.uk/2/hi/events/asia_nuclear_crisis/analysis/92942.stm; BBC News, "US lifts India and Pakistan sanctions," September 23, 2001, http://news.bbc.co.uk/2/hi/americas/1558860.stm.

6. Nuclear Lunatics

1. Robert Jay Lifton, Eric Olson, *Living and Dying* (London: Wildwood House, 1974), 120; Richard Rhodes, *The Making of the Atom Bomb, 25th Anniversary Edition* (New York: Simon & Schuster, 2012), 676.

2. William Langewiesche, "The Wrath of Khan," *The Atlantic,* November 1, 2005, http://www.theatlantic.com/magazine/archive/2005/11/the-wrath-of-khan/304333/.

3. Robert Jay Lifton, *Destroying the World to Save It: Aum Shinrikyo, Apocalyptic Violence, and the New Global Terrorism,* (New York: Holt, 2000), 194, 183, 20.

4. Langewiesche, "The Wrath of Khan."

5. Michael Ortiz Hill, "Dreaming the End of the World: Apocalypse as a Rite of Passage," see http://www.dhushara.com/book/explod/nuclears/ort/ortiz.htm.

6. Hill, "Dreaming the End of the World."

7. Brig. Gen. Thomas F. Farrell's comments appear in a July 18, 1945 War Department memo written by General Leslie Groves. See "The First Nuclear Test in New Mexico," *American Experience,* http://www.pbs.org/wgbh/americanexperience/features/primary-resources/truman-bombtest/.

8. Project of the Nuclear Age Peace Foundation, "Nuclear Files: Timeline of the Nuclear Age: 1945," http://www.nuclearfiles.org/menu/timeline/timeline_page.php?year=1945.

9. Dr. Khidhir Hamza, with Jeff Stein, *Saddam's Bombmaker: The Terrifying Inside Story of the Iraqi Nuclear and Biological Weapons Agenda* (New York: Touchstone, 2000), 123–24.

10. General Curtis E. LeMay (ret.) with McKinlay Kantor, *Mission with LeMay: My Story,* (New York: Doubleday, 1965), 495–96.

11. Union of Concerned Scientists, "UCS Statement on 50th Anniversary of Eisenhower's 'Atoms for Peace' Speech," December 8, 2003, *www.ucsusa.org*; Union of Concerned Scientists, "Preventing Nuclear Terrorism," *www.ucsusa.org*.

12. Leonard Weiss, "Atoms for Peace," *Bulletin of the Atomic Scientists,* vol. 59, no. 6 (November–December 2003): 41–42, *thebulletin.org*.

13. Richard Brennan and Anna Husarska, International Rescue Committee's Health Unit, "Inside Congo, an Unspeakable Toll," *Washington Post*, July 16, 2006, http://www.washingtonpost.com/wp-dyn/content /article/2006/07/14/AR2006071401389.html; Finbarr O'Reilly, "Rush for Natural Resources Still Fuels War in Congo," Reuters, August 9, 2004, *news .yahoo.com*; Chris McGreal, "Missing keys, holes in fence and a single padlock: welcome to Congo's nuclear plant," *The Guardian*, November 23, 2006, http://www.guardian.co.uk/world/2006/nov/23/congo.chrismcgreal.

14. Kenneth A. Thompson, *Gerard Smith on Arms Control* (Lanham, MD: University Press of America, 1987), 110–17.

15. President Dwight D. Eisenhower's "Atoms for Peace" speech to the United Nations General Assembly is reprinted by World Nuclear University at http://www.world-nuclear-university.org/about.aspx?id=8674&terms=at oms%20for%20peace.

16. Mike Nartker, "U.S., Russian Scientists Exploring Collaboration on Floating Nuclear Power Plants," Global Security Newswire, August 27, 2004, http://www.nti.org/gsn/article/us-russian-scientists-exploring-col laboration-on-floating-nuclear-power-plants/; Alissa de Carbonnel, "Can Nuclear Power Plants Float?" Reuters, April 18, 2011, http://www.reuters .com/article/2011/04/18/nuclear-industry-floating-idAFLDE73D27 K20110418; Robert Einhorn, Rose Gottemoeller, Fred McGoldrick, Daniel Poneman, Jon Wolfsthal, "The U.S.–Russia Civil Nuclear Agreement: A Framework for Cooperation," Center for Strategic & International, May 2008, 41, http://csis.org/files/media/csis/pubs/080522-einhorn-u.s.-russia -web.pdf; Global Security Newswire, "Russia Starts Work on Floating Nuclear Power Plant," April 19, 2007, http://www.nti.org/gsn/article/russia -starts-work-on-floating-nuclear-power-plant/; Martin Matishak, "Floating Nuclear Reactors Could Fall Prey to Terrorists, Experts Say," Global Security Newswire, August 31, 2010, http://www.nti.org/gsn/article/floating-nuclear -reactors-could-fall-prey-to-terrorists-experts-say/; Goska Romanowicz, "Russian Floating Nuclear Reactors Spark Contamination Fears," March 2, 2006, http://www.edie.net/news/3/Russian-floating-nuclear-reactors-spark -contamination-fears/11138/; Preeti Bhattacharji, "Terrorist Havens:

Philippines," Council on Foreign Relations, June 1, 2009, http://www.cfr
.org/philippines/terrorism-havens-philippines/p9365.

17. World Nuclear News, "Reactors Ready for First Floating Plant,"
August 7, 2009, http://www.world-nuclear-news.org/NN-Reactors_ready
_for_first_floating_plant-0708094.html; Martin Matishak, "Floating Nuclear
Reactors Could Fall Prey to Terrorists, Experts Say." Oak Ridge National
Nuclear Laboratory (TN), "Definition of Weapons-Usable Uranium-233,"
March 1998, http://www.ornl.gov/info/reports/1998/3445606041609.pdf.

18. Mike Nartker, "U.S., Russian Scientists Exploring Collaboration on
Floating Nuclear Power Plants."

19. Robert Einhorn, Rose Gottemoeller, Fred McGoldrick, Daniel Poneman, and Jon Wolfsthal, "The U.S.–Russia Civil Nuclear Agreement: A
Framework for Cooperation."

20. Einhorn, Gottemoeller, McGoldrick, Poneman, and Wolfsthal, "The
U.S.–Russia Civil Nuclear Agreement."

21. Goska Romanowicz, "Russian Floating Nuclear Reactors Spark Contamination Fears."

22. Alissa de Carbonnel, "Can Nuclear Power Plants Float?" Another
recent, really good NTI article on the subject is "Isolated Criticality: Russia's
Floating Nuclear Power Plants, Concepts and Concerns," written by Thomas
Young, November 5, 2010, http://www.nti.org/analysis/articles/russias
-floating-nuclear-power-plants/.

23. General Curtis E. LeMay (ret.) with McKinlay Kantor, *Mission with
LeMay: My Story*, 495–96.

24. Robert Scheer, *With Enough Shovels: Reagan, Bush and Nuclear War*,
Updated Edition (New York: Vintage Books, 1983), 18–22.

25. John McPhee, *The Curve of Binding Energy* (New York: Farrar, Straus
and Giroux, 1980), 4–6.

26. Peter J. Kunznick, "Scientists on the Stump," *Bulletin of the Atomic
Scientists*, vol. 60, no. 6 (November–December, 2004); "1968 Presidential
General Election Results," http://uselectionatlas.org/RESULTS/national.
phpyears=1968.

27. Peter J. Kuznick, "Scientists on the Stump."

28. "The Davy Crockett," The Brookings Institute, www.brookings.edu/projects/archive/nucweapons/davy.aspx; Robert Burns "Veterans Recall Huge Nuclear Arsenal of 1950s," *Los Angeles Times*, December 1, 1991.

29. William Burr, "To Have the Only Option That of Killing 80 Million People Is the Height of Immorality: The Nixon Administration, the SIOP, and the Search for Limited Nuclear Options, 1969–1974," National Security Archive Electronic Briefing Book No. 173, http://www.gwu.edu/~nsarchiv/NSAEBB/NSAEBB173/; Jon Else, "Tomgram: Jon Else on the Museum of Attempted Suicide," National Institute, August 12, 2004, http://www.tomdispatch.com/post/1680/.

30. John Podhoretz, "Crazy Korea Cures," *New York Post*, December 27, 2002, http://www.nypost.com/p/news/opinion/opedcolumnists/item_urxWSWWU8WJksZqz0scdiP.

31. Charles Krauthammer, "The Japan Card," *Washington Post*, January 3, 2003, A19.

32. Agence France-Presse, "Iraq Could Eventually Have Civilian Nuclear Power: US Official," June 9, 2004, http://www.spacewar.com/2004/040608230221.m2bj3j7d.html; Radio Free Europe, Radio Liberty, "U.S. Received Little for What It Spent in Iraq," GlobalSecurity.org, March 6, 2013, http://www.globalsecurity.org/wmd/library/news/iraq/2013/iraq-130306-rfer101.htm?_m=3n%2e002a%2e748%2ezn0ao04n6e%2eoiv.

33. Agence France-Presse, "Iraq Could Eventually Have Civilian Nuclear Power."; Radio Free Europe, Radio Liberty, "U.S. Received Little for What It Spent in Iraq."

34. Adapted from Peter Goodchild, *Edward Teller: The Real Dr. Strangelove* (Cambridge, MA: Harvard University Press, 2004).

35. NASA, "Solar Physics," Marshall Space Center, http://solarscience.msfc.nasa.gov/interior.shtml; Daniel Clery, "After ITER, Many Other Obstacles for Fusion Power," *Science Magazine/Science Insider*, January 17, 2013, http://news.sciencemag.org/scienceinsider/2013/01/after-iter-many-other-obstacles-.html.

36. Clery, "After ITER, Many Other Obstacles for Fusion Power."

37. Clery, "After ITER, Many Other Obstacles for Fusion Power." Union of Concerned Scientists, "Energy Trends," revised February 18, 2003.

38. European Patent Office, http://worldwide.espacenet.com/publication Details/biblio?CC=GB&NR=817681&KC=&FT=E&locale=en_EP; Armin Grünwald, Reinhard Grünwald, Dagmar Oertel, Herbert Paschen, "Thermonuclear Fusion," TAB report no. 075, Berlin 2002, http://www.tab -beim-bundestag.de/en/publications/reports/ab075.html

39. Armin Grünwald, Reinhard Grünwald, Dagmar Oertel, Herbert Paschen, "Thermonuclear Fusion."; Soo Bin Park, "South Korea Makes Billion-Dollar Bet on Fusion Power," *Scientific American,* January 2003, http://www.scientificamerican.com/article.cfm?id=south-korea-makes -billion-dollar-bet-fusion-power&print=true.

40. Associated Press, "Iran Sets 2020 Target for Fusion Reactor," August 30, 2010, reprinted by Salon.com at http://www.salon.com/2010/08/30 /iran_nuclear_reactor/.

PART III   And He Opened Up the Bottomless Pit

1. The Fatal Fallacy of Nuclear Homeland Security

1. Nicholas D. Kristof, "An American Hiroshima," *New York Times,* August 11, 2004, http://www.nytimes.com/2004/08/ll/opinion/an-american-hi roshima.html.

2. Robert Jay Lifton, *Death in Life: Survivors of Hiroshima* (Chapel Hill, NC: UNC Press, 1991), 32–42, 69.

3. Lynn Eden, "City on Fire," *Bulletin of the Atomic Scientists,* vol. 60, no. 1 (January–February 2004), 32–43.

4. Richard L. Garwin, "A Nuclear Explosion in a City or an Attack on a Nuclear Reactor," National Academy of Engineering, Summer 2010, http:// www.nae.edu/Publications/Bridge/19804/19892.aspx.

5. David Hoffman, "The Little Nukes That Got Away," *Foreign Policy,* May 8, 2012, http://hoffman.foreignpolicy.com/posts/2012/05/08/the_little _nukes_that_got_away.

2. The Fatal Fallacy of Fortifying a Nuclear Firetrap

1. Yochi J. Dreazen, "Nuclear Plants May Be Vulnerable to Terrorists," *National Journal,* Global Security Newswire, March 18, 2011, http://www.nti.org/gsn/article/nuclear-plants-may-be-vulnerable-to-terrorists/; Global Security Newswire, "Terror Suspect's Manual of Western Targets Included Nuclear Plants, British Prosecutor Says," January 12, 2006, http://www.nti.org/gsn/article/terror-suspects-manual-of-western-targets-included-nuclear-plants-british-prosecutor-says/; Mark Thompson, with reporting by Bruce Crumley, "Are These Towers Safe?" *Time,* June 20, 2005, http://www.time.com/time/magazine/article/0,9171,1071249,00.html; Yochi J. Dreazen, "Special Report: Aftermath of Terror Warning of Attack at Nuclear Plant Further Rattles Already Jumpy U.S.," *Wall Street Journal,* October 19, 2001.

2. *CBSNews.com,* "U.S. Knew of Sharif Mobley, US Nuclear Official Says," October 4, 2010, http://www.cbsnews.com/2100-201_162-6293288.html; Scott Shane, "Worker Spoke of Jihad, Agency Says," *New York Times,* October 4, 2010; Scott Shane, "Worker Spoke of Jihad Agency Says."

3. Malia Rulon, "Gov't to End Public Nuclear Updates," Associated Press, August 4, 2004, http://groups.yahoo.com/group/FPE/message/32594?var=1.

4. Eric Lipton and Benjamin Weiser, "Threats and Responses: The Plots; Qaeda Strategy Is Called Cause for New Alarm," *New York Times,* August 5, 2004, http://www.nytimes.com/2004/08/05/us/threats-and-responses-the-plots-qaeda-strategy-is-called-cause-for-new-alarm.html.

5. Lipton and Weiser, "Threats and Responses: The Plots; Qaeda Strategy Is Called Cause for New Alarm."

6. Lipton and Weiser, "Threats and Responses: The Plots; Qaeda Strategy Is Called Cause for New Alarm."

7. Shaun Gregory, "Terrorist Tactics in Pakistan Threaten Nuclear Weapons Safety," Combating Terrorism Center at West Point, June 1, 2011, http://www.ctc.usma.edu/posts/terrorist-tactics-in-pakistan-threaten-nuclear-weapons-safety.

8. Matthew L. Wald, "Responsibility for Defending Nuclear Plants Is Debated," *New York Times,* April 5, 2006, http://www.nytimes.com/2006/04/05/washington/05nuke.html?pagewanted=print.

9. Mark Thompson, with reporting by Bruce Crumley, "Are These Towers Safe?"

10. Keith Bradsher and Hiroko Tabuchi, "Greater Danger Lies in Spent Fuel Than in Reactors," *New York Times*, March 17, 2011, http://www.nytimes.com/2011/03/18/world/asia/18spent.html; James M. Acton and Mark Hibbs, "Why Fukushima Was Preventable," Carnegie Endowment for International Peace, March 6, 2012, http://carnegieendowment.org/2012/03/06/why-fukushima-was-preventable.

11. Juergen Baetz, "Insurance Cost vs. Nuclear Power Risk, Associated Press, May 1, 2011.

12. Rory Kennedy, "Indian Point: Imagining the Unimaginable," HBO documentary, September 8, 2004; Anita Gates, "Seeing a Mushroom Cloud in New York," *New York Times*, September 9, 2004, http://tv.nytimes.com/2004/09/09/arts/television/09gate.html.

13. Rebecca Leung, "Nuclear Insecurity," *60 Minutes, cbsnews.com*, December 5, 2007, http://www.cbsnews.com/8301-18560_162-599957.html.

14. Anne-Marie Cusac, "Fire Hazard: Bush Leaves Nuclear Plants at Risk," *Progressive*, vol. 68, no. 8, August 2004.

3. A Terrorist Armageddon

1. Dan Verton, *Black Ice: The Invisible Threat of Cyber-Terrorism* (Emeryville, CA: McGraw Hill/Osborne, 2003), 1–15.

2. Verton, *Black Ice*, 5.

3. Verton, *Black Ice*, 17–30, 21–24.

4. Verton, *Black Ice*, 17–30, 21–24.

5. Paul Boatin, "Slammed!" *www.wired.com*, July 20, 2003.

6. David E. Sanger, "Obama Order Sped up Wave of Cyberattacks Against Iran," *New York Times*, June 1, 2012, http://www.nytimes.com/2012/06/01/world/middleeast/obama-ordered-wave-of-cyberattacks-against-iran.html.

7. Verton, *Black Ice*, 1–15.

8. Carlo Kopp, "The Electromagnetic Bomb—A Weapon of Electrical Mass Destruction," Chronicles Online Journal, http://www.airpower.maxwell.af

.mil/airchronicles/cc/apjemp.html; Jim Wilson, "E-Bomb," *Popular Mechanics* 179, no. 9 (September 2001), 50–53. Reprinted by Free Republic at http://www.freerepublic.com/focus/f-news/561183/posts; Verton, *Black Ice*, 99–101.

9. Kopp, "The Electromagnetic Bomb—A Weapon of Electrical Mass Destruction."; Wilson, "E-Bomb."

10. Dan Vergano, "One EMP burst and the world goes dark," *USA Today*, October 27, 2010, http://usatoday30.usatoday.com/tech/science/2010-10-26-emp_N.htm.

11. Elisabeth Bumiller and Thorn Shanker, "Panetta Warns of Dire Threat of Cyberattack on U.S.," *New York Times*, October 11, 2012, http://www.nytimes.com/2012/10/12/world/panetta-warns-of-dire-threat-of-cyberattack.html.

12. Bumiller and Shanker, "Panetta Warns of Dire Threat of Cyberattack on U.S."

13. Bumiller and Shanker, "Panetta Warns of Dire Threat of Cyberattack on U.S."

14. David E. Sanger, David Barboza, and Nicole Perlroth, "Chinese Army Unit Is Seen as Tied to Hacking Against U.S.," *New York Times*, February 18, 2013, http://www.nytimes.com/2013/02/19/technology/chinas-army-is-seen-as-tied-to-hacking-against-us.html.

15. Sanger, Barboza, and Perlroth, "Chinese Army Unit Is Seen as Tied to Hacking Against U.S."

16. Herman Kahn, *Thinking About the Unthinkable* (New York: Avon, 1964), 60–61.

17. Global Security Newswire, "The Indo-China War of 1962," http://www.globalsecurity.org/military/world/war/indo-prc_1962.htm.

PART IV   *Quis Custodiet Ipsos Custodes?*

1. Nuclear Conflicts-of-Interest

1. George Shultz as told to Bob Herbert, "Spoils of War," *New York Times*, April 10, 2003, http://www.nytimes.com/2003/04/10/opinion/spoils-of-war.html.

2. George P. Shultz, William J. Perry, Henry A. Kissinger, and Sam Nunn, "A World Free of Nuclear Weapons," *Wall Street Journal,* January 4, 2007, http://online.wsj.com/article/SB116787515251566636.html.

3. See http://www.ge.com/company/leadership/board-of-directors; Bob Sechler, "Penske, Lafley and Nunn Leaving GE's Board," *The Wall Street Journal,* March 11, 2013.

4. Bechtel Corporation, "Milestones," http://www.bechtel.com/milestones.html; Bechtel Corporation, "Bechtel Responds to Inaccuracies in Media Coverage of the USAID Iraq Infrastructure Reconstruction Program Award," http://www.bechtel.com/2003-04-29.html, updated from 2003 to comment on George Shultz's April 2006 retirement from the board of directors.

5. See http://www.nndb.com/people/065/000057891/ Perry; http://www.lanl.gov/science-innovation/science-programs/civilian-nuclear-programs/_assets/docs/AdvancedNuclearFinal_8_15.pdf.

6. See http://publicintelligence.net/kissinger-associates-inc/.

7. Bob Herbert, "Spoils of War."

8. Peter Cohan, "Big Risk: $1.2 Quadrillion Derivatives Market Dwarfs World GDP," *DailyFinance.com,* June 9, 2010, http://www.dailyfinance.com/2010/06/09/risk-quadrillion-derivatives-market-gdp/; Kevin Phillips, *American Theocracy: The Peril and Politics of Radical Religion, Oil, and Borrowed Money in the 21st Century* (New York: Viking, 2007), 298–318.

9. Timothy Noah, "When Did Trickle-Down Get Respectable?" *New Republic,* September 19, 2011, http://www.newrepublic.com/blog/timothy-noah/95098/when-did-trickle-down-get-respectable; William Greider, "The Education of David Stockman," *The Atlantic,* December 1, 1981, http://www.theatlantic.com/magazine/archive/1981/12/the-education-of-david-stockman/305760/3/.

10. Ken Zweibel, James Mason, and Vasilis Fthenakis, "The Grand Solar Plan [Preview]: By 2050 solar power could end U.S. dependence on foreign oil and slash greenhouse gas emissions," *Scientific American,* January 2008, http://people.bu.edu/sobieraj/articles/SolarGrandPlan_Jan08_SciAm.pdf.

11. Zweibel, Mason, and Fthenakis, "The Grand Solar Plan [Preview]."

12. Zweibel, Mason, and Fthenakis, "The Grand Solar Plan [Preview]."

13. Juan Cole, "The Incredibly Shrinking Cost of Solar Power," Informed Comment, http://www.juancole.com/2013/05/incredible-shrinking-projects .html, April 4, 2013.

14. Juan Cole, "The Incredibly Shrinking Cost of Solar Power."

15. Tony Seba, "Solar Has Improved Unit Costs by 1,000 Times Relative to Nuclear," http://tonyseba.com/disruption/solar-has-improved-unit-costs -by-1000-times-relative-to-nuclear/, April 25, 2013.

16. *National Geographic,* "Wind Power," http://environment.nationalgeo graphic.com/environment/global-warming/wind-power-profile/.

17. Hannele Holttinen, et al., "Design and Operation of Power Systems with Large Amounts of Wind Power, First Results of IEA Collaboration," Global Wind Power Conference, September 18–21, 2006, Adelaide, Australia, http://www.ieawind.org/annex_XXV/Meetings/Oklahoma/IEA%20 SysOp%20GWPC2006%20paper_final.pdf.

18. Martin Rosenberg, "Harvesting Solar Power in Space," *Energybiz,* September–October 2008, http://energycentral.fileburst.com/EnergyBizOn line/2008-5-sep-oct/Tech_Frontier_Solar_Space.pdf.

19. Tim Hornyak, "Farming Solar Energy in Space: Shrugging Off Massive Costs, Japan Pursues Space-based Solar Arrays," *Scientific American,* July 1, 2008, http://www.scientificamerican.com/article.cfm?id=farming -solar-energy-in-space&print=true.

20. Author interview with Major General Sid Shachnow, U.S. Special Forces (ret.).

2. The Door of Death

1. Arnold J. Toynbee, *A Study of History,* Abridgement of Volumes I–VI by D. C. Somervell and VII–X © 1957, renewed © 1985 by Robert Somervell, Mary Brautaset and Lawrence Toynbee (New York: Oxford University Press [Dell Publishing, Laurel edition, 1965]), vols. I–VI, 320.

2. Toynbee, *A Study of History,* vols. I–VI, 261–62.

3. Toynbee, *A Study of History,* vols. I–VI, 320 and vol. VII–X, 354.

4. Toynbee, *A Study of History,* vols. I–VI, 320.

5. Toynbee, *A Study of History,* vols. I–VI, 320.

6. Oswald Spengler, *The Decline of the West* (New York: Knopf), 413–14.

Appendix 1: Why I Wrote *The Nuclear Terrorist*

1. Herman Kahn, *Thinking About the Unthinkable* (New York: Avon, 1964), 60–61.

2. *GlobalSecurity.org,* "Russian National-Level Nuclear Weapons Storage," July 24, 2011, http://www.globalsecurity.org/wmd/world/russia/storage.htm.

3. World History Center, "Union of Soviet Socialist Republics," http://history-world.org/union_of_soviet_socialist_republ.htm.

4. Graham T. Allison, Owen R. Coté, Jr., Richard A. Falkenrath, and Steven E. Miller, *Avoiding Nuclear Anarchy: Containing the Threat of Loose Russian Nuclear Weapons and Fissile Material* (Cambridge, MA: MIT Press, 1996), 1–5.

5. Craig Whitlock, "Homemade, Cheap and Dangerous," *Washington Post,* July 4, 2007, http://www.washingtonpost.com/wp-dyn/content/article/2007/07/04/AR2007070401814.html; Gilmore J. Childers, Henry J. DePippos, "Senate Judiciary Committee Hearings: Foreign Terrorists in America: Five Years After the World Trade Center," *http://web.archive.org,* February 24, 1998; Lawrence Wright, *The Looming Tower: Al-Qaeda and the Road to 9/11* (New York: Knopf, 2006), 176.

6. Allison, et al., *Avoiding Nuclear Anarchy,* 222–23.

7. Allison, et al., *Avoiding Nuclear Anarchy,* 222–23.

8. Luis Alvarez, *Adventures of a Physicist* (New York: Basic Books, 1989), 125.

9. Eric Pianin and Bill Miller, "Nuclear Arms Plants' Security Lax, Report Says," *Washington Post,* January 23, 2002, http://www.washingtonpost.com/wp-dyn/articles/A22106-2002Jan22.html; Mark Hertsgaard, "Nuclear Insecurity," *Vanity Fair,* November 2003.

10. U.S. General Accounting Office, "Quick and Secret Construction of Plutonium Reprocessing Plants: A Way to Nuclear Weapons Proliferation?" Report by the Comptroller General of the United States, October 6, 1978, http://archive.gao.gov/f0902c/107377.pdf.

11. U.S. General Accounting Office, "Quick and Secret Construction of Plutonium Reprocessing Plants: A Way to Nuclear Weapons Proliferation?"

12. Mark Cooper, "Nuclear liability: The market-based, post-Fukushima case for ending Price-Anderson," *Bulletin of the Atomic Scientists,* October 5, 2011, http://www.thebulletin.org/print/web-edition/features/nuclear-liability-the-market-based-post-fukushima-case-ending-price-anderson; Juergen Baetz, "Insurance Cost vs. Nuclear Power Risk," Associated Press, May 1, 2011.

13. Julio Godoy, "Energy: Nuclear Does Not Make Economic Sense Say Studies," Inter Press Service, February 12, 2010, http://www.ipsnews.net/2010/02/energy-nuclear-does-not-make-economic-sense-say-studies/.

14. David Biello, "Spent Nuclear Fuel: A Trash Heap Deadly for 250,000 Years or a Renewable Energy Source?" *Scientific American,* January 28, 2009, http://www.scientificamerican.com/article.cfm?id=nuclear-waste-lethal-trash-or-renewable-energy-source; Andrew Sowder, "Used Nuclear Fuel Management: The Back End of the Fuel Cycle," *Health Physics News,* January 2010, http://hps.org/; Ralph Anderson, chief health physicist at the Nuclear Energy Institute (NEI), quoted in Biello's "Spent Nuclear Fuel: A Trash Heap Deadly for 250,000 Years or a Renewable Energy Source?" *Scientific American,* January 28, 2009; Michael Winter, "NRC Clears Way for Scrapping Yucca Mt. Nuke Dump," *USA Today,* September 11, 2011, http://content.usatoday.com/commumties/ondeadline/post/2011/09/nrc-clears-way-for-scrapping-yucca-mt-nuke-dump-/1; Rebecca Leung, "Yucca Mountain," *60 Minutes,* February 11, 2009 http://www.cbsnews.com/8301-18560_162-579696.html; Pierre Sadik, "Radioactive Roads and Rails: Hauling Nuclear Waste Through Our Neighborhoods," a report of the U.S. PIRG Education Fund and Penn Environment Research and Policy Center, June 2002, p. 12, https://pincdn.s3.amazonaws.com/assets/5F7uHwbKhTsl_oc6mfPtfg/RadioactiveRoadsandRails.pdf.

15. Winter, "NRC Clears Way for Scrapping Yucca Mt. Nuke Dump."

16. Global Security Newswire, "U.S. Marketers Visited Saudi Arabia, As Trade Talks Underway," *nti.org*, February 1, 2013; Dean Nelson, "Hillary Clinton: US to build nuclear plants in India," *The Telegraph*, July 20, 2009, http://www.telegraph.co.uk/news/worldnews/asia/india/5872836/Hillary-Clinton-US-to-build-nuclear-plants-in-India.html; United Press International, "Emirates, Saudis Drive for Nuclear Power," September 21, 2012, http://www.upi.com/Business_News/Energy-Resources/2012/09/21/Emirates-Saudis-drive-for-nuclear-power/UPI-30481348241422/; Louis Charonneau, "Iraq gets U.N. green light for civil nuclear program," Reuters, December 15, 2010, http://www.reuters.com/article/2010/12/15/us-iraq-un-idUSTRE6BD63620101215; Eric Lichtblau and Eric Schmitt, "Cash Flow to Terrorists Evades U.S. Efforts," *New York Times*, December 5, 2010, http://www.nytimes.com/2010/12/06/world/middleeast/06wikileaks-financing.html.

17. Louis Charonneau, "Iraq gets U.N. green light for civil nuclear program."

18. Richard Behar, "Rummy's North Korea Connection," *Fortune*, vol. 147, issue 9, May 12, 2003, http://money.cnn.com/magazines/fortune/fortune_archive/2003/05/12/342316/; Randeep Ramesh, "The Two Faces of Rumsfeld," *The Guardian*, May 9, 2003, http://www.guardian.co.uk/world/2003/may/09/nuclear.northkorea.

19. Associated Press, "Cheney Once Pressed for Halliburton-Iran Trade," October 9, 2004; *60 Minutes*, "Doing Business with the Enemy," January 25, 2004, *cbsnews.com*; *Newsweek*, "Business As Usual?" February 16, 2005; Colum Lynch, "Halliburton's Iraq Deals Greater Than Cheney Has Said, Affiliates Had $73 Million in Contracts," *Washington Post*, June 23, 2001. See http://www.globalpolicy.org/component/content/article/170/42166.html.

20. Leslie Wayne, "Elder Bush in Big GOP Cast Toiling for Top Equity Firm," *New York Times*, March 5, 2001, http://www.nytimes.com/2001/03/05/us/elder-bush-in-big-gop-cast-toiling-for-top-equity-firm.html; Craig Unger, *House of Bush, House of Saud: The Secret Relationship Between the World's Two Most Powerful Dynasties* (New York: Scribner, 2004), 166–68.

21. John Buchanan and Stacey Michael, "Bush: Nazi Dealings Continued Until 1951," *New Hampshire Gazette*, vol. 248, no. 3, November 3, 2003. See

http://www.globalresearch.ca/bush-nazi-dealings-continued-until-1951
-federal-documents/1176; Herbert Parmet, "What Should We Make of the
Charge Linking the Bush Family Fortune to Nazism?" History News Network, November 17, 2003, http://hnn.us/node/1811.

Appendix 2: The Fatal Fallacy of Serving Two Gods

1. Matthew 6:12, English Standard Version
2. Revelation 9:20, English Standard Version
3. Revelation 13:17, English Standard Version

BIBLIOGRAPHY

Books

Allison, Graham T., et al. *Avoiding Nuclear Anarchy: Containing the Threat of Loose Russian Nuclear Weapons and Fissile Material*. Cambridge, MA: MIT Press, 1996.

Alvarez, Luis. *Adventures of a Physicist*. New York: Basic Books, 1989.

Baer, Robert. *Sleeping with the Devil: How Washington Sold Our Soul for Saudi Crude*. New York: Three Rivers Press, 2003.

Bodansky, Yossef. *Bin Laden: The Man Who Declared War on America*. Roseville, CA: Prima Lifestyles, 2001.

Eliot, T. S. *The Waste Land*.

English Standard Version *Holy Bible*.

Goodchild, Peter. *Edward Teller: The Real Dr. Strangelove*. Cambridge, MA: Harvard University Press, 2004.

Gordon, Michael R., and General Bernard E. Trainor. *COBRA II: The Inside Story of the Invasion and Occupation of Iraq*. New York: Vintage, 2007.

Hamza, Khidhir. *Saddam's Bomb-maker: The Terrifying Inside Story of the Iraqi Nuclear and Biological Weapons Agenda*. New York: Touchstone, 2000.

Hasan, S. E. "International Practice in High-Level Nuclear Waste Management" in *Concepts and Applications in Environmental Geochemistry*, ed. by D. Sarkar, R. Datta, and R. Hannigan. Oxford: Elsevier, 2007.

Johnsen, Gregory D. *The Last Refuge: Yemen, al-Qaeda, and America's War in Arabia*. New York: W. W. Norton, 2013.

Kahn, Herman. *Thinking About the Unthinkable*. New York: Avon, 1964.

Kaplan, Robert D. *The Coming Anarchy: Shattering the Dreams of the Post Cold War*. New York: Vintage, 2001.

King James Version *Holy Bible*.

LeMay, Curtis, with McKinlay Kantor. *Mission with LeMay: My Story*. New York: Doubleday, 1965.

Lifton, Robert Jay. *Death in Life: Survivors of Hiroshima*. Chapel Hill, NC: University of North Carolina Press, 1991.

———. *Destroying the World to Save It: Aum Shinrikyo, Apocalyptic Violence, and the New Global Terrorism*. New York: Holt, 2000.

Lifton, Robert Jay, and Eric Olson. *Living and Dying*. London: Wildwood House, 1974.

McPhee, John. *The Curve of Binding Energy*. New York: Farrar, Straus and Giroux, 1980.

Phillips, Kevin. *American Theocracy: The Peril and Politics of Radical Religion, Oil, and Borrowed Money in the 21st Century*. New York: Viking, 2007.

Reader's Companion to American History—1968. Boston: Houghton Mifflin, 1968.

Rhodes, Richard. *The Making of the Atom Bomb, 25th Anniversary Edition*. New York: Simon & Schuster, 2012.

Sanger, David E. *Conceal and Confront, Obama's Secret Wars and Surprising Use of American Power*. New York: Crown, 2012.

Scheer, Robert. *With Enough Shovels: Reagan, Bush and Nuclear War*. New York: Random House, 1982.

Spector, Leonard. *Nuclear Proliferation Today*. Cambridge, MA: Ballinger, 1984.

Spengler, Oswald. *The Decline of the West*. New York: Knopf, 1932.

Suskind, Ron. *The Price of Loyalty: George W. Bush, the White House and the Education of Paul O'Neill*. New York: Simon & Schuster, 2004.

Thompson, Kenneth A., and Gerard Smith. *On Arms Control*. Lanham, MD: University Press of America, 1987.

Toynbee, Arnold J. *Study of History*. Volumes I–VI and Volumes VII–X. Abridgement of Volumes I–VI by D. C. Somervell and VII–X, Oxford

University Press, New York/Oxford (Dell Publishing, Laurel edition) © 1957, renewed © 1985 by Robert Somervell, Mary Brautaset, and Lawrence Toynbee.

Unger, Craig. *House of Bush, House of Saud: The Secret Relationship Between the World's Two Most Powerful Dynasties.* New York: Scribner, 2004.

Verton, Dan. *Black Ice: The Invisible Threat of Cyber-Terrorism.* Emeryville, CA: McGraw Hill/Osborne, 2003.

Wright, Lawrence. *The Looming Tower: Al-Qaeda and the Road to 9/11.* New York: Knopf, 2006.

Articles and Web Sites

Acton, James M., and Mark Hibbs. "Why Fukushima Was Preventable." *Carnegie Endowment for Peace,* March 2012.

"Aircraft Threats to Nuclear Plants." *Union of Concerned Scientists*, March 25, 2005. www.ucsusa.org.

Ali, Mayed. "The Close Combat at PNS Mehran." *The News International,* May 25, 2011.

Alvarez, Robert. "Five Reasons Not to Invest in Nuclear Power." *Huffington Post*, February 17, 2010.

———. "In a Perfect World Fukushima Would Halt Nuclear Renaissance in its Tracks." *Focal Points Blog/Foreign Policy in Focus*, March 16, 2011.

Anderson, Zac, and Robert Eckhart. "FBI Investigated Another Sarasota Link to 9/11." *Sarasota Herald-Tribune*, September 8, 2011.

Anderson, Ralph, quoted in David Biello's "Spent Nuclear Fuel: A Trash Heap Deadly for 250,000 Years or a Renewable Energy Source?" *Scientific American*, January 28, 2009.

"A. Q. Khan and Onward Proliferation from Pakistan." *International Institute for Strategic Studies (IISS.)*

"Arab Countries Look to Nukes." *Reuters*, November 5, 2006. www.reuters .com.

Arora, Vishal. "Prescription for Failure: The Need for Addressing Corruption in India." *Harvard College Global Health Review*, October 19, 2011. www.hcs.harvard.edu/hghr/online/india-corruption/.

Baetz, Juergen. "Insurance Cost vs. Nuclear Power Risk." Associated Press, May 1, 2011.

Bahree, Megha. "Child Labor." *Forbes*, March 10, 2008. www.forbes.com.

Baker, Russ W. "Iraqgate: The Big One That (Almost) Got Away: Who Chased It—and Who Didn't." *Columbia Journalism Review*, March/April 1993.

Bakr, Amena. "Egypt to Issue Nuclear Plants Tender by End January." *Reuters*, January 16, 2011. www.reuters.com.

Barlett, Donald L., and James B. Steele. "Iraq's Crude Awakening." *Time*, May 19, 2003. www.time.com.

Battle, Joyce. "Shaking Hands with Saddam Hussein: The U.S. Tilts Toward Iraq, 1980–1983." *National Security Archive Electronic Briefing Book No. 82.* February 25, 2003. George Washington University National Security Archive.

"Bechtel Responds to Inaccuracies in Media Coverage of the USAID Iraq Infrastructure Reconstruction Program Award." Updated from 2003 to comment on George Shultz April 2006 retirement from the directors board. www.bechtel.com/2003-04-29.html.

Beeston, Richard. "Nuclear Steps Put Region on Brink of Most Fearful Era Yet." *The Times*, November 4, 2006. www.timesonline.co.uk.

Behar, Richard. "Rummy's North Korea Connection." *Fortune*, April 28, 2003. www.independent-media.tv.

Bencivenga, Jim. "The Other News Rumsfeld Made." *Christian Science Monitor*, December 9, 2004. www.csmonitor.com.

Biello, David. "Spent Nuclear Fuel: A Trash Heap Deadly for 250,000 Years or a Renewable Energy Source?" *Scientific American*, January 28, 2009.

Blitzer, Wolf, quoting his September 8, 2002 interview with Condoleezza Rice. "Search for the 'Smoking Gun,'" *CNN*. January 10, 2003. www.cnn.com.

Bradsher, Keith and Hiroko Tabuchi. "Greater Danger Lies in Spent Fuel Than in Reactors." *New York Times*, March 17, 2011. www.nytimes.com.

Brennan, Richard and Anna Husarska. "Inside Congo, an Unspeakable Toll." *Washington Post*, July 16, 2006. www.washingtonpost.com.

"A Brief History of Reprocessing and Cleanup in West Valley, NY." *Union of Concerned Scientists*, December 2007. www.ucsusa.org.

Brill, Steve. "AFTER: How America Confronted the September 12 Era." Quoted from Nat Hentoff's "Is Ashcroft Fit for Office?" June 27, 2003. www.truthout.com, http://archive.truthout.org/article/nat-hentoff-is -ashcroft-fit-for-office.

Broad, William J., and David E. Sanger. "Eye on Iran, Rivals Pursuing Nuclear Power." *New York Times*, April 15, 2007. www.nytimes.com.

Broad, William J., John Markoff, and David E. Sanger. "Israeli Test on Worm Called Crucial in Iran Nuclear Delay." *New York Times*, January 15, 2011. www.nytimes.com.

Broder, John M. "Environmental Advocates Are Cooling on Obama." *New York Times*, February 18, 2010. www.nytimes.com.

Buchanan, John. "Bush: Nazi Dealings Continued Until 1951." *New Hampshire Gazette*, November 7, 2003. www.nhgazette.com.

Bumiller, Elisabeth, and Thom Shanker. "Panetta Warns of Dire Threat of Cyberattack on U.S." *New York Times*, October 11, 2010. www.nytimes.com.

"Bush: Nazi Dealings Continued Until 1951." *New Hampshire Gazette*, November 7, 2003. www.nhgazette.com.

"Business As Usual?" *Newsweek*, February 16, 2005. www.msnbc.msn.com.

Cala, Andres. "Drive Toward Low-Carbon Future Stalls." *New York Times*, October 25, 2011. www.nytimes.com.

Caldicott, Helen. "How Nuclear Apologists Mislead the World Over Radiation." *The Guardian/UK*, April 11, 2011.

Charonneau, Louis. "Iraq Gets U.N. Green Light for Civil Nuclear Program." *Reuters*, December 15, 2010. www.reuters.com.

Chavkin, Sasha, and Sheri Fink. "US Nuclear-Disaster Preparedness Hobbled by Uncertain Chain of Command." *Pro Publica*, April 8, 2011.

"Cheney Once Pressed for Halliburton-Iran Trade." Associated Press, October 9, 2004.

"Cheney to Pitch Nuclear Reactors During China Trip." Associated Press, April 9, 2004. www.msnbc.msn.com.

Childers, Gilmour J., and Henry J. DePippos. "Senate Judiciary Committee Hearings: Foreign Terrorists in America: Five Years After the World Trade Center." February 24, 1998. http://web.archive.org.

Choudhury, Shankhadeep. "India Warns Rumsfeld Against U.S. Arms Sales to Pakistan." *Los Angeles Times*, December 10, 2004. www.latimes.com.

Clayton, Mark. "Stuxnet Malware Is 'Weapon' Out to Destroy . . . Iran's Busheher Nuclear Plant?" *Christian Science Monitor*, September 21, 2010. www.csmonitor.com.

——. "Stuxnet Worm: Private Security Experts Want US to Tell Them More." *Christian Science Monitor*, October 3, 2010. www.csmonitor.com.

"Cleric Says American 'Devils" Must Die." *UPI*, November 8, 2010. http://www.upi.com/Top_News/World-News/2010/11/08/Cleric-says-American-devils-must-die/UPI-61991289245343.

Clery, Daniel. "After ITER, Many Other Obstacles for Fusion Power." *Science Magazine/Science Insider*, January 17, 2013. http://news.sciencemag.org/scienceinsider/2013/01/after-iter-many-other-obstacles-.html.

Cohan, Peter. "Big Risk: $1.2 Quadrillion Derivatives Market Dwarfs World GDP." *Daily Finance*, June 9, 2010. www.dailyfinance.com/2010/06/09/risk-quadrillion-derivatives-market-gdp/.

Cockburn, Alexander. "Lessons of Fukushima." *The Nation*, March 26, 2012.

Cole, Juan. "The Incredibly Shrinking Cost of Solar Power." *Informed Comment*, April 4, 2013. http://www.juancole.com/2013/05/incredible-shrinking-projects.html.

"Congress Mulls India Nuclear Deal." *BBC News*, October 27, 2005. news-vote.bbc.co.uk.

"Construction of Flamville EPR Begins." *World Nuclear News*, December 4, 2007. www.wnn.com.

Cooper, Mark. "Nuclear liability: The Market-Based, Post-Fukushima Case for Ending Price-Anderson." *Bulletin of the Atomic Scientists*, October 5, 2011. www.thebulletin.org/print/web-edition/features/nuclear-liability-the-market-based-post-fukushima-case-ending-price-anderson.

Cusac, Anne-Marie. "Fire Hazard: Bush Leaves Nuclear Plants at Risk." *The Progressive*, August 2004.

"Cutting James Baker's Ties." *New York Times*, December 12, 2003. www.nytimes.com.

Daly, Corbett B. "U.S., India Formally Sign Nuclear Reprocessing Pact." *Reuters*, July 30, 2010. www.reuters.com.

"Davis-Besse." *Union of Concerned Scientists*, http://www.ucsusa.org/assets /documents/nuclear_power/davis-besse-ii.pdf.

"Davis-Besse: The Reactor with a Hole in Its Head." *Union of Concerned Scientists*, http://www.ucsusa.org/assets/documents/nuclear_power /acfnx8tzc.pdf.

De Carbonnel, Alissa. "Can Nuclear Power Plants Float?" *Reuters*, April 18, 2011. http://in.reuters.com/article/2011/04/18/idINIndia-564027 20110418.

"Definition of Weapons-Usable U-233." *Oak Ridge National Nuclear Laboratory*, March 1998. http://www.ornl.gov/info/reports/1998 /3445606041609.pdf.

"Design and Operation of Power Systems with Large Amounts of Wind Power, First Results of IEA Collaboration." *Global Wind Power Conference*, September 18–21, 2006. http://www.ieawind.org/annex_XXV/Meet ings/Oklahoma/IEA%20SysOp%20GWPC2006%20paper_final.pdf.

Dreazen, Yochi J. "Special Report: Aftermath of Terror Warning of Attack at Nuclear Plant Further Rattles Already Jumpy U.S." *Wall Street Journal*, October 19, 2001.

———. "Nuclear Plants May Be Vulnerable to Terrorists." *National Journal, Global Security Newswire*, March 18, 2011. www.nti.org.

Drew, Christopher, and Heather Timmons. "Wealthy and Worried, India Is Rich Arms Market." *New York Times*, November 4, 2010. www.nytimes .com.

Dowd, Maureen. "The Asbestos President." *New York Times*, April 1, 2001. www.nytimes.com.

Dvorak, Phred, and Mitsuru Obe. "Japan Plots 40-Year Nuclear Cleanup." *Wall Street Journal*, December 22, 2011.

Eden, Lynn. "City on Fire." *Bulletin of the Atomic Scientists*, Vol. 60, January /February 2004.

Einhorn, Robert, et al. "The U.S.-Russia Civil Nuclear Agreement: A Framework for Cooperation; Center for Strategic & International."

May 2008. http://csis.org/files/media/csis/pubs/080522-einhorn-u.s .-russia-web.pdf.

Eisenhower, Dwight. "Atoms for Peace" Speech. *World Nuclear University.* http://www.world-nuclear-university.org/about.aspx?id=8674&terms =atoms%20for%20peace.

"Emirates, Saudis Drive for Nuclear Power." *UPI*, September 21, 2012. www .upi.com.

"Energy Trends." *Union of Concerned Scientists.* http://www.ucsusa.org /clean_energy/our-energy-choices/energy-trends.html.

Engelhardt, Tom. "To Have the Only Option That of Killing 80 Million People is the Height of Immorality: The Nixon Administration, the SIOP, and the Search for Limited Nuclear Options, 1969–1974." *National Security Archive Electronic Briefing Book No. 173*, November 23, 2005. http://www.gwu.edu/~nsarchiv/NSAEBB/NSAEBB173/.

Entous, Adam. "Saudi Arms Deal Advances." *Wall Street Journal*, September 12, 2010.

European Patent Office, http://worldwide.espacenet.com/publicationDetails /biblio?CC=GB&NR=817681&KC=&FT=E&locale=en_EP.

Fackler, Martin. "Flow of Tainted Water Is Latest Crisis at Japan Nuclear Plant." *New York Times*, April 29, 2013. www.nytimes.com.

"Fact Sheet on Improvements Resulting from Davis-Besse Incident." *NRC Fact Sheet*, September 2009. www.nrc.gov/reading-rm/doc-collections /fact-sheets/fs-davis-besse-improv.html.

Farah, Douglas. "Al Qaeda's Finances Ample, Say Probers: Worldwide Failure to Enforce Sanctions Cited." *Washington Post*, December 14, 2003. www.washingtonpost.com.

"Finland's Olkiluoto 3 Nuclear Plant Delayed Again." *BBC News Europe*, July 16, 2012.

Finn, Peter. "The Post-9/11 Life of an American Charged with Murder." *Washington Post*, September 4, 2010.

Fitzpatrick, Mark. "Dr. A. Q. Khan and the Rise and Fall of Proliferation Network." *International Institute for Strategic Studies (IISS)*, 2007.

Follman, Mark. "Did the Saudis Know About 9/11?" *Salon*, October 18, 2003. www.salon.com.

Fox, Jon. "Physicists Back Claim that US-Indian Deal Could allow for 509 New Indian Nuclear Weapons a Year." *Global Security Network*, August 23, 2006. www.nti.org.

"France Doubles Down On Commitment to Flamanville Nuclear Project." *NPI*, Nuclear Power International, December 6, 2012.

Frantz, Douglas, and Catherine Collins. "Those Nuclear Flashpoints Are Made in Pakistan." *Washington Post*, November 11, 2007.

Francis, David. "Expert Warns Risks of India-US Nuclear Pact." *Global Security Newswire*, March 22, 2006. www.nti.org.

"From Kashmir to the FATA: The ISI Loses Control [Pakistan Primer Pt. 2]." *Global Bearings*, October 28, 2011.

Garwin, Richard L. "A Nuclear Explosion in a City or an Attack on a Nuclear Reactor." *National Academy of Engineering*, Summer 2010. http://www.nae.edu/Publications/Bridge/19804/19892.aspx.

Gates, Anita. "Seeing a Mushroom Cloud in New York." *New York Times*, September 9, 2004. www.nytimes.com.

"Global Trends 2015." www.cia.gov/terrorism/global_trends_2015.html.

Godoy, Julio. "Energy: Nuclear Does Not Make Economic Sense Say Studies." *Inter Press Service*, February 12, 2010.

Goldberg, Jeffrey, and Marc Aminder. "The Ally from Hell." *The Atlantic*, December 2001.

Goodspeed, Peter. "Pakistan's Nuclear Arsenal May Be 'Compromised.'" *National Post*, August 25, 2011.

Gravitz, Alisa. "The Top Ten Reasons We Don't Need More Nukes." *Institute for Policy Studies*, March 1, 2010. www.commondreams.org/view /2010/03/01-8?print.

Green, Jim. "Nuclear Weapons and 'Fourth Generation,' Nuclear Power." *Energy Bulletin*, August 25, 2009. www.energybulletin.net/49949.

Gregory, Shaun. "Terrorist Tactics in Pakistan Threaten Nuclear Weapons Safety." *Combating Terrorism Center at West Point*, June 1, 2011. http://

www.ctc.usma.edu/posts/terrorist-tactics-in-pakistan-threaten-nuclear
-weapons-safety.

Grossman, Elaine M. "Preliminary U.S.-Saudi Nuclear Trade Talks Set for
Next Week." *Global Security Newswire*, July 28, 2011.

Grossman, Karl. "The Big Lie: One Year After Fukushima, Nuclear Cover
Up Revealed." March 5, 2012. www.commondreams.org.

———. "The Big Lies Fly High: Fukushima and the Nuclear Establishment,"
June 16, 2011. www.counterpunch.org.

———. "Nuclear Disaster and Obama's Disastrous Response," March 31,
2011. www.commondreams.org.

———. "NRC's Pro-Nuke Spin on Evacuation Zone," May 5, 2011. www
.commondreams.org.

Grunwald, Armin, et al. "Thermonuclear Fusion." *TAB report no. 075*, 2002.
http://www.tab-beim-bundestag.de/en/publications/reports/ab075.html.

"Gunmen Attack Army Camp, Kill Seven." *International Herald Tribune*,
July 9, 2012. http://tribune.com.pk/story/405717/attack-on-army-camp
-in-gujrat-kills-six-soldiers/.

Gupta, A. K. "Prize of the Century: Major Oil Companies Ready to Claim
Iraqi Resources." *The Independent*, February 27, 2007. http://www.in
dypendent.org/2007/02/27/prize-century-major-oil-companies-ready
-claim-iraqi-resources.

Hanamirian, Jocelyn. "Analysis: U.S.-India Nuke Deal Revisited." *United
Press International*, July 18, 2006. www.washtimes.com.

Hayers, Dr. Jarod. "Fukushima and the Politics of Nuclear Energy." *Sam
Nunn School of International Affairs, Georgia Institute of Technology*,
December 13, 2011. www.gatech.academia.edu.

Heinatz, Stephanie. "Army Brig. Gen. Mark Scheid, an Early Planner of the
War, Tells About Challenges of Invasion and Rebuilding." *The Daily
Press* (Hampton Roads, VA), September 8, 2006.

Heller, Jean. "TIA Now Verifies Flight of Saudis." *St. Petersberg Times*, June
9, 2004. www.sptimes.com.

Herbert, Bob. "Spoils of War." *New York Times*, April 11, 2003. www.ny
times.com.

Hertsgaard, Mark. "Mushroom Cloud Over Denver?" *Salon*, April 12, 1999. http://www.salon.com/1999/04/12/whistleblower.

———. "Nuclear Insecurity." *Vanity Fair*, November 2003.

Hill, Michael Ortiz. "Dreaming the End of the World: Apocalypse as a Rite of Passage." http://www.dhushara.com/book/explod/nuclears/ort/ortiz.htm.

Hodge, Nathan. "Maverick Colonel Blames US Army's 'Sycophantic' Culture and Heavy-Handedness for Failures in Iraq." *Financial Times*, June 9, 2004. www.ft.com.

Hoffman, David. "The Little Nukes That Got Away." Foreign Policy, May 8, 2012. http://hoffman.foreignpolicy.com/posts/2012/05/08/the_little _nukes_that_got_away.

Holt, Mark, and Anthony Andrews. "Nuclear Power Plant Security and Vulnerabilities." *Congressional Research Service*, August 28, 2010. http:// www.fas.org/sgp/crs/homesec/RL34331.pdf.

Hoodbhoy, Pervez. "Myth-Building: The 'Islamic' Bomb." *Bulletin of the Atomic Scientists*, June 1993. www.thebulletin.org.

Hornyak, Tim. "Farming Solar Energy in Space: Shrugging Off Massive Costs, Japan Pursues Space-based Solar Arrays." *Scientific American*, July 1, 2008. http://www.scientificamerican.com/article.cfm?id=farming -solar-energy-in-space&print=true,

Hundley, Tom. "Pakistan and India: Race to the End." *Pulitzer Center on Crisis Reporting*, September 5, 2012. http://www.foreignpolicy.com /articles/2012/09/05/race_to_the_end.

"India and Pakistan: Tense Neighbors." *BBC News*, December 16, 2001. www .news.bbc.co.uk.

"India: Historic Ruling Against 'Sodomy' Laws, the First Step to Equality." *Amnesty International*, July 2, 2009. www.amnesty.org.

"India Involved in Illicit Nuclear Activities: US Think Tank." *Agence France-Press*, March 11, 2006. www.news.yahoo.com.

"India: Malnutrition Report." *World Bank*. www.web.worldbank.org.

"India to Ramp Up Nuclear Fuel Production." *Global Security Newswire*, April 10, 2007. http://www.nti.org/gsn/article/india-to-ramp-up-nuclear -fuel-production/.

"India Victory in 65, 71 and 99." *Pakistan Defense*. http://www.defence.pk
/forums/military-history-strategy/47077-indian-victory-65-71-1999-a.html.

"India—Will Sanctions Bite?" *BBC News*, June 1, 1998. http://news.bbc.co
.uk/2/hi/events/asia_nuclear_crisis/analysis/92942.stm.

"The Indo-China War of 1962." *Global Security Newswire*. http://www
.globalsecurity.org/military/world/war/indo-prc_1962.htm.

"Iran Denies Cyberattack Hurt Nuclear Program—But Expert Isn't Sure."
CNNWorld, September 29, 2010.

"Iran Sets 2020 Target for Fusion Reactor." Associated Press, August 30, 2010.

"Iraq Could Eventually Have Civilian Nuclear Power: US Official."
Agence France-Presse, June 9, 2005. http://www.spacewar.com/2004
/040608230221.m2bj3j7d.html.

Jahn, George. "Stuxnet Virus Penetrates Nuclear Plant, May Cause
Chernobyl-like Disaster." Associated Press, January 31, 2011. See http://
www.csmonitor.com/World/Latest-News-Wires/2011/0131/Stuxnet
-virus-penetrates-nuclear-plant-may-cause-Chernobyl-like-disaster.

Johnsen, Gregory D. "The Wrong Man for the C.I.A." *New York Times*, November 19, 2012. www.nytimes.com.

Johnston, William Robert. "Database of Radiological Incidents and Related
Events." November 19, 2011. www.johnstonsarchive.net/nuclear/rade
vents/index.html.

"Jon Else on the Museum of Attempted Suicide." *Tomgram, National Institute*, August 12, 2004. www.tomdispatch.com.

Joshi, Manoj. "Could India Have Won the China War?" *Times of India*,
November 24, 2002. http://articles.timesofindia.indiatimes.com/2002
-11-24/india/27306736_1_air-power-tibet-air-operations.

Kaplan, Fred. "Rolling Blunder: How the Bush Administration Let North
Korea Get Nukes." *Washington Monthly*, May 2004.

Kelly, Tim, and David Dolan. "Japan Eyes State-Backed Insurer to Save
Tepco." *Reuters*, April 15, 2011.

Klare, Michael. "Bush-Cheney Energy Strategy: Procuring the Rest of the
World's Oil." Foreign Policy in Focus, January 2004, http://www.com
mondreams.org/views04/0113-01.htm.

———. "More Blood, Less Oil: The Failed U.S. Mission to Capture Iraqi Petroleum." TomDispatch.com, September 21, 2005.

Klein, Naomi. "James Baker's Double Life." *The Nation*, November 1, 2004. http://www.thenation.com/article/james-bakers-double-life.

———. "Reparations in Reverse." *Globe and Mail*, October 15, 2004. www.globalpolicy.org. Also see CommonDreams.org, http://www.common dreams.org/views04/1015-01.htm.

Koplow, Douglas. "Nuclear Power: Still Not Viable Without Subsidies." *Union of Concerned Scientists*, February 2011. www.ucsusa.org.

Kopp, Carlo. "The Electromagnetic Bomb—A Weapon of Electrical Mass Destruction." Chronicles Online Journal, http://www.airpower.maxwell .af.mil/airchronicles/cc/apjemp.html; www.cs.monash.edu.au/-carlo.

Krauthammer, Charles. "The Japan Card." *Washington Post*. January 3, 2003.

Kristof, Nicholas D. "An American Hiroshima." *New York Times*, August 11, 2004. www.nytimes.com.

Kuznick, Peter J. "Scientist on the Stump." *Bulletin of the Atomic Scientists*, November/December 2004. www.thebulletin.org.

Lague, David. "Russia Covets China Nuclear Deals." *International Herald Tribune*, April 15, 2006. www.iht.com.

Langewiesche, William. "The Wrath of Khan." *The Atlantic*, November 1, 2005. http://www.theatlantic.com/magazine/archive/2005/11/the-wrath-of -khan/304333/.

Langner, Ralph. "Why Attack When We Can't Defend?" *New York Times*, June 4, 2012. www.nytimes.com.

Lapidos, Juliet. "Atomic Priesthoods, Thorn Landscapes and Munchian Pictograms." *Slate*, November 16, 2009. www.slate.com.

Lemos, Robert. "A Way to Attack Nuclear Plants." *MIT Technology Review*, September 29, 2010. http://www.technologyreview.com/news/420970/a -way-to-attack-nuclear-plants/.

Leventhal, Paul. "Getting Serious About Proliferation." *Bulletin of the Atomic Scientists*, Vol. 40, No. 3, March 1984.

Lewis, Michael. "The Access Capitalists." *New Republic*, October 18, 1993. http://www.newrepublic.com/article/politics/the-access-capitalists.

Lichtblau, Eric. "Saudi Arabia May Be Tied to 9/11, 2 Ex-Senators Say." *New York Times*, February 29, 2012. www.nytimes.com.

Lichtblau, Eric, and Eric Schmitt. "Cash Flow to Terrorists Evades U.S. Efforts." *New York Times*. December 5, 2010. www.nytimes.com.

Lipton, Eric. "Ties to Obama Aided in Access for Big Utility." *New York Times*, August 22, 2012. www.nytimes.com.

Lipton, Eric and Benjamin Weiser. "Qaeda Invests Years to Plan Terror Attacks." *New York Times*, August 5, 2004. www.nytimes.com.

Lister, Tim. "WikiLeaks Cables Assess Terrorism Funding in Saudi Arabia, Gulf States." CNNWorld, December 6, 2010. www.cnn.com.

Lochbaum, David. "The NRC and Nuclear Plant Safety in 2010: A Brighter Spotlight Needed." *Union of Concerned Scientists*, March 3, 2011.

Lovins, Amory. "The Nuclear Illusion." *Rocky Mountain Institute*, August 1, 2008.

Lyman, Dr. Edwin S. "Impacts of a Terrorist Attack at Indian Point Nuclear Power Plant." *Union of Concerned Scientists*, September 2004. www.ucsusa.org.

———. "Nuclear Plant Protection and Homeland Security." *Union of Concerned Scientists*. www.ucsusa.org.

———. "Testimony to the Subcommittee on Clean Air, Climate Change and Nuclear Security Committee on Environment and Public Works, United States Senate." *Union of Concerned Scientists*, May 26, 2005. www.ucsusa.org.

Lynch, Colum. "Halliburton's Iraq Deals Greater Than Cheney Has Said, Affiliates Had $73 Million in Contracts." *Washington Post*, June 23, 2001. www.washingtonpost.com.

Madrigal, Alexis. "Solar Company Says Its Tech Can Power 90 Percent of Grid and Cars." *Wired*, March 6, 2008.

Mahapatra, Rajesh. "Rumsfeld Warned on Arms Sale." Associated Press, December 10, 2004.

"Maps and Charts of Iraqi Oil Fields." *Judicial Watch*, March 7, 2006. www.judicialwatch.org/printer_iraqi-oil-maps.shtml.

"March 2013 Update: US covert actions in Pakistan, Yemen and Somalia."

The Bureau of Investigative Journalism, April 2, 2013. http://www.the bureauinvestigates.com/2013/04/02/march-2013-update-us-covert -actions-in-pakistan-yemen-and-somalia/.

Margolis, Eric. "The Nuclear New-Boy We Should Be Watching Is India." April 27, 2013. http://ericmargolis.com/2013/04/the-nuclear-new-boy -we-should-be-watching-is-india/.

Markoff, John. "A Code for Chaos." *New York Times,* October 2, 2010. www .nytimes.com.

Masood, Salman and Ismail Khan. "Taliban Militants Attack Pakistani Base." *New York Times*, February 2, 2013. www.nytimes.com.

Matishak, Martin. "Floating Nuclear Reactors Could Fall Prey to Terrorists, Experts Say." Global Security Newswire, August 13, 2010. www .nti.org.

Mazzetti, Mark, Charlie Savage and Scott Shane. "How a U.S. Citizen Came to Be in America's Cross Hairs." *New York Times*, March 9, 2013. www .nytimes.com.

McCain, John. "Rogue State Rollback." *Weekly Standard*, January 20, 2003. www.weeklystandard.com.

McGeary, Johanna. "Confessions of a Terrorist." *Time,* August 31, 2003. http://www.time.com/time/magazine/article/0,9171,480226,00.html.

McGlinchey, Dan. "Iran: Russian Nuclear Assistance Motivated by Economic Needs." *Global Security Newswire*, February 27, 2003. www.nti.org.

McGreal, Chris. "Missing Keys, Holes in Fence and A Single Padlock: Welcome to Congo's Nuclear Plant." *The Guardian*, November 23, 2006. http://www.guardian.co.uk/world/2006/nov/23/congo.chrismc greal.

Meyer, Josh. "Classified 9/11 Report Said to 'Damn' Saudi Officials: Some Who Saw Pages Say Riyadh Government Gave Money to Hijackers." *Los Angeles Times,* August 2, 2003. www.latimes.com.

———. "2 Allies Aided Bin Laden, Say Panel Members." *Los Angeles Times,* June 20, 2004. www.latimes.com.

Michaels, Jim. "6 Months After U.S. Combat Troops Left, Can Iraq Go It Alone?" *USA Today,* June 6, 2012. www.usatoday.com.

"Milestones." http://www.bechtel.com/milestones.html.

"Militants Kill Pakistani Soldiers in Attack on Base." *BBC News*, March 31, 2010. http://news.bbc.co.uk/2/hi/south_asia/8596226.stm.

Mintz, John. "Saudi Anti-Terror Efforts Criticized." *Washington Post*, June 15, 2004. www.washingtonpost.com.

Mufson, Steven. "Another Push for Nuclear Power." *Washington Post*, December 17, 2007. http://www.washingtonpost.com/wp-dyn/content /article/2007/12/17/AR2007121701886.html.

Munger, Frank. "Y-12 Protesters Arraigned for Federal Trespassing; More Charges Could Follow." July 30, 2012. www.knoxvillenews.com, http:// www.knoxnews.com/news/2012/jul/30/y-12-protesters-arraigned-for -federal-more-could/.

Myers, Lisa. "Influence Peddling Charged Over Iraq's Debt." October 13, 2004. http://www.nbcnews.com/id/6242360/.

Nader, Ralph. "No Nukes." February 13, 2010. http://www.commondreams .org/view/2010/02/13.

Nelson, Dean. "The US Agreed to Build Two Nuclear Power Stations and Supply Sophisticated Weaponry to India When Hillary Clinton Visited New Delhi." *Telegraph*, July 20, 2009. www.telegraph.co.uk.

"New Documents Spotlight Reagan-era Tensions Over Pakistani Nuclear Program." *National Security Archive: George Washington University*, April 27, 2012. http://www.gwu.edu/~nsarchiv/nukevault/ebb377/.

"N. Korea Re-Opens Nuclear Facilities, Agency Says." *PBS Online News Hour*, December 24, 2002. http://www.pbs.org/newshour/updates/nkorea _12-24-02.html.

Noah, Timothy. "When Did Trickle-Down Get Respectable?" *New Republic*, September 19, 2011.

"North Korea 'To Restart Yongbyon Nuclear Reactor'." *BBC News Asia*, April 2, 2013. http://www.bbc.co.uk/news/world-asia-21999193.

"The NRC and Nuclear Power Plant Safety in 2010: A Brighter Spotlight Is Needed." *Union of Concerned Scientists*, March 17, 2011. www.ucsusa.org.

"Nuclear Files: Timeline of the Nuclear Age: 1945." *Project of the Nuclear*

Age Peace Foundation. http://www.nuclearfiles.org/menu/timeline /timeline_page.php?year=1945.

"Nuclear Power: Adequate Insurance Too Expensive." Associated Press, April 21, 2011.

"Nuclear Power in the USA." *World Nuclear News*, March 2012. www.world -nuclear.org/info/inf41.html.

"Nuclear Power Joint Fact-Finding." *The Keystone Center*, June 2007. http:keystone.org.

"Nuclear Reactor Security." *Union of Concerned Scientists*, March 30, 2005. www.ucsusa.org.

"Nuclear Reprocessing: Dangerous, Dirty and Expensive." *Nuclear Reprocessing Fact Sheet*, Union of Concerned Scientists, April 5, 2011. www .ucsusa.org.

"Nuclear Reprocessing Fact Sheet." *Union Of Concerned Scientists*, December 8, 2003.

"Nuclear Terrorism Fact Sheet." *Harvard: Kennedy School, Belfer Center for Science and International Affairs*, October 1, 2006. http://www.nuclear summit.org/files/FACT_SHEET_Final.pdf.

"Obama Approves Raising Permissible Levels of Nuclear Radiation in Drinking Water. Civilian Cancer Deaths Expected to Skyrocket." *Public Employees for Environmental Responsibility (PEER), Global Research News*, April 14, 2013. http://www.globalresearch.ca/obama-approves -raising-permissible-levels-of-nuclear-radiation-in-drinking-water -civilian-cancer-deaths-expected-to-skyrocket/5331224.

"Obama Renews Commitment to Nuclear Energy." Associated Press, February 16, 2010.

Olson, Mary. "Reprocessing Is Not the 'Solution' to the Nuclear Waste Problem." *Nuclear Information and Resource Service*, January 2006. www.nirs.org.

"160 Saudis Flew Home After 9/11." *Pittsburgh Tribune-Review*, March 30, 2004.

Onishi, Norimitsu, and Ken Belson. "Culture of Complicity Tied to

Stricken Nuclear Plant." *New York Times*, April 26, 2011. http://www
.nytimes.com/2011/04/27/world/asia/27collusion.html.

O'Reilly, Finbarr. "Rush for Natural Resources Still Fuels War in Congo."
Reuters, August 9, 2004.

"Pakistan, India Could Receive U.S. F-16s." Global Security Newswire,
March 15, 2005.

Park, Soo Bin. "South Korea Makes Billion-Dollar Bet on Fusion Power."
Scientific American, January 2013. http://www.scientificamerican.com
/article.cfm?id=south-korea-makes-billion-dollar-bet-fusion-power
&print=true.

Parks, Michael. "Chernobyl Lies By Soviets Confirmed—Contaminated
Meat, Milk Mixed with Other Supplies." *Seattle Times/Los Angeles
Times*, April 25, 1992.

Parmet, Herbert. "What Should We Make of the Charge Linking the Bush
Family Fortune to Nazism?" *History News Network*, November 17, 2003.
www.hnn.us.

Parry, Tom. "We Plant 'Bomb' on Nuke Train." *Daily Mirror*, July 21, 2006.
www.mng.org.uk.

"Peaceful Nuclear Technology Can Be Effective 'Deterrent,' IAEA Chief
ElBaradei Warns." *Global Security Newswire*, December 10, 2004. www
.nti.org.

Perlroth, Nicole, and David E. Sanger. "New Computer Attacks Traced to
Iran, Officials Say." *New York Times*, May 24, 2013. www.nytimes.com.

Peters, Ralph. "Dubya's Grovel." *New York Post*, August 9, 2002. www
.nypost.com.

Pianin, Eric, and Bill Miller, "Nuclear Arms Plants' Security Lax, Report Says:
Mock 'Commandos' Were Able to Beat Safeguards at U.S. Facilities About
Half the Time." *Washington Post*, January 23, 2002. washingtonpost.com.

Pica, Erich. "Don't Jump to Conclusions About Nuclear Reactors: Look at
the Facts and Say No." *Huffington Post*, April 3, 2011. www.huffington
post.com.

"Plutonium Proliferation and MOX Fuel." *Nuclear Information and Re-*

source Service: Reactor Watchdog Project. www.nirs.org/factsheets
/moxproliferation.htm.

Podhoretz, John. "Crazy Korea Cures." New York Post, December 27, 2002.
www.nypost.com.

Podvig, Pavel. "Consolidating Fissile Materials in Russia's Nuclear Complex." May 2009. www.fissilematerials.org.

Pollack, Joshua, and George Perkovich. "The AQ Khan Network and Its
Fourth Customer." Carnegie Endowment for International Peace, January 23, 2012. www.carnegieendowment.org.

Prather, Gordon. "Condi's Diplomatic Triumph." December 23, 2006. www
.antiwar.com.

"Prevalence of Child Marriage in India High Fertility Risks." ScienceDaily,
March 9, 2009. www.sciencedaily.com.

"Preventing Nuclear Terrorism." Union of Concerned Scientists. www
.ucsusa.org.

"Quick and Secret Construction of Plutonium Reprocessing Plants: A Way
to Nuclear Weapons Proliferation?" U.S. General Accounting Office, Report by the Comptroller General of the United States, October 6, 1978.

Quigley, Fran. "How the US Turned Three Pacifists into Violent Terrorists."
www.counterpunch.org, May 15, 2013. http://www.counterpunch.org
/2013/05/15/how-the-us-turned-three-pacifists-into-violent-terrorists/.

Rabin, Kyle. "9/11 Report Reveals Al Qaeda Ringleader Contemplated a NY-
area Nuclear Power Plant as Potential Target." Energy Bulletin, July 25,
2004. www.EMS.org.

"Radioactive Roads and Rails." Nuclear Information Resource Service. www
.nirs.org.

"Radioactive Wastes: Myths and Realities." World Nuclear Association, June
2006. www.world-nuclear.org/info/inf103.htm/.

Ramesh, Randeep. "The Two Faces of Rumsfeld." The Guardian, May 9, 2003.

———. "Rumsfeld Link to Sale of Reactors to North Korea." The Guardian,
May 10, 2003.

"Reactors Ready for Floating Plant." World Nuclear News, August 7, 2009.

http://www.world-nuclear-news.org/NN-Reactors_ready_for_first _floating_plant-0708094.html.

Regan, Tom. "Daily Update: Hatfill, While Under Investigation for Anthrax, Trained US Intelligence Agents for Bioweapons Searches." *Christian Science Monitor*, July 3, 2003. www.scmonitor.com.

Rennie, David. "Rumsfeld Calls for Regime Change in North Korea." *Daily Telegraph*, April 22, 2003.

"Researchers: Cyber Spies Break into Govt Computers." *USA Today/AP*, March 29, 2009.

"Rice Offers India Nuclear Help, But Objects to Natural Gas Line." *Sydney Morning Herald*, March 18, 2006. www.smh.com.au.

Riedel, Bruce. "Saudi Arabia: Nervously Watching Pakistan." *The Brookings Institution*, January 28, 2008.

Roberts, Sam. "In 2025, India to Pass China in Population, U.S. Estimates." *New York Times*, December 15, 2009. http://www.nytimes.com/2009/12 /16/world/asia/16census.html?_r=0.

Roche, Elizabeth. "India Upgraded Security at Nuclear Facilities Amid Terror Warnings." *Agence France-Presse*, September 5, 2006.

"Rocky Flats Plant." *US EPA*, www.epa.gov/region8/superfund/co/rky flatsplant/.

Romanowicz, Goska. "Russian Floating Nuclear Reactors Spark Contamination Fears." March 2, 2006. http://www.edie.net/news/news_w4w .asp?id=11138.

Rosenberg, Martin. "Harvesting Solar Power in Space." *Energybiz*, September/October 2008. http://energycentral.fileburst.com/EnergyBizOnline /2008-5-sep-oct/Tech_Frontier_Solar_Space.pdf.

Rulon, Malia. "Gov't to End Public Nuclear Updates." Associated Press, August 4, 2004. www.newsday.com.

Rumsfeld, Donald. "Commission to Assess the Ballistic Missile Threat to the United States." www.fas.org.

Ruppe, David. "Govt. Report Critiques Bush Nuclear Deal with India." *Global Security Newswire*, August 16, 2005. www.nti.org.

——. "U.S. Deal Would Aid Indian Nuclear Weapons, Expert Says." *Global Security Newswire*, October 13, 2005. www.nti.org.

——. "U.S.-Indian Deal Would Violate NPT, Critics Say." *Global Security Newswire*, June 21, 2006.

"Russian Floating Nuclear Reactors Spark Contamination Fears." March 2, 2006. www.edie.net/news /news_story.asp?id=11138.

"Russian National-Level Nuclear Weapons Storage." *Global Security Newswire*, July 24, 2011. http://www.globalsecurity.org/wmd/world/russia /storage.htm.

"Russia Starts Work on Floating Nuclear Power Plant." *Global Security Newswire*, April 19, 2007. www.nti.org, 4/19/07

Ruthven, Malise. "Excremental India." *The New York Review of Books*, May 13, 2010.

Saletan, William. "Nuclear Incest: Did Industry-Government Collusion Contribute to Japan's Nuclear Disaster?" *Slate,* April 28, 2011. www.slate.com.

"Sanders Asks Obama for Nuclear Moratorium." March 20, 2011. http://www.sanders.senate.gov/newsroom/news/?id=cdf18d5d-a5d5-4c30 -8e00-ac12a82751d7.

Sanger, David E. "Obama Order Sped up Wave of Cyberattacks Against Iran." *New York Times*, June 1, 2012. www.nytimes.com.

Sanger, David E., David Barboza, and Nicole Perlroth. "Chinese Army Unit Is Seen as Tied to Hacking Against U.S." *New York Times*, February 18, 2013. www.nytimes.com.

"Saudi Arabia: Nuclear." *Global Security Newswire.* http://www.nti.org /country-profiles/saudi-arabia/nuclear/.

Sayah, Reza. "Hostages at Pakistani Army HQ Released." *CNN Asia*, October 11, 2009. http://www.cnn.com/2009/WORLD/asiapcf/10/10/pakistan .shootings/index.html.

Seba, Tony. "Solar Has Improved Unit Costs by 1,000 Times Relative to Nuclear." April 25, 2013. http://tonyseba.com/disruption/solar-has-im proved-unit-costs-by-1000-times-relative-to-nuclear/.

Sewell, Abbey. "Letters Show Rift Over San Onofre Nuclear Repairs." *Los*

Angeles Times, May 19, 2013. http://articles.latimes.com/2013/may/19/local/la-me-san-onofre-20130520.

Shah, Saeed. "Terrorist Attack in Pakistan Shows How Vulnerable It Is." *McClatchy Newpapers*, October 11, 2009. http://www.mcclatchydc.com/2009/10/11/76954/terrorist-attack-in-pakistan-shows.html#story link=cpy.

Shane, Scott. "Worker Spoke of Jihad, Agency Says." *New York Times*, October 4, 2010. http://www.nytimes.com/2010/10/05/us/05mobley.html.

Shorrick, Tim. "Crony Capitalism Goes Global." *The Nation*, March 14, 2002. www.thenation.com.

Shukla, Shublakshmi. "India Probes Corruption in Flagship Health Programme." *The Lancet*, Volume 379, Issue 9817. February 25, 2012.

Shultz, George P., William J. Perry, et al. "A World Free of Nuclear Weapons." *Wall Street Journal*, January 4, 2007. www.online.wsj.com.

"Solar Physics." *NASA Marshall Space Center*, http://solarscience.msfc.nasa.gov/interior.shtml.

Sowder, Dr. Andrew. "Used Nuclear Fuel Management: The Back End of the Fuel Cycle." *Health Physics News*, January 2010.

Speier, Richard. "U.S. Space Aid to India: On a 'Glide Path' to ICBM Trouble?" *Arms Control Today*, March 2006. www.armscontrol.org.

Strickland, Eliza. "What Went Wrong in Japan's Nuclear Reactors." *IEEE Spectrum*, March 16, 2011.

"Stuxnet Could Trigger Atomic Calamity, Intel Report Warns." *Global Security Newswire*, February 1, 2011. www.nti.org.

"Stuxnet Malware Mystery Deepens: Another Hint of Israeli Origins." *Huffington Post*, October 1, 2010. www.huffingtonpost.com.

Sudarasan, Raghavan. "U.S.-Aided Attack in Yemen Thought to Have Killed Aulaqi, 2 al-Qaeda leaders." *Washington Post*, December 24, 2009. http://www.washingtonpost.com/wpdyn/content/article/2009/12/24/AR2009122400536.html,12/24/09.

Sullivan, John. "NRC Waives Enforcement of Fire Rules at Nuclear Plants." *Pro Publica*, May 11, 2011.

Summers, Anthony and Robbyn Swan, "The Kingdom and the Towers,"

Vanity Fair, http://www.vanityfair.com/politics/features/2011/08/9-11 -2011-201108, August 2011.

Talmadge, Eric. "The First 24 Hours Shaped Japan Nuke Crisis." Associated Press, July 2, 2011.

"Terrorist Havens: Philippines." *Council on Foreign Relations*, June 1, 2009. http://www.cfr.org/philippines/terrorism-havens-philippines/p9365.

"Terror Strikes Hint at Pakistani Nuke Security Gaps." *Global Security Newswire*, June 14, 2011. www.nti.org.

"Terror Suspect's Manual of Western Targets Included Nuclear Plants, British Prosecutor says." *Global Security Newswire*, November 12, 2006. See Agence France-Presse, November 11, 2006. www.nti.org.

"Thanks to Cheap Natural Gas, America's Nuclear Renaissance Is on Hold." *The Economist*, June 1, 2013.

Thompson, Mark and Bruce Crumley. "Are These Towers Safe?" *Time*, June 20, 2005. www.time.com.

Totten, Shay. "Nuclear Regulatory Commission: Nuclear Watchdog or Lapdog?" *New England Center for Investigation*. May 6, 2011.

"Two Months Before 9/11, an Urgent Warning to Rice." *Washington Post*, October 1, 2006. http://www.washingtonpost.com/wp-dyn/content /article/2006/09/30/AR2006093000282.html.

"UCS Statement on 50th Anniversary of Eisenhower's 'Atoms for Peace' Speech." *Union of Concerned Scientists*, December 8, 2003. www.ucsusa .org.

Unger, Craig. "The Great Escape." *New York Times*, June 1, 2004. http:// www.nytimes.com/2004/06/01/opinion/the-great-escape.html.

"Union of Soviet Socialist Republics." *World History Center*. http://history -world.org/union_of_soviet_socialist_republ.html.

Unnithan, Sandeep. "US Decision to Sell P-3C Orion Strike Aircraft to Pakistan Shocks India." *India Today*, December 16, 2004. www.indiatoday.in.

"The Untouchables." *Frontline*. www.pbs.org/wgbh/pages/frontline/un touchables/.

"US Embassy Warns U.S. Citizens in Saudi Arabia." *Washington Post/ Reuters*, June 13, 2004.

"US Knew of Sharif Mobley, US Nuclear Official Says." *CBS*, October 4, 2010. www.CBSNews.com.

"US Lifts India and Pakistan sanctions." *BBC News*, September 23, 2001.

"U.S. Marketers Visited Saudi Arabia, As Trade Talks Underway." *Global Security Newswire*, February 1, 2013. www.nti.org.

"U.S. Received Little for What It Spent in Iraq." *Radio Free Europe, Radio Liberty*, March 6, 2013. www.globalsecuritynewswire.org, http://www.globalsecurity.org/wmd/library/news/iraq/2013/iraq-130306-rferl01.htm?_m=3n%2e002a%2e748%2ezn0ao04n6e%2eoiv.

"U.S., Russian Scientists Exploring Collaboration on Floating Nuclear Power Plants." *Global Security Newswire*, August 27, 2004. www.nti.org.

Vallette, Jim, with Steve Kretzmann and Daphne Wysham, "Crude Vision: How Oil Interests Obscured U.S. Government Focus on Chemical Weapons Us by Saddam Hussein." Based on documents obtained from the Government's National Archives and the non-profit National Security Archive, Sustainable Energy & Economy Network, Institute for Policy Studies: IPS, March 2003.

Vancko, Ellen. "Room for Debate: A Comeback for Nuclear Power? Better Environmental Options." *New York Times*, February 16, 2010. www.nytimes.com.

Vergano, Dan. "One EMP Burst and the World Goes Dark." *USA Today*, October 27, 2010.

Vidal, John. "Ukraine Raises $785 to Seal Chernobyl Under New 'Shell'." *The Guardian*, April 19, 2011. www.guardian.co.uk.

Von Hippel, Frank N. "Plutonium and Reprocessing of Spent Fuel." *Science*, Volume 293, Number 5539, September 28, 2001. See http://www.sciencemag.org/content/293/5539/2397.summary.

Wald, Matthew L. "Court Forces a Rethinking of Nuclear Fuel Storage." *New York Times*, June 8, 2012. www.nytimes.com.

———. "A Nation Challenged: Nuclear Security; Suicidal Nuclear Threat Is Seen at Weapons Plants." *New York Times*, January 23, 2002. www.nytimes.com.

———. "Nuclear Power Gets a Strong Push from the White House." *New York Times*, January 22, 2010. www.nytimes.com.

———. "Responsibility for Defending Nuclear Plants Is Debated." *New York Times*, April 5, 2006. www.nytimes.com.

———. "Security Questions Are Raised by Break-In at Nuclear Site." *New York Times*, August 7, 2012.

———. "US Loans for Reactors in China Draw Objections." *New York Times*, February 28, 2005. www.nytimes.com.

Waller, David. "Atoms for Peace: A Perspective from the IAEA." *The International Atomic Energy Agency*, December 8, 2003. www.IAEA.org.

Walsh, Declan. "WikiLeaks Cables Portray Saudi Arabia as a Cash Machine for Terrorists." *The Guardian*, December 5, 2010. www.guardian.co.uk.

Warner, Melanie. "What Do George Bush, Arthur Levitt, Jim Baker, Dick Darman, and John Major All Have in Common?" *Fortune*, March 18, 2002.

Wasserman, Harvey. "America's Eggshell Nukes." *Huffington Post*, November 15, 2010. www.huffingtonpost.com.

———. "Is Fukushima Now Ten Chernobyls Into the Sea?" May 26, 2011. commondreams.org.

———. "Los Angeles to San Onofre: 'Not So Fast!'" *Huffington Post*, April 29, 2013. http://www.huffingtonpost.com/harvey-wasserman/los-angeles-to-san-onofre_b_3167482.html.

———. "People Died at Three Mile Island." March 9, 2009. www.counterpunch.org.

Wayne, Leslie. "Elder Bush in Big GOP Cast Toiling for Top Equity Firm." *New York Times*, March 5, 2001. www.nytimes.com.

"Waziristan Raid: Taliban 'Kill Eight Pakistan Soldiers'." *BBC News*, August 29, 2012. http://www.bbc.co.uk/news/world-asia-19407661,

Weisman, Steven R. "Saudi Arabia Longtime Ambassador to the U.S. Is Resigning." *New York Times*, July 21, 2005. www.nytimes.com.

Weiss, Leonard. "Atoms for Peace." *Bulletin of the Atomic Scientists*, November/December 2003. www.thebulletin.org.

"Westinghouse Sold to Toshiba for $5.4B." *Pittsburgh Business Times*,

February 6, 2006. http://www.bizjournals.com/pittsburgh/stories/2006/02/06/daily3.html.

Whitlock, Craig. "Homemade, Cheap and Dangerous—Terror Cells Favor Simple Ingredients in Building Bombs." *Washington Post*, July 4, 2007.

Wilson, Jim. "E-Bomb," *Popular Mechanics*, September 2001. www.popularmechanics.com/science/military/2001/9/e-bomb.

"Wind Power." *National Geographic*. http://environment.nationalgeographic.com/environment/global-warming/wind-power-profile/.

Winter, Michael. "NRC Clears Way for Scrapping Yucca Mt. Nuke Dump." *USA Today*, September 11, 2011.

Wit, Joel. "The North Korea Deal That Wasn't." April 2, 2013. http://www.foreignpolicy.com/articles/2013/04/02/the_north_korea_deal_that_wasnt_yongbyon.

Wonacott, Peter. "Lawless Legislators Thwart Social Progress in India." *Wall Street Journal*, May 4, 2007. http://online.wsj.com/article/SB117823755304891604.html.

Zeibel, Ken, James Mason, and Vasilis Fthenakis. "The Grand Solar Plan: By 2050 Solar Power Could End U.S. Dependence on Foreign Oil and Slash Greenhouse Gas Emissions." *Scientific American*, January 2008. http://people.bu.edu/sobieraj/articles/SolarGrandPlan_Jan08_SciAm.pdf.

Zeller, Tom Jr. "With US Nuclear Plants Under Scrutiny, Too, a Report Raises Safety Concerns." *New York Times*, March 17, 2011. www.nytimes.com.

———. "Nuclear Agency Beset by Lapses." *New York Times*, May 7, 2011. www.nytimes.com.

Zia, Amir. "Pakistan Tests Medium-Range Nuclear-Capable Missile." *Reuters*, December 8, 2004. www.reuters.com.

Television Programs

Carollo, Kim. "Radiation from Japan Disaster Found in Kelp Along California Coast." *ABC News*. April 10, 2012. http://abcnews.go.com/blogs/health/2012/04/10/radiation-from-japan-disaster-found-along-calif-coast/.

"Cyber War: Sabotaging the System." *CBS News*. CBS. November 6, 2009. http://www.cbsnews.com/8301-18560_162-5555565.html.

"Doing Business with the Enemy." *60 Minutes*. CBS. January 25, 2004. www
.cbsnews.com.

"The First Nuclear Test in New Mexico." See Brig. Gen. Thomas F. Farrell's
comments in a July 18, 1945, War Department memo written by General Leslie Grove. *American Experience*. PBS. http://www.pbs.org
/wgbh/americanexperience/features/primary-resources/truman-bomb
test/.

Kennedy, Rory. "Indian Point: Imagining the Unimaginable." Rory Kennedy. HBO documentary. September 8, 2004.

Leung, Rebecca. "Yucca Mountain." *60 Minutes*. CBS. February 11, 2009,
http://www.cbsnews.com/8301-18560_162-579696.html.

Meet the Press with Tim Russert. Interview with Vice President Dick Cheney.
MSNBC. March 16, 2003. See transcript at https://www.mtholyoke.edu
/acad/intrel/bush/cheneymeetthepress.htm.

Myers, Lisa. "Saudi Prince: Zionism to Blame for Terror Attack." Lisa Myers. *Nightly News with Tom Brokaw*. NBC News. June 15, 2004. http://
www.msnbc.msn.com/id/5218227/.

Rossin, A. David. "U.S. Policy on Spent Fuel Reprocessing: The Issues."
Frontline. PBS. http://www.pbs.org/wgbh/pages/frontline/shows/reac
tion/readings/rossin.html.

"Who Is Osama bin Laden?" *BBC World News*. BBC. September 18, 2001.
http://news.bbc.co.uk/2/hi/south_asia/155236.stm.

Testimony and Remarks

Cheney, Richard. Remarks before the Senate Armed Services Committee,
September 11, 1990.

Ferguson, Charles D. *Philip D. Reed Senior Fellow for Science and Technology,
Council on Foreign Relations, Testimony to Committee In Science and Technology*. U.S. House of Representatives Hearing on "Advancing Technology
for Nuclear Fuel Recycling: What Should Our Research, Development,
and Demonstration Strategy Be?" June 17, 2009. http://www.gpo.gov/fdsys
/pkg/CHRG-111hhrg50172/pdf/CHRG-111hhrg50172.pdf.

Mueller, Robert. Senate Intelligence Committee testimony, February 16, 2005.

Shachnow, Sid. Major General, U.S. Special Forces (ret.) interview.

Tenet, George. "The Worldwide Threat 2004: Challenges in a Changing Global Context." Testimony before the Senate Select Committee on Intelligence on February 24, 2004. Quoted from Allison, Graham. *Nuclear Terrorism: The Ultimate Preventable Catastrophe*, New York: Holt, 2005.

Watergate Tapes, March 9, 1971.

Other Cited Links

www.brookings.edu/projects/archive/nucweapons/davy.aspx)

www.ge.com/company/leadership/board-of-directors

www.lanl.gov/science-innovation/science-programs/civilian-nuclear-programs/_assets/docs/AdvancedNuclearFinal_8_15.pdf

www.nndb.com/people/065/000057891/Perry

www.nti.org/analysis/articles/russias-floating-nuclear-power-plants/

www.publicintelligence.net/kissinger-associates-inc/

INDEX

reprocessing, nuclear waste, 48–50, 67, 114, 242
Revelation 9:20–21, 109
Rice, Condoleezza, 115, 155, 156, 157–58
Rice, Megan, 26–28
Rocky Flats facility, 25
Rumsfeld, Donald, 113–14, 126, 141–44,
 146–47, 158–60, 163–64
Russia
 Catalytic Nuclear War and, 237
 floating nuclear reactors from, 174–76
 Iran nuclear relationship with, 29, 122–23
 Iraq War impact on, 122–23
 nuclear facility security in, 25, 175
 nuclear proliferation, 157, 174–76
 nuclear weapons of, 190
 U.S. cyber attack from, 79–80

safety
 of Fukushima cleanup effort, 100, 101–3
 ITER, 182–83
 nuclear facility, 63, 87–89, 197–98
 of nuclear reactors, 176
 nuclear waste storage and transportation,
  38, 44–45, 49, 50, 173, 243
 radiation and, 98
Sanders, Bernie, 106–7
Saudi Arabia
 Afghanistan and, 131
 Bush, George W., administration and, 133–38
 Bush family profiting from, 115–16, 134–35
 9/11 and, 134, 135–39
 nuclear bomb for, 69–70
 nuclear program of, 116, 122
 Pakistan, terrorism, and, 131–32
 Pakistani nuclear industry and, 116, 122
 al Qaeda links to, 67–68, 130–33, 138–39
 Taliban relationship with, 130, 131–32, 134
 terrorism and links to, 130–40
 U.S. and U.S. officials' collusion with,
  115–16, 130–31, 133–40, 233
 U.S. arms sales to, 68
 U.S. debt owned by, 216, 217
 U.S. nuclear power technology sold to, 31,
  66, 68, 243
 U.S. perception in, 139–40

security
 cyber attack, 78–79, 204
 of HEU, 217–18
 at Indian nuclear facilities, 151
 at Indian Point facility, 196
 mock-intrusion trials for, 60–61, 62, 240–41
 NRC on, 60–64
 nuclear industry undermining, 23–24,
  61–62, 78–79, 195
 nuclear waste storage and transportation,
  41, 42, 43, 44
 private enterprise and U.S. national, 203
 Russian nuclear facility, 25, 175
 U.S. nuclear bomb-fuel storage site, 25,
  26–28, 30, 193–94, 232, 240–41
 U.S. nuclear facility, 22, 23–24, 25, 26–28,
  60–64, 79, 192–93, 195–96, 232
Shelby, Richard, 130–31
Shultz, George, 213, 214
Single Integrated and Operational Plan
 (SIOP), 179–80
small vengeful power, 236–37
Smith, Gerard C., 172
Sokolski, Henry, 150, 153, 157, 160–61
solar power, 55, 220–23, 225
South Korea, 183–84
Special Service Group (SSG), 17
Spengler, Oswald, 229–30
SSG. See Special Service Group
Stuxnet, 74–78, 202
Sugaoka, Kei, 85–86
Suskind, Ron, 126–27

Taliban, 130, 131–32, 134
Teller, Edward, 181
Telvent DMS, 204–5
Tepco. See Tokyo Electric
Terminal High Altitude Area Defense missile
 defense systems (THAAD), 68
terrorism, terrorists, and terrorist attacks.
  See also cyber attacks; nuclear terrorism
  and terrorists; al Qaeda
 Islamist, 22–23, 70, 151, 238
 nature of, 193–94
 New York City as target of, 188, 192